CALLED TO SERVE

PLACES AND PEOPLE

A Walking Tour of St. Olaf College

See Part II: Biography

- **A** **Manitou Field House** *(Ade Christenson, Chapter 12)*
- **B** **Ellingson Hall** *(Emil Oscar Ellingson, Chapter 8)*
- **C** **Christiansen Hall of Music** *(F. Melius Christiansen, Chapter 6)*
- **D** **Boe Memorial Chapel** *(Lars W. Boe, Chapter 5)*
- **E** **Rolvaag Memorial Library** *(Ole Edvart Rølvaag, Chapter 7)*
- **F** **Ditmanson Wing** *(Harold Ditmanson, Chapter 15)*
- **G** **Kierkegaard Library** *(Howard V. and Edna H. Hong, Chapter 14)*
- **H** **Berntsen Memorial Garden Classroom** *(John Berntsen, Chapter 10)*
- **I** **Flaten Hall** *(Arnold Flaten, Chapter 13)*
- **J** **Larson Hall** *(Agnes Larson, Chapter 11)*
- **K** **Hilleboe Hall** *(Gertrude Hilleboe, Chapter 9)*

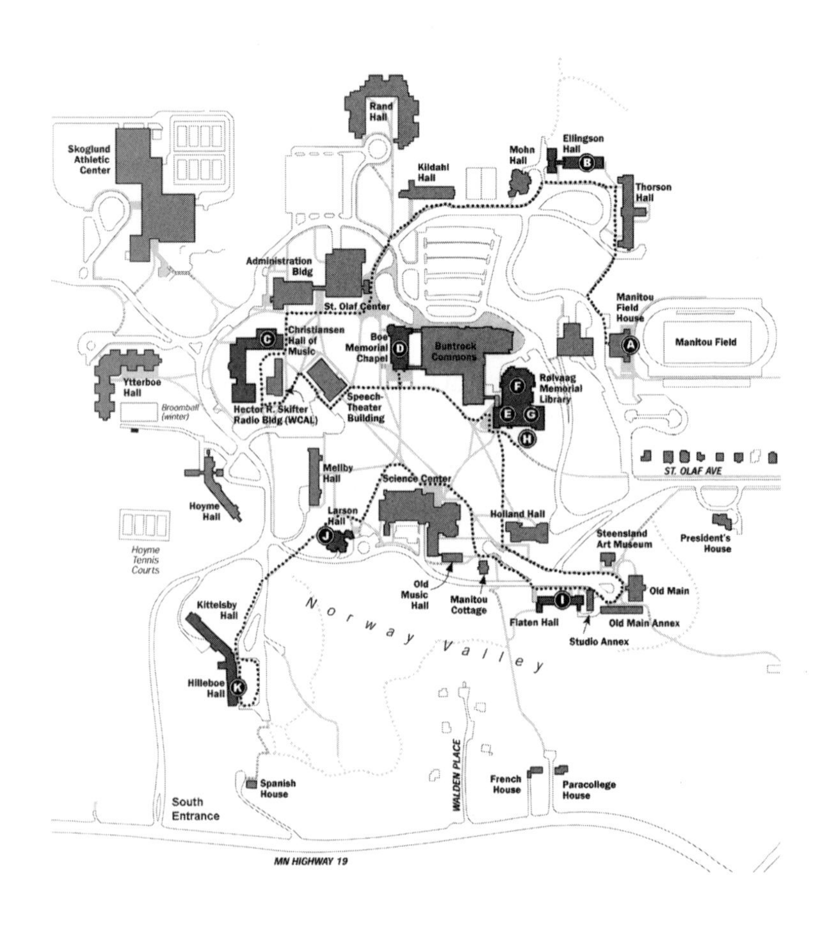

CALLED TO SERVE

St. Olaf and the Vocation of a Church College

Pamela Schwandt
Editor

Gary De Krey and L. DeAne Lagerquist
Coeditors

St. Olaf College

CALLED TO SERVE

Book design and typesetting: Peregrine Graphics Services
Cover design: Joseph Bonyata
Cover art : John Maakestad
Frontispiece map: Steven Edwins

The paper used in this publication meets the minimum requirements for American National Standard for Information Sciences—Permanence of Paper for Printed Library Materials, ANSI Z329.48–1984.

Manufactured in the United States of America 6-0001-1621-7

CONTENTS

FOREWORD

Martin E. Marty

"I want to thank my family and Lord Buddha for . . ." The thanker was one of two students asked to represent others at an honors lunch at St. Olaf College in Northfield, Minnesota. A "boat person" who came as a boy from Vietnam—where his father was killed in the war—to Faribault, Minnesota, and then to St. Olaf, he told me that he disappointed his family back home. He did not practice Buddhism, but its thought world was his. And he was much at home at St. Olaf, a "college of the church" with a Lutheran provenance.

He could have attended religion classes taught by a Hindu, in the company of, yes, more Lutheran students than students of any other religion, but with a strong Roman Catholic presence and, again yes, too few Jews and more Asians—in other words, in a religious and cultural mix. Since the campus is an hour south of downtown Minneapolis and St. Paul, like all schools similarly situated, it attracts fewer "multicultural" students than it would like. But the school compensates by encouraging extended foreign exposure and boasts that it has far more students doing their "year abroad" than any other liberal arts college in the nation.

In sum: St. Olaf welcomes diversity in religion and culture.

At the same time, the college declares forthrightly on page one of its publications and in lines borrowed from a faculty statement of 1987 that it is "a four-year college of the Evangelical Lutheran Church in America, [providing] an education committed to the liberal arts, rooted in the Christian gospel, and incorporating a global perspective." That statement represents more than lip service and mouthed missiology. (I am reminded of Samuel Goldwyn's statement that "an oral agreement is not worth the paper it's printed on.")

Wake up any regent of the college at 3 A.M. and he or she could recite that statement; all of them do make efforts to help the school live up to it. I know, because I am one of them. We see this mission and intention worked out in all the basic regent decisions, especially when electing a president and approving top leadership.

The other bearer of tradition, the main bearer of tradition in day-to-day life—along with administration and staff and alumni and students—is, of course, faculty. I wouldn't risk waking a faculty member at 3 A.M. for anything. And I wouldn't expect all the members of this diverse faculty or any faculty to come to complete agreement about the meanings and applications of a mission statement it has prepared and signed. But a criterion in faculty selection, whether Catholic, Jew, other believer, or nonbeliever, is that the candidate be friendly to the stated mission.

You can see from the above that there is no expectation that to be bearers of this tradition and innovators on the basis of it, you have to be of Norwegian descent or culture (as I am not) or Lutheran (as I am). While dealing with faculty committees in the selection of a new St. Olaf president several years ago, I found Baptists, Catholics, and others at least as attentive to the genius, ethos, shape, and intention of this "college of the church" as many Lutherans might ever be. (I am reminded of a statement by a Lutheran magazine editor years ago, commenting on a survey of faiths in America. Asked whether Lutherans believe theirs is the only true faith, he answered, "Yes, but they do not believe that they hold it alone.")

When risking a faith on a college, where pluralism, criticism, and experimentalism rule more than overt confessionalism and creedalism, no one expects to find agreement on "the only true faith" about what a college of this sort should be, teach, or embody. But the essays in this book show how our contemporaries on and off campus wrestle with the issue.

This book is for the St. Olaf family, dispersed around the world, but not just for them. It is designed to be a mirror for the more than two dozen Evangelical Lutheran Church in America peer colleges and universities, all of whom wrestle with similar issues. Without doubt, it will be of interest to leaders in the secular academy and the general public and especially to people at Catholic, mainstream Protestant, and evangelical institutions of higher learning, none of whom have these issues down cold. (If any of them claim to, they are not doing their daily homework.)

Why concentrate on one school instead of writing a generic book of essays on colleges, church-related colleges, or Lutheran church-related colleges? What different expectations does the specific instance raise instead of the general?

Let me back up for a moment. Before I was involved with the Board of Regents, St. Olaf's then-president, the chair of the Board of Regents, and a veteran board member had me to lunch to probe my interest and explain their criteria for membership. When I pleaded that my agenda and calendar were crowded and asked why should I add this, one of them said: You may have visited hundreds of campuses, written in general terms about higher education, and read many theories about that world, but aside from the school where you teach, do you really know what these other schools are like?

I was a satisfied customer of St. Olaf, having been close to two sons who had found the college. But I did not really know it. By joining the board I did get partially to know it up close, from the angle of one kind of up-closeness.

Such is the case with readers who may never have seen this place. We are learning today to follow case studies and case stories, to find exemplars, to come in close to places and situations. This book is such a close-up. What use is to be made of it, beyond the greater St. Olaf community? I like to quote editor William Sloan's advice to individuals: If you write autobiography, don't think that readers are saying, "Tell me about you." Each is saying, "Tell me about me, as I am using you as a mirror."

That could sound narcissistic, but it has more to do with exemplarity, guidance, and experiment than with self-obsession. So most readers will not say, "Tell me about St. Olaf." They will say, "Tell me about our interests, as we are using you as a mirror, seeking reflection and perspective as we are."

I am tempted now to weigh in on the main theme of the book: that this college has as its vocation the pursuit of vocation. But we leave that to the authors. Do know that *vocation* is a big word in Lutheran circles. It translates the concept of being called and of calling into various zones of extraordinary and ordinary life. Not all readers will care about all the biographies on these pages. But concretely these essays embody and exemplify various ways of responding to a call, finding a vocation. Something the authors hope every student, every faculty member and staffer, every alumnus and alumna, keeps on doing all his or her days.

But don't let me keep you longer. Let the authors make their observations and state their case.

INTRODUCTION

Pamela Schwandt

Ed Sövik, the distinguished architect and one of the contributors to this volume, has described how his firm approached the remodeling of Old Main seventeen years ago. They did the interior renovation in careful period detail, and today the whole is one of the jewels of the campus. In 1877 the interior had been built very plainly, with no frills and few decorative elements; the fledgling school had no money to spare. Pastor Bernt Julius Muus, however, paid the contractor fifty dollars extra to build the foundations of The Main two feet down into the solid sandstone "so that it can withstand the ravages of time." The sturdy brick structure erected on those foundations withstood those ravages well and was a good candidate for renovation, according to Ed Sövik. He said that in the 1982 remodeling "our job was to figure out what those original builders would have done with the place if they had more money and better technology."

This book arose out of a comparable concern for foundations and for the remodeling that takes place daily on any college campus, through hap or intention, a cumulative remodeling that can quickly alter the original shape of the school beyond recognition. In the summer of 1995, a group of St. Olaf faculty members attended a conference supported by the Evangelical Lutheran Church in America and titled "The Vocation of a Lutheran College." As a result of the discussion at that conference and later, they established the St. Olaf Forum, designed to foster campus conversation about the importance of the college's religious heritage for its academic work. They were concerned about changes in the faculty at St. Olaf in recent decades, many of whom had no experience with church-related higher education. That year the St. Olaf Forum sponsored faculty discussions with visiting scholars who had written on the subject of church-related colleges, and the next year they established a mentoring program between old and new faculty, which was paid for by a grant from the Lilly Fellows Program at Valparaiso University. That grant also included a plan for commissioning four to six essays about the mission and heritage of St. Olaf. These essays were to be bound into a pamphlet that could be presented to new faculty and administrators. Gary De Krey and DeAne Lagerquist, who wrote the grant, asked me to edit the pamphlet. Early in 1997 the essays were commissioned, but by then the plan had begun to expand. It slowly metamorphosed into a book of essays in four distinct parts, each of them exploring a question about the college.

"Part I: The Living Tradition" contains the four essays originally conceived as a separate pamphlet and attempts to answer the question: "What is the religious, ethnic, and historical background of St. Olaf?" In the first essay, Walter C. Sundberg writes about the origins of Luther's reformation of the Church, about the doctrines and beliefs that distinguish Lutherans from other Christian denominations, and about those that most Christians hold in common. In the second essay, Darrell Jodock explores the relationship between Luther's ideas about education and the many liberal arts colleges founded by Lutherans in America. In the third essay, Michael B. Aune writes about the contending ideas among Norwegian American Lutheran synods that form a background to the founding of St. Olaf and its early years: questions about the kind of education their colleges should offer to young people and its purpose, about the desirable degree of secularity and ethnicity in them, about the effects of Americanization on ethnic and religious identity, questions that still have currency for newly arrived immigrants to this country. In the last essay in this section, Robert L. Nichols writes about changes he has observed at St. Olaf over the past quarter century he has been teaching here, changes in the relationship between college, church, and world.

In "Part II: Biography" eleven writers offer short essays on a variety of people who have left their distinctive mark on today's St. Olaf College. These include administrators such as President Lars W. Boe and Dean of Women Gertrude Hilleboe; faculty members such as F. Melius Christiansen, Ole Rølvaag, E. O. Ellingson, Agnes Larson, Ade Christenson, Arne Flaten, and Harold Ditmanson, who shaped departments or institutions for which the college is renowned; and John Berntsen, the groundskeeper and steward of campus upkeep and beauty for more than half a century. Because the list of people whose biographies might be included in this section was impossibly long, we decided on two criteria for inclusion: those who were no longer alive and those whose names have been given to places on the campus, thinking that for newcomers this brief list might be configured into a map and become an introductory history of the college. After we had narrowed our list to ten, we realized that if we stuck to our original rules, there would be a serious gap in the book. If we included only biographical subjects who were no longer living, there would be accounts of the St. Olaf Choir and of the Norwegian American Historical Association;[1] but there would be no account of another institution similarly unique to St. Olaf and of international importance, the Howard V. and Edna H. Hong Kierkegaard Library, or of its founders. They are very much alive and still translating from Danish to English, as they have been doing for sixty years. Our colleague Bill Narum put it this way: "You have to include the Hongs! Their work is known all over the world!"

"Part III: Vocation" contains eleven memoirs by a variety of people who have worked or studied at St. Olaf: by a former president of St. Olaf and by the academic dean serving now; by a woman who was interned in the Philippines during World War II by the Japanese and then served as a missionary to Japan for thirty years; by an executive in the health insurance and organ transplant industry who studied philosophy at St. Olaf and theology at Luther Seminary; by a songwriter and performer, by a high school English teacher, by a recent alumna who works in the college Admissions Department; by two teachers at St. Olaf—of piano performance and of American studies—who are still shaking their heads in amazement over the calling they have heard and followed; by two pastors, one who works with inner-city congregations, the other whose father and grandfather were pastor and missionary and who changed her career plans at least twice in response to a powerful calling. All these people describe the ways in which they see their lives of work and family as a calling to serve God.

In "Part IV: The Future" each of five scholars responds to the question: "How can church colleges best serve students in the present world, particularly a college with St. Olaf's history and background?" We assembled the essays for the first three parts (all of these about St. Olaf, written by people with ties to this particular college) and sent them to four scholars without ties to St. Olaf. They, along with our president, Mark Edwards, had agreed to read the manuscript and write essays in response. They all did their undergraduate work at schools other than St. Olaf, and three of them have spent most of their teaching careers at church colleges other than Lutheran. Robert Benne is Lutheran and now teaches at a Lutheran college in Virginia, Roanoke College. David J. O'Brien is Roman Catholic and teaches at the College of the Holy Cross in Massachusetts. Shirley Hershey Showalter and Keith Graber Miller are Mennonite and they serve at Goshen College in Indiana, she as president and he as a teacher of religion and philosophy. Nicholas

Wolterstorff is Dutch Reformed and, before moving to Yale University, taught for thirty years at his alma mater, Calvin College in Michigan.

Although the collection had expanded in size and so we imagined had its audience, we instructed our writers to keep firmly in mind the original audience for the essays, people newly arrived to work at St. Olaf who may have no knowledge or understanding of its mission and heritage. This, then, is how the book came into being.

I'll say a general word here about the writers, although a paragraph about each individual contributor is included at the end of the volume. We tried to offer a mixture of inside knowledge and outside perspective. Those who wrote essays for Parts I and IV do not work at St. Olaf, with one exception in each part; however, the three nonresident scholars in Part I, "The Living Tradition," all graduated from St. Olaf. Parts II and III, the biographies and vocation essays, are by people with deep roots in St. Olaf. The writers of the biographies have a connection to the subjects of their essays. They write about teachers, friends, colleagues, predecessors, or subjects of longtime research, and theirs is a labor of love. Every single one of these writers answered my request for a biographical essay with an immediate and unhesitating "Yes," and asked for details of length and deadline later. This connection, this readiness is true also for the two who contributed the map and the artwork for the cover.

Recently I read a sermon preached by a friend on Matthew 4:1-11, the temptations of Christ. After she discussed each of the three scenes in that text, she sounded the same note: "Jesus is not just saying 'no' to the tempter's offer; he is saying 'yes' to something more important. He is saying 'yes' to a relationship with the living God. He is saying 'yes' to God's mission for him." She underlines an unassailable truth that gets muted in the clamor of our lives, individual and institutional: that if we are to say "yes" to one thing, we must say "no" to another. We cannot have it all, and we cannot be all things to all people. The difficulty comes in understanding what "yes" correlates with what "no," in making first the connections and then the choices, in convincing ourselves that we really must choose. What is it that St. Olaf, a 125-year-old college of the Lutheran Church, can do best in today's world? How best can we now describe its mission? And in order to say "yes" to this mission, to what must the college then say "no"?

St. Olaf has always changed as its constituents and the world around it have changed. The editors hope that this volume might encourage members of the college to oversee its future change in the spirit of the Sövik firm's remodeling of Old Main, which reveals in visible, tangible form how a knowledge of the past can serve the present and the future. We hope the book might equip them "to figure out what those original builders would have done with the place" if they had been looking into the dawn of the twenty-first century.

NOTE

1. The Norwegian-American Historical Association early began doing seriously and methodically what other ethnic immigrant groups later realized they too needed to do: to preserve, classify, translate, and make available documents about their history in the new world, as well as interpret and disseminate the information. NAHA has become a pattern for other such associations. We asked Solveig Zempel to include some description of the beginnings of NAHA in her biographical essay of Ole Rølvaag. The contributions of Agnes Larson to this institution are also mentioned in her biography.

PART I:

The Living Tradition: What is the religious, ethnic, and historical background of St. Olaf?

1.
WHAT DOES IT MEAN TO BE LUTHERAN?

Walter C. Sundberg

Beginnings

Between 1450 and 1550, a series of events deeply affected the future of Western Europe. Among these were the invention of modern printing by movable type, the beginning of modern physics, the discovery of the New World, the establishment of sea trade with India and the Far East, the rise of ethnic and national feeling that challenged the inherited political arrangements of the Middle Ages, and the full flowering of Renaissance Humanism in Italy and its spread to the north.

In the midst of these tumultuous developments, the western church found itself in theological and social upheaval. The papacy had been held captive for political reasons in the French city of Avignon between 1302 and 1378. This situation led to the election of a rival pope in Rome. Between 1378 and 1417 there were two popes and for a brief period three popes. Critics of the church such as John Wycliffe (1329–1384) in England asserted that the very principle of the clerical hierarchy was unscriptural and therefore false. In Bohemia, Jan Hus (1373–1415) was burned at the stake because he condemned ecclesiastical corruption. As the sixteenth century began, the authority of the Roman Catholic Church was at a low ebb. The decisive attack came from an unexpected quarter: an obscure monk and theological professor in the Electorate of Saxony named Martin Luther (1483–1546).

The catalyst for Luther's rebellion was Roman Catholic teaching concerning indulgences, a widespread practice in the church that requires explanation. In the age of faith that came before modern Europe, people believed intensely in the threat of divine judgment. Jesus' admonition, "Repent for the kingdom of heaven is at hand" (Matthew 4:17), was taken with the utmost seriousness. To obey Christ's command, the church obligated Christians to avail themselves of the sacrament of penance at least once a year. In making penance, believers would lay bare their souls before a priest in confession, receive absolution or forgiveness, which only the priest could grant, and then carry out the duty of satisfaction by performing certain works to atone for sin. These works could be done while one lived on earth. They were also undertaken, according to Catholic teaching, after death, as one's soul was purged of sin in Purgatory.

The practice of penance slowly got out of control. People became obsessed with the details of their errant behavior. They correlated sins and satisfactions. The gift of forgiveness was quantified. Perhaps most dangerously of all, the church came to believe that priestly mediation of forgiveness was the exclusive means of divine grace.

The practice of penance led to extreme behavior. Some Christians adopted harsh, disciplined lives, punishing their bodies. Others would make long pilgrimages to churches all over Europe to worship relics from the Holy Land. Many believed that the best way to please God was to retreat from the world into the cloister.

The average believer refused to renounce the world for a monastery or undertake a costly pilgrimage to a distant shrine. However, the quantitative definition of grace implied by the doctrine of penance opened the possibility of placing a cash value on forgiveness. In this context the practice of indulgences became popular. The church taught that believers could pay for satisfaction with money instead of deeds. The priestly hierarchy encouraged indulgences to pay for its ambitious building programs, the chief of which was the construction of St. Peter's in Rome. Using high-powered salesmen such as the infamous Dominican monk Johannes Tetzel (1465–1519), the church claimed:

As soon as the coin in the coffer rings,
The soul from purgatory springs.

The monk Martin Luther attacked indulgences in his "95 Theses" of October 31, 1517. In the "Theses," Luther calls religious salesmen like Tetzel "hawkers who cajole money" (Thesis 51).[1] Luther knew that in the desire to fill the coffers of the church, the word of God was being distorted. He declared: "The true treasure of the church is the most holy gospel of the glory and grace of God" (Thesis 62). Against indulgences Luther asserted that it is the gospel alone that forgives and makes free:

> Any truly repentant Christian has a right to full remission of penalty and guilt, even without indulgence letters.
> Any true Christian, whether living or dead, participates in all the blessings of Christ and the church; and this is granted him by God, even without indulgence letters. (Theses 36 and 37)

Luther called into question a church authority that would seek, for the sake of money, to restrict the declaration of the grace that comes from God alone:

> The unbridled preaching of indulgences makes it difficult even for learned men to rescue the reverence which is due the pope from the slander or from the shrewd questions of the laity. Such as: "Why does not the pope empty purgatory for the sake of the holy love and the dire need of the souls that are there if he redeems an infinite number of souls for the sake of miserable money with which to build a church? The former reasons would be most just; the latter is most trivial." (Theses 81 and 82)

Luther's posting of the "95 Theses" was a courageous act of a person of faith willing to take on the teaching of the church for the sake of what he believed to be authentic Christian faith. Within three weeks, the "95 Theses" were copied and distributed throughout German lands.

"Angels" of Authority

It was Luther's attack on the authority of the priesthood that made him a schismatic and heretic in the eyes of the Roman church. Luther believed, according to Scripture, that, "even if we, or an angel from heaven, should preach to you a gospel contrary to that which we preached to you, let him be accursed" (Galatians 1:8). The gospel of Jesus Christ is its own authority. No matter how impressive the spokesman for the gospel may seem to be—even if it is an angel!—our allegiance should not be given uncritically or automatically. The only authority that ultimately matters is the content of the gospel. All else is secondary. Luther sought to obey this radical admonition of Scripture in all matters. Commenting on I John 1:5 ("This is the message we have heard from him and proclaim to you, that God is light and in him is no darkness at all"), Luther expresses his conviction bluntly: "What is not Christ is not light. As often as I hear 'the fathers, Augustine, Jerome, the councils,' I ask: 'Is there also a proclamation?' If not, I say: 'Be off!' "[2]

This stance separated Lutherans from the Roman Catholic Church in no uncertain terms. Catholicism claimed that the hierarchy of the priesthood centered in the office of bishop and especially that the papacy is the guarantee to orthodox Christian faith; that the pope is the Vicar of Christ on earth; that the priesthood, obedient to the papacy, receives its authority from the Apostle Peter whom Jesus called the "rock" (Matthew 16:16-20). To Luther, this was a false reading of Scripture. The gospel is never a matter of human jurisdiction. Christ's word is not physically represented by a male priesthood. If it were, then the church would be built on sand. Peter denied the Lord and disobeyed him; so have Christians down through the ages. The only true "rock" is Christ himself (1 Corinthians 10:4). He alone died for our sins and reconciles us to the Father. He needs no other representatives than his word and sacraments of Baptism and the Lord's Supper. This Christ is the "living stone, though rejected by mortals yet chosen and precious in God's sight" (1 Peter 2:4). It is Christ who, by faith, makes all of us, male and female, "like living stones . . . built into a spiritual house, to be a holy priesthood, to offer spiritual sacrifices acceptable to God" (2:5). The church does indeed have an important focus in a priesthood. But it is a priesthood of all believers directly subject to the gospel.

In the earliest years of the Reformation, Luther found himself in conflict not only with Rome but also with "radical reformers" who taught that the true community of faith is made up of believers who experience personal conversion. These reformers taught a wide variety of doctrines, the effect of which was to exhort Christians to make a self-conscious commitment to Christ that expresses itself in outward behavior. Some insisted that Baptism is for adults, not infants, because only an adult can make a responsible decision for Christ. Others placed special emphasis on the gift of speaking in tongues, interpreting this gift as a necessary sign of new life in the Holy Spirit. Some stressed that moral discipline is not only the fruit of faith, but the necessary proof that faith is genuine. Luther argued that the general effect of these teachings is to bind faith to certain works. These works become the "angels" of authority.

Personal Faith and the Doctrine of Justification

Against the teachings of such radical reformers, Lutherans affirm infant Baptism as the divine tradition of the church. They reject reliance on outward works as means of faith. This does not mean that Lutherans are indifferent to the notion that faith involves personal commitment to the Lord and obedience to his teaching. One cannot be a Christian simply by attending worship and engaging in the ritual performance of the sacraments. Commenting on John 15:10 ("If you keep my commandments, you will abide in my love"), Luther writes:

> It behooves everyone to search his heart and examine himself. Let no one bank on thoughts like these: "I am baptized and am called a Christian. I hear God's Word and go to the Sacrament." For here Christ Himself separates the false Christians from those who are genuine, as if He were saying: "If you are true believers in Me and are in possession of My treasure, it will surely become evident that you are My disciples. If not, do not

> imagine that I will acknowledge and accept you as My disciples. You will never cheat and deceive any but yourselves—to your eternal shame and harm. Christ and the Gospel will surely not be cheated and defrauded."
>
> Christ found this admonition necessary, and it must constantly be repeated in Christendom, because we see that there are always many Christians of this sort among us. Christ is determined not to have or to acknowledge any false Christians. In Matthew 7.23 He passes a terrible sentence on them, when He says that on the Day of Judgment He will address them with the words: "I never knew you; depart from Me you evildoers." Such false Christians would fare far better if they were heathen and non-Christians. Then they would at least not do harm to Christianity with their offensive example and would not disgrace and blaspheme the holy name of Christ and of His Word.[3]

Luther placed before believers the duty of explicit faith (*fides explicata*). A believer is called by the Word of God out of custom, lethargy, and formal obedience to a clerical hierarchy into the fullness of an individual relation to Jesus as Lord and Master. This is a personal faith. Nothing can substitute for it. Why? Because true religion has to do with personal faith; anything less is not religion. Luther makes this point most clearly in his famous exposition of the First Commandment in *The Large Catechism*: "Thou shalt have no other gods." "What is it," he asks, "to have a god? . . . A god is that to which we look for all good and in which we find refuge in every time of need. To have a god is nothing else than to trust and believe with our whole heart."[4] Whatever a person gives his whole heart to is religion. Anything less is not religion. Lutherans teach that a personal relationship to God involves the honest recognition that we fail to live up to our commitments of faith. Christian life cannot be realistically defined as uninterrupted progress in sanctification. Genuine believers fall into sin every day. This is why good works can never be the basis of a saving relationship to God. Our failure to obey God, however, can be an opportunity for renewal. Sin reveals a person's true self. If acknowledged, it can strip away illusion and pride. A person learns about weakness, vulnerability, and the depth of iniquity. He or she begins to know how much they need the mercy and understanding of others. The gospel proclaims that God accepts people despite their failed commitments. All that God requires is that we come before him in true repentance.

This is the heart of the teaching of Jesus. It appears in the parable of the Prodigal Son. The father in the parable accepts his wayward son, returned in repentance from "a far country" where he has squandered his birthright. He accepts his son despite his failure. Indeed, before his son has even reached the house, "his father saw him and had compassion, and ran and embraced him and kissed him" (Luke 15:20). The gospel teaches that God forgives us even though we fail him. Through the atonement of his Son, he receives us: "And Jesus said, 'Father forgive them; for they know not what they do'" (Luke 23:34). If we turn to God in our plight, he will turn to us. We have a place to go. God rejoices in our homecoming.

This is a joyous message. But there are those who find it hard to receive. The elder brother in the parable cannot comprehend his father's lavish attention to the prodigal son (Luke 15:25-30). While he too must have made mistakes in life, he remembers only his accomplishments: "'Lo, these many years I have served you, and I never disobeyed your command'" (v. 29). Thus, "he was angry and refused to go in" (v. 28).

Like the elder brother, all of us tend to link our identity as individuals to our accomplishments. We follow the custom of society to admire those who are successful. We want success. We desire recognition and reward for our works. This viewpoint encourages us to forget our failures all too quickly. It makes us judge others harshly. Most seriously of all, it prevents us from recognizing our dependence on God.

To understand ourselves as prodigal sons and not as elder brothers is essential to the task of Christian proclamation. It is judged by Lutherans to be of the greatest importance. In theological terms, Lutherans define the error illustrated by the elder brother as "works righteousness." They oppose to it the insight of the prodigal son that divine grace extends to the ungodly through Jesus Christ. This teaching they call "justification by grace through faith." In their primary confessional document, the Augsburg Confession from the year 1530, this teaching is described as follows:

> It is also taught among us that we cannot obtain forgiveness of sin and righteousness before God by our own merits, works, or satisfactions, but that we receive forgiveness of sin and become righteous before God by grace, for Christ's sake, through faith, when we believe that Christ suffered for us and that for his sake our sin is forgiven and righteousness and eternal life are given to us. For God will regard and reckon this faith as righteousness. . . .[5]

The teaching of justification by grace through faith is expressed here in official doctrinal language of the church. It is ultimately grounded in the New Testament. It is the central teaching of Lutheranism: that which gives this particular church a reason for being among the churches of Jesus Christ. Without the teaching of justification, there would be no reason for the Lutheran church to exist as a separate denomination.

Lutherans in the Catholic Tradition

Lutherans regard themselves as part of the "great unanimity"[6] of Christianity through the ages. They hold a number of central teachings in common with the vast majority of other Christian churches—teachings about Scripture, the Trinity, the sacraments, and love for the neighbor—although not all Christian churches interpret these teachings exactly alike.

Scripture: Lutherans believe "that the prophetic and apostolic writings of the Old and New Testaments are the only rule and norm according to which all doctrines and teachers alike must be appraised and judged."[7] Lutherans understand the Bible to be the "word of God." Following the Bible, they commonly speak of the word of God in three senses. The word is first of all Jesus Christ himself who was "in the beginning . . . with God" and "was God" (John 1:1). This same word "became flesh and dwelt among us" (v. 14). Second, the word of God is the written Bible, the sixty-six books of the Old and New Testaments. The Bible ensures the accuracy and fidelity of the church to the gospel. It protects the people of God from false teaching, cultural accommodation, and subjectivity. It also tells them the rich and various story of God's work of salvation. The Bible is the record of divine revelation. It is the final authority for all preaching and teaching. No doctrine, tradition, priest, or self-anointed evangelist supplements it or overrules it. Hence the meaning of the Reformation slogan, *sola scriptura*: Scripture alone!

Third, the word of God is the message about Jesus Christ, his life, death, and resurrection, which is the subject of the New Testament and to which the Old Testament bears witness as it recounts God's work of salvation among the people Israel. In this sense, the "word of God" means the same as the "gospel": the good news of Jesus Christ which is proclaimed by believers (see 1 Peter 1:24-25; Philippians 1:12-14). It is of the essence of the word of God in this sense to be spoken. It must be preached and heard, taught and learned, prayed and sung. It is not to be confined to the letter of written documents or the wooden repetition of memorized verses.

This third sense of the word of God as spoken is especially important for Lutherans. Jesus and the apostles were above all public proclaimers. Certainly they drew upon the written scriptures of the time (that is, the Old Testament) but they did so in living speech. As Luther puts it:

> In the New Testament, preaching must be done orally and publicly, with the living voice, to produce in speech and hearing what prior to this lay hidden in the letter and secret vision. . . . That is why Christ did not write his doctrine himself, as Moses did his, but transmitted it orally, and also

> commanded that it should be orally continued giving no command that it should be written.

Luther derives a lesson from this fact:

> So it is not at all in keeping with the New Testament to write books on Christian doctrine. Rather in all places there should be fine, goodly, learned, spiritual, diligent preachers without books, who extract the living word from the old Scripture and unceasingly inculcate it into the people, just as the apostles did. For before they wrote, they first of all preached to the people by word of mouth and converted them, and this was their real apostolic and New Testament work.[8]

This sense of the word of God, coming out of the meaning of Scripture itself, protects Lutherans from the danger of an inflexible biblicism. God's word is a light that must shine anew. It must be proclaimed to every generation in a living voice that is in dialogue with history and culture.

The Trinity: Lutherans confess the Trinitarian faith of the "one, holy, catholic, and apostolic" church. They call God "Father, Son, and Holy Spirit." This is the name of God which Jesus exhorts Christians to proclaim in Baptism as disciples are made (Matthew 28:19). Lutherans, like most Christian churches, profess the standard of faith as established in the Apostles', Nicene, and Athanasian Creeds.

The Sacraments: Lutherans receive the sacraments of Baptism and the Lord's Supper. Sacraments are specific, external signs that convey divine grace instituted by Christ himself. The sacraments employ the common elements of water, bread, and wine transformed by the word of God into means of salvation.

Baptism is the entrance way into the church. Following ancient Christian practice, Lutherans baptize infants, interpreting this act as an appropriate symbol of the priority of God's work of salvation in the life of each believer through the Holy Spirit. God saves us; we do not save ourselves. Baptism begins the journey of faith and it is to be acknowledged daily in the Christian life as a comfort to the repentant sinner:

> To appreciate and use Baptism aright, we must draw strength and comfort from it when our sins or conscience oppress us, and we must retort, "But I am baptized!" and if I am baptized, I have the promise that I shall be saved and have eternal life, both in soul and body.[9]

Christ also instituted the Lord's Supper "on the night when he was betrayed" (1 Corinthians 11:23). The Lord's Supper is the true body and blood of Christ given in sacrifice for us beginning on that night long ago. It nourishes the repentant believer throughout life, bringing the assurance of forgiveness of sins and the presence of God in what is often a dark and hostile world.

Preaching the gospel and receiving the sacraments is the work of the church. Where gospel and sacraments are done, there the church is to be found. According to the Augsburg Confession:

> For the true unity of the church it is enough to agree concerning the teaching of the Gospel and the administration of the sacraments. It is not necessary that human traditions or rites and ceremonies, instituted by men, should be alike everywhere.[10]

This definition of the church is truly ecumenical. The church does not need a certain sign on the door. It does not need a specific form of church government. The church is the word of God, the sacraments of Baptism and the Lord's Supper, and sinners seeking God's grace.

Love for the Neighbor: In solidarity with all Christians, Lutherans declare that true faith is active in love for the neighbor. As Jesus sought the outcast and outsider in his ministry, so the church seeks them in its ministry. The church is called to serve people in human as well as spiritual needs. Luther explains this responsibility in no uncertain terms in his exposition of the Fifth Commandment—"Thou shalt not kill"—in his *Large Catechism*:

> this commandment is violated not only when a person actually does evil, but also when he fails to do good to his neighbor, or, though he has the opportunity, fails to prevent, protect, and save him from suffering bodily harm or injury.[11]

Often the best way to serve the neighbor is through the callings or vocations that we hold. Our secular occupations and tasks are ordained by God to serve his purposes of justice and order. While social responsibility is vital to the life of the church, Lutherans do not commonly advocate a particular political party or ideology. The kingdom of Christ and the kingdoms of the world do not combine in such a way that a political party or legislative program can claim to represent Christ's will and thus demand a Christian's allegiance. No matter what our political point of view, what is important is the motivation that determines our social engagement. Christians are called to love the neighbor. "Truly I say to you, as you did it to one of the least of these my brethren, you did it to me" (Matthew 25:39).

There are 220 Lutheran churches worldwide with a total membership of approximately 60 million people. The largest concentration of Lutherans is in Europe (38 million). The single largest Lutheran church is the Church of Sweden (7.6 million people). Next to Europe, the United States has the most significant concentration of Lutherans (8.6 million) with the Evangelical Lutheran Church in America having the greatest share (5.2 million). After the United States comes Africa with 5.6 million Lutherans, the majority to be found in Namibia, Tanzania, South Africa, Ethiopia, and Madagascar. Lutherans are also well represented in Indonesia (3.1 million members).

What the future holds for the Lutheran tradition is unclear. Next to the Roman Catholic Church (1.9 billion), the Orthodox churches (174 million), the Anglican Communion (78 million), and Pentecostal churches (400 million according to some estimates), Lutheranism accounts for a relatively modest portion of the Christian population. The greatest threat facing Lutheranism at the present time is the erosion of membership in its home base in Europe, where secularization is an unrelenting force. The greatest challenge for Lutheranism is whether or not it can adapt its theological tradition to the dynamic religious environment in America, Asia, and Africa while retaining a hold on its historic identity as a confessional church.

NOTES

1. See Jaroslav Pelikan and Helmut Lehman, eds., *Luther's Works*, 55 vols. (St. Louis: Concordia; Philadelphia: Fortress, 1955–1986) 31: 25–33. Hereafter cited as *LW*.
2. *LW* 30: 226–227.
3. *LW* 24: 250.
4. Theodore G. Tappert, tr. and ed., *The Book of Concord* (Philadelphia: Fortress, 1959) 365.
5. *The Book of Concord* 30.
6. *The Book of Concord* 27.
7. *The Book of Concord* 464.
8. *LW* 52: 205f.
9. *The Book of Concord* 442.
10. *The Book of Concord* 32.
11. *The Book of Concord* 390f.

2. THE LUTHERAN TRADITION AND THE LIBERAL ARTS COLLEGE: HOW ARE THEY RELATED?

Darrell Jodock

In our day two difficulties beset colleges related to the Lutheran church. One difficulty is a steadily decreasing understanding of the educational-theological outlook upon which the colleges were founded. Previously it was sustained and nourished by the shared experience of Lutheran faculty, staff, and students, but such commonality is vanishing. Its disappearance is an unintended, and perhaps even unanticipated, side effect of the colleges' otherwise laudable efforts to diversify their faculty and staff. The second difficulty is a growing confusion among all constituencies, especially among students and their parents, about the character of the liberal arts. Frequently students and their parents see themselves as consumers. In exchange for tuition payments they expect to receive training and access to a better job. They do not expect to be engaged, transformed, or set free. Thus the threat is twofold: in jeopardy are both a healthy, deeply rooted identity and a lively orientation to the liberal arts.

Observers who lack the shared experience mentioned above often find the colleges related to the Lutheran church puzzling. They wonder why these schools have retained their ties to the church when so many institutions begun by other denominations have not. These observers tend to assume that a church relation is inherently stifling, since it yokes the college with a partner that is either anti-intellectual or authoritarian. Perhaps this assumption is what a student tour guide feared when responding to a visitor's question: "Yes, the college is related to the Lutheran church, but it doesn't make any difference." Well, does it?

We begin by asking: why have Lutherans prized education? After all, education is not a high priority for every denomination.[1] In the 1940s and 1950s, Amish parents went to jail rather than allow their children to attend school beyond the eighth grade.[2] Today neither Amish clergy nor teachers in their elementary schools have more than an eighth-grade education. This is not to say that the Amish disparage learning—only that formal schooling is not prized. Likewise, the Pentecostal tradition has often valued the gifts of the Spirit so highly as to make formal education secondary. Ordination into the ministry, for example, is usually not contingent on a college and a seminary degree.

Why have Lutherans valued education? One factor, although not the only one, is the character and influence of its founder. As a monk pledged to obedience, Martin Luther was sent by his superiors to earn his master's and his doctorate in theology.[3] Already a priest, with a Th.D. in hand he was appointed a professor as well. The reform movement which soon became known as "Lutheran" emerged out of the university. Not only were the famous "95 Theses" originally posted for debate on the bulletin board of the University of Wittenberg, and not only did the academic debates that followed form and shape Luther's ideas, but his ideas themselves were the product of an intense *intellectual* as well as a religious struggle.

Luther's religious difficulties are well known. While a monk he made diligent use of every religious practice available to him—chastity, poverty, obedience, pilgrimages, penance, communion, prayer, fasting, meditation, Bible study, veneration of relics—but he still felt as if he had not done enough to warrant the grace of God. He had, after all, been taught the theology of Gabriel Biel, which stipulated that the believer must *facere quod in se est*, must do whatever he or she could to please God, and only then would God's grace make up for whatever was lacking.[4]

Alongside this religious turmoil and intimately involved with it was an intellectual struggle; Luther noticed that Augustine (the influential fifth-century theologian after whom his own order had been named) had a quite different view of predestination than did Gabriel Biel. This discrepancy, so at odds with the medieval ideal of doctrinal consensus among the teachers of the church, intensified his study of the Scriptures and led eventually to Luther's exegetical insight that "the righteousness of God" was a gift rather than a demand. That insight was as much a scholarly discovery as it was a religious breakthrough.[5] Luther's teaching and ongoing academic research helped him refine this new understanding of the biblical message and work out its theological as well as its pastoral implications.

In addition to the character of the founder, another consideration should be mentioned. Lutherans have prized education because they are a confessional church. Their denominational identity is defined not by a particular structure (for example, bishops or papacy), nor by a particular set of rituals, nor by a particular piety or ethical standard, but by a set of theological principles. Those principles are enunciated in statements formulated in the sixteenth century, the most important of which are the Augsburg Confession and Luther's *Small Catechism*. In order to serve as guidelines, these confessional documents need to be understood, interpreted, and applied to changing circumstances. Moreover, the central element in this confessional identity is a distinction between "the Law and the Gospel," between a communication in the name of God that is received as a demand and a communication in the name of God that is heard as "good news"—that is, as a promise and reassurance of God's favor. Because the distinction has to do not only with what is said but ultimately with what is conveyed, the distinction cannot be captured in a formula. It must be discerned: theological, historical, biblical, and pastoral education is most often the best way to gain this skill of discernment.

All of this would lead one to expect that Lutherans value educated clergy and leaders, and this is in fact the case. Such considerations explain why Lutherans established seminaries and why they built academies and preparatory schools for clergy, but why did they establish colleges whose purpose included the education of laity? And why were church-related colleges a high enough priority that Lutheran immigrants in the United States started them very early—that is, while they were facing so many other pressing problems as they settled in a new land?

Their vision of college education was built on the foundations of a religious outlook. In order to outline that vision, we will identify a cluster of characteristics which, when taken together, suggest its profile. For the sake of clarity and analysis, these features will be considered separately, but they are ultimately all interlocking. None can be understood in isolation from the others, and no single feature by itself identifies a college rooted in the Lutheran tradition. Each is part of one overall vision regarding the character and purpose of education. All five are decisively shaped by the theological principles in which they are rooted, and each is influenced by *how* it interlocks with the others.

It will quickly become apparent that the characteristics are not themselves distinctive. They are shared with many other institutions of higher education. What *is* distinctive is their grounding. In what follows we will explore this grounding and point out its contemporary significance.

A college related to the Lutheran tradition exhibits the following five interlocking characteristics.

1. It serves the community and educates community leaders.

2. It strives for academic excellence.
3. It honors freedom of inquiry.
4. It embraces the ideal of the liberal arts.
5. It organizes itself as a community of discourse.

It Serves the Community and Educates Community Leaders

Some proponents of church colleges see little distinction between parish education and college education. On their view, the purpose of the college is to train adult church members according to a pattern of doctrinal formation consistent with the teachings of the church and a pattern of moral formation consistent with its ideal lifestyle. In other words, for them the college exists primarily to serve the church. As an arm of the church its purpose is to produce good, dedicated members.

Although one would not want to claim that these purposes are totally absent from the tradition we are examining, its emphasis clearly lies elsewhere.

Again, let us begin with Martin Luther. Seven years after the posting of his "95 Theses," he became concerned enough about the state of education in Germany to write an open letter to the city councils, encouraging them to establish public schools—not only for young men but also (amazingly for that day) for young women—and to establish libraries, even at great public expense. His priorities are evident in that open letter:

> Now the welfare of a city does not consist solely in accumulating vast treasures, building mighty walls and magnificent buildings, and producing a goodly supply of guns and armor. Indeed, where such things are plentiful, and reckless fools get control of them, it is so much the worse and the city suffers even greater loss. A city's best and greatest welfare, safety, and strength consist rather in its having many able, learned, wise, honorable, and well-educated citizens.[6]

A healthy community, he is convinced, needs "able, learned, wise, honorable, and well-educated citizens." His overarching concern is primarily the well-being of the community.

Luther extols the virtues of learning languages because they enable people to understand the Scriptures; in this way, clearly, education does serve the church and its purposes, but then he goes on:

> if . . . there were no souls, and there were no need at all of schools and languages for the sake of the Scriptures and of God, *this one consideration*

> *alone* would be sufficient to justify the establishment everywhere of *the very best schools* for both boys and girls, namely, that in order to maintain its temporal estate outwardly *the world must have good and capable men and women*, men able to rule well over land and people, women able to manage the household and train children and servants aright. Now such men must come from our boys, and such women from our girls. *Therefore, it is a matter of properly educating and training our boys and girls to that end.*[7]

The well-being of the community depends on having men and women who are able "to rule" and "to manage" and to discern right from wrong. The community needs educated leaders. In addition to helping people read the Bible and perform religious tasks, education so much enhances the good of the community that "this one consideration alone" is sufficient to justify its support.

Cannot then people train their own children? Yes, he answers, but:

> Even when the training is done to perfection and succeeds, the net result is little more than a certain enforced outward respectability; underneath, they are nothing but the same old blockheads, unable to converse intelligently on any subject, or to assist or counsel anyone. But if children were instructed and trained in schools, or wherever learned and well-trained schoolmasters and schoolmistresses were available to teach the languages, the other arts, and history, they would then hear of the doings and sayings of the entire world, and how things went with various cities, kingdoms, princes, men, and women. Thus, they could in a short time set before themselves as in a mirror the character, life, counsels, and purposes—successful and unsuccessful—of the whole world from the beginning; on the basis of which they could then draw the proper inferences and in the fear of God take their own place in the stream of human events. In addition, they could gain from history the knowledge and understanding of what to seek and what to avoid in this outward life, and be able to advise and direct others accordingly.[8]

The community as a whole will benefit if people understand the course of human events enough to "draw the proper inferences" and know "what to seek and what to avoid in this outward life." Such a contribution is one that schools can make and parents alone cannot accomplish. What persons educated at these schools need in order to serve the community, according to Luther, is what I would call "wisdom"—that is, the ability to make proper judgments, to deal with knotty human issues, and to discern what can be said or done to be of help to individuals and/or communities. Unfortunately, there is not enough time in one person's life, or even in two generations, to learn what is needed from experience; with the help of "learned and well-trained schoolmasters and schoolmistresses" wisdom needs to be gathered from the accumulated experiences of humankind down through the ages.

Not only did Luther himself indicate that the purpose of education is to serve the community; such an idea is also consistent with basic Lutheran teaching. One aspect of this teaching is a distinction between the "two kingdoms" or "two governances" of God. That important distinction also comes from Luther, who frequently identified two different kinds of ruling that are exercised by God.[9] One kind occurs in the gospel, when God shows mercy, forgives, and accepts an individual back into fellowship. Here the goal is personal reconciliation. The other kind of governance occurs when God works through social structures to bring order and justice to the world—when God works through governments, families, communities, economic systems, and so on, in order to restrain those who would harm others and in order to provide the necessities of life to all. Here the goal is justice. The same God is at work in both ways, so it is a mistake (regrettably not always avoided by those who have invoked this teaching) to separate the two, and it is likewise a mistake to assume that they translate easily into a simple endorsement of the separation of church and state. While not to be separated, the two governances of God are to be distinguished, lest one try to rule a country by mercy alone when compulsion may sometimes be necessary, or lest the gospel be perverted into a social philosophy.

In terms of this distinction, college education serves primarily the second form of divine governance. Its purpose is to enable young men and women to discern what makes for justice and what preserves and enhances human dignity. In fact, when asked once what I would most desire for every graduate of a college related to the Lutheran church, assuming the comprehension of some body of knowledge, my answer was, "A passion for justice." It was a Lutheran answer. The college graduate with a passion for justice and some understanding of human beings will make a significant contribution in his/her workplace, family, and neighborhood. Whenever this passion for justice emerges, a central purpose of education, as understood from the Lutheran tradition, has been served.

The principle that education serves the community is also undergirded by another closely related Lutheran emphasis: a sense of vocation. According to Luther, God's adoption of human beings is a free, unmerited gift. For him, the expected response to that gift is, yes, gratitude to God; but this gratitude, surprisingly enough, is not to be channeled directly into obedience, piety, and devotion to God but instead primarily into service to the neighbor. Luther does not intend for the believer to be "looking over his shoulder," wondering whether his/her actions are meeting with God's approval. Luther intends rather that the believer so focus on the needs of a neighbor as not to be thinking of anything else. The believer has been freed *from* worry about one's own status in part in order to be freed *for* a lively preoccupation with the person in need. Every child of God is "called" into this service. It can be exercised in a variety of ways, through parenting, through serving in government, through one's work (if it does indeed benefit the community; exploiting workers, customers, or the environment is not the content of a vocation!), through one's charitable activities, and so on. The Lutheran tradition directs the energies of believers outward. Thus, educating for justice is also educating for service. To educate for the benefit of the community is also to encourage a sense of vocation.

In passing, we should point out that the word *vocation* has recently been so corrupted that it is often used to designate a self-serving career. The latter concept is an expression of the prevailing ethos in America, which is individualistic in a way that the Lutheran tradition is not. A genuine sense of vocation, as understood above, is increasingly out of step with the attitudes and self-understanding commonly found in our society. To have a vocation is to see one's life and work as avenues of service to God, the community, and the world, not merely as ways to pursue one's own goals.

This section has asserted that the primary purpose of a college related to the Lutheran tradition is to serve the community and to educate community leaders. This characteristic is rooted in Martin Luther's own philosophy of education and based on two theological principles: vocation and the distinction between the "two kingdoms" of God.

It follows that a college related to the Lutheran tradition may serve the community—and often does so—by educating persons who are not themselves Lutheran. If its primary purpose were to train church members, admitting, educating, and graduating persons who are not members of its own denomination would be a shortcoming, but when its fundamental purpose is to serve the community, the appropriate benchmark is instead the number of wise, good, and able citizens of whatever religious background that it graduates. Its task is to instill a sense of the whole, to cultivate the priority of service, and to equip persons with wisdom as well as knowledge. Given contemporary society's propensity for individualism, instant gratification, and job skills, this is no small task!

It Strives for Academic Excellence

I begin with an observation seemingly some distance removed from academic excellence, but one that helps locate its theological foundation.

A basic metaphor underlies the whole of the Lutheran tradition. Rather than using impersonal images for God, such as "the wind (spirit)," "the force," or "the rock," Luther (drawing on the Bible) assumes that God can best be understood with images drawn from interpersonal relations, images such as "prince," "father," "bridegroom," or a neighbor from whom one is estranged. God's relationship with humans is of course not the same as that between two human beings, so these interpersonal images function as metaphors. Underlying them is a root metaphor that portrays and understands God as if God were a fellow human being with whom one is estranged and then reconciled, with whom one experiences the complex interactions of nurture and rebellion, of guilt and forgiveness, of fear and trust, of freedom and responsibility. To put this matter differently, for Luther and his followers Christianity is not primarily a set of beliefs or a code of ethics; it is primarily a dynamic set of interpersonal relationships, including a restored family tie with God, freely granted by God's adoption, and along with it a renewed kinship with other human beings. As specified in a whole series of concrete images, the basic conception of religion and of God's interaction with humans is interpersonal, familial, and communal; and faith is trust in this God, not the acceptance of church doctrines. Although Luther's approach has become commonplace wherever the Bible has exercised influence, it is far from universal and thus deserves our notice. One should add that nature is not excluded, for reconciliation with God and other human beings results also in a restored relationship with creation. As God's gift, the natural world is to be stewarded and tended rather than exploited or abused. However, even here the basic metaphor remains interpersonal and communal, because the stewarding and tending are undertaken in response to God and for the good of all. The personal rather than the impersonal has conceptual priority.

For Lutherans the priority of the personal gives urgency to academic excellence. Before explaining this point, however, let me make another preliminary observation.

Interpersonal relations are complex enough to defy straightforward definition. They invite seemingly contradictory descriptions. The pervasiveness of this basic metaphor has thus enabled Luther and Lutherans to affirm and live with paradoxes that have discomforted others. Luther could talk about believers being simultaneously justified and sinners. He could talk about God's being both hidden and revealed. Lutherans have even settled intense, long-lasting theological controversies about predestination and free will by saying, paradoxically, that *both* predestination *and* free will are right![10] Similarly, they have said, in the context of the Eucharist, that bread and wine remain bread and wine and yet, paradoxically, are also the body and blood of Christ. The list of such paradoxes could go on and on. All of these tensions have been possible because truth is measured not merely by abstract standards such as internal consistency but by its fidelity to the other with whom the community of believers has an ongoing relationship. Indeed, the truth of an idea or a statement is measured by its effect on relationships (God/human, human/human, and human/nature) as well as by its accuracy.

Lutherans live with paradoxes because for them reality is at root interpersonal and communal. Because ideas affect humans and their relationships, Lutherans also hold that ideas matter. Ideas mattered to Luther himself: one cluster of theological ideas confused his relationship to God, another set him free to "let God be God" and to feel that he "had entered paradise itself through open gates."[11] Ideas matter because they affect the way people everywhere are treated. It was, after all, a set of ideas regarding the inferiority of other peoples that prompted the perpetrators of the Holocaust to murder some 11,000,000 noncombatants. In the 1930s an idea regarding collectivization induced Stalin to starve out the Ukrainian peasants and not stop until some 3,000,000 of them were dead. A set of ideas regarding the "manifest destiny" of the United States prompted European settlers in this land to destroy Native Americans by the thousands. If someone gets the *idea* that the group to which I belong no longer deserves to live, my security is in serious jeopardy. Contrary to the contemporary attitude that sometimes unthinkingly declares one idea to be as good as another, ideas do matter. They matter because people matter.

If ideas are important, and if the purpose of education is to serve the community, then academic excellence is a priority. The college needs to strive to "get it right" in order to help people distinguish between what contributes to justice and what does not. In order to "get it right" academically a college needs at least to be solid or "good," but the standard I have suggested is still higher: a college should exhibit academic *excellence*. At stake in the distinction between solidity and excellence is leadership—leadership in the community and leadership in the academy. Such leadership involves a level of critical engagement intense enough to uncover new insights into our world: to uncover those as yet unrecognized developments that contribute to justice or to injustice and to distinguish, ever more clearly and perceptively, those forces that foster human degradation from those that support human dignity.

The assumptions of the culture in which a person lives are like the air that a person breathes; those assumptions affect us all in ways and on levels of which we are not conscious. It takes academic excellence to break through those assumptions and to challenge us to discern and face squarely their implications for our own lives and for the lives of others elsewhere on our planet. For this, it is not enough to be "good"; for this, academic excellence is needed. In the end, such excellence is important because and to the degree that it serves wisdom and because and to the degree that it serves the community, not necessarily because it meets the criteria that happen to prevail at the moment in the academy or in any particular discipline or profession.

It Honors Freedom of Inquiry

I begin with a reminder that the most famous of Martin Luther's teachings was his emphatic insistence on the free, unmerited character of God's adoption of human beings. God does not adopt humans because of their prior goodness or their prior faith, or because of their correct thinking or the way they have or have not subscribed to the status quo. Affirming such an unmerited adoption by God has several important implications.

One is a sense of humor—that is, a readiness not to take things *too* seriously. The unmerited character of God's favor suggests that humans should not take themselves too seriously (as if they possess some characteristic or quality that others do not), or take their politics, their economic success, their academic disciplines, their piety, or their theology too seriously—indeed, not even take the Bible *too* seriously. As much as Luther emphasized the religious importance of the Bible, he was quite ready to doubt that Moses authored the first five books of the Bible,[12] to call James an "epistle of straw,"[13] and to joke about removing James from the canon and replacing it with the *Loci Communes*, the exposition of Christian teachings written by his faculty colleague, Philip Melanchthon. His readiness to "play" with the canon reveals something of the distinctive flavor of the Lutheran tradition. Each of the things mentioned above—politics, economics, theology, the Scriptures—is important but not ultimate. A sense of humor means not regarding as ultimate anything of secondary or limited importance.

Humans who are gratuitously adopted can afford to be critical of every aspect of life. No "sacred cows" exist that are immune from careful scrutiny; everything is open for investigation. Traditional Roman Catholics get nervous when the magisterium of the church is investigated. Conservative Protestants get nervous when the Bible is investigated. There is nothing comparable that makes (or at least ought to make) Lutherans nervous if and when it is placed under critical scrutiny.

John Updike, raised as a Lutheran in Shillington, Pennsylvania, has given voice to this outlook:

> God is the God of the living, though His priests and executors, to keep order and to force the world into a convenient mold, will always want to make Him the God of the dead, the God who chastises life and forbids and says No. What I felt, in that basement Sunday school of Grace Lutheran Church in Shillington, was a clumsy attempt to extend a Yes, a blessing, and I accepted that blessing. . . . Having accepted that old Shillington blessing, I have felt free to describe life as accurately as I could, with especial attention to human erosions and betrayals. What small faith I have has given me what artistic courage I have. My theory was that God already knows everything and cannot be shocked. And only truth is useful. Only truth can be built upon.[14]

The divine "Yes" of the gospel sets people free to search for the truth, no matter how messy it may turn out to be. Because humans have no basis for any sort of claim on God, nothing needs to be protected.

No inherited ideas or practices are exempt from critique and evaluation. Religion itself can be critiqued because it is capable of getting in the way of the gospel, indeed even of becoming destructive of the very human dignity it was intended to preserve. The state can be critiqued. To the distress of presidents and deans, the college itself can be critiqued. Whenever loyalty to a learned profession gets in the way of education, it can be critiqued. Every area can be investigated. The results of such investigations may vary in value, but nothing stands in the way of their undertaking. The net effect is freedom of inquiry.

These observations about a sense of humor lead to another closely related implication. Because theology and religious practice cannot place limits upon the freedom of God's initiatives toward humans, a college with such a sense of humor is automatically ecumenical and automatically interested in interfaith understanding. Contrary to the prevailing tendencies of our society, however, this ecumenicity and commitment to interfaith understanding does not issue from indifference or empty tolerance. Religious differences are to be explored, not ignored, because they are but another way of understanding and serving the community. Although religious truth is important and God can be known, humility should prevail because the ultimate cannot be exhaustively captured in any penultimate formulation.[15]

Likewise, a college related to the Lutheran tradition appreciates both the sciences, as they analyze and investigate the world, and the humanities, as they seek human wisdom. Disagreements may abound and problems need to be worked out, but there is no fundamental conflict between science and religion when the teachings of each are approached with a sense of humor. Conflict emerges only when either takes itself too seriously.

Given the theological tradition which we have been exploring, freedom of inquiry is *possible* because no inherited ideas or practices are immune from critique and evaluation. Nothing in this world is so ultimate that it cannot be investigated and/or criticized. However, it is not enough to say that it is possible. Freedom of inquiry is also *needed* and should be encouraged. To discover the reason, we must refer back to our first characteristic: it is needed and encouraged *because freedom of inquiry serves the community.* The purpose of academic investigation is to discern how well individuals, institutions, or ideologies are serving the common good and to suggest and explore proposals with greater promise for improving the life of the community and its members. Thus the reason for the scrutiny, the purpose of the inquiry, is not to foster cynicism or to gain for the critic some elevated status as an "individual in the know." Criticism is not an end in itself but a moment in the quest for truth, for that which edifies and enhances humane living.

The framework suggested here thus provides for criticism a purpose and an urgency without prescribing for it any restrictions or limits.

It Embraces the Ideal of the Liberal Arts

In our day the meaning of the phrase, "the liberal arts," is often misunderstood. Many adolescents and others assume that it means courses taken from a diversity of disciplines, so that a college becomes a sort of academic buffet where one is permitted or even obligated to sample a certain range of offerings. Although liberal arts colleges in fact often do insist on some breadth of study and exposure to a variety of disciplines, the primary thrust of "the liberal arts" has nothing directly to do with diversity or distribution requirements. The adjective *liberal* in the phrase, "the liberal arts," means "freeing." The liberal arts are those studies which set the student free—free from prejudice and misplaced loyalties and free for service, wise decision making, community leadership, and responsible living.

Given the assumptions prevalent in our society, we must stress that the kind of freedom under discussion here is not simply an unencumbering of the student. It is not just a freedom *from* restraints that stifle individual liberty but also a freedom *for* creative, ethically sensitive, responsible participation in a community. The goal of the liberal arts is not simply self-expression but a kind of transformation—indeed, a transformation disquieting enough to be daunting for many students. Such an education endeavors to wean them (and their teachers!) from their comfortable, uncritical allegiance to societal assumptions and to entice them into both an intense curiosity regarding the worlds beyond their own experience and an intense desire to make their corner of the globe a better place in which to live. The student who is liberally educated is quite often a different person at graduation than he or she was at enrollment. Likewise, the teacher who is truly engaged in the liberal arts is quite often a different person than he or she was in graduate school. Because the goal is genuine freedom (which goes well beyond political freedom) and because people are not in fact free, accomplishing or approximating the goal involves changing people—faculty and students alike. The objective is not merely to "meet the needs of students" or to "help them achieve their own goals"; the objective is to set them free—free "from" and free "for."

Strangely enough, critics in his own day assailed Luther both for ascribing too little freedom to humans and for giving them too much. The first criticism came because he denied that persons were free or able to make themselves pleasing to God; hence he authored the vigorous defense of religious unfreedom found in *The Bondage of the Will*,[16] one of only two of his many writings that he thought deserved to be preserved.[17] The second criticism came because he objected to coercion in matters of the spirit[18] and granted the community of believers what critics considered to be too much freedom. Members of the community of faith, he thought, should be free to decide together the interpretation of the Bible, the selection of clergy, the choice of devotional practices, and the specific application of ethical principles.

The teachings that elicited the second criticism are of importance here. In his treatise "The Freedom of a Christian," Luther set forth one of his famous paradoxes: "A Christian is a perfectly free lord of all, subject to none. A Christian is a perfectly dutiful servant of all, subject to all."[19] The Christian is free *from* religious requirements imposed by anyone else but simultaneously free *for* service to the neighbor and the community. If the community needs a mayor or even a hangman, Luther recommends that a person volunteer. Service to the community has such a high priority that one should serve it even if doing so may threaten one's own moral purity.

> Therefore, if you see that there is a lack of hangmen, constables, judges, lords, or princes, and you find that you are qualified, you should offer your services and seek the position, that the essential governmental authority

> may not be despised and become enfeebled or perish. The world cannot and dare not dispense with it.
>
> Here is the reason why you should do this: In such a case you would be entering entirely into the service and work of others, which would be of advantage neither to yourself nor your property or honor, but only to your neighbor and to others.[20]

Luther was continually thrusting the people outward into the community. Their calling was always to build it up, to make sure that justice prevails and human dignity is protected. And, as can be seen in the passages previously cited from his open letter "To the Councilmen," he was convinced that education equips people to discern what actually does contribute to the well-being of the community.

If such is the freedom Luther ascribes to the believer, if Lutheran principles support freedom of inquiry, and if wisdom is the intended outcome of education, then it comes as no surprise that this tradition affirms the ideal of the liberal arts. That is, it endorses, as the intended outcome of education, the freeing of human beings.

Luther's references in his open letter to "the languages, the other arts, and history" that should be taught by "learned and well-trained schoolmasters and schoolmistresses" and to "the doings and sayings of the entire world" about which the students should hear suggest a study not only of human history but also of the geographical breadth that would today be called "global education." Included in his outlook is a readiness to explore all cultures, past and present, for any possible wisdom that can be found there.[21]

The purposes of education influence its character. If its purposes are informed by the ideals of the liberal arts, then the goal of teaching, of assignments, and of courses is not primarily technical training or the acquisition of a specific body of knowledge (as valuable as those may be) but instead the development of the student as a free person. The development of this kind of freedom includes the capacity to investigate, assess findings, and draw conclusions, the wisdom to understand their impact on human beings, a mature ethical sensitivity and understanding, an awareness of the importance of religion, a commitment to justice, and the developed ability to articulate insights in such a way as to be ready to manage and to lead.

Whenever "freedom" is under discussion, a word of caution is necessary. American society continues to be heavily influenced by an outlook, rooted in the Enlightenment, which ascribes to individual human beings a capacity not present in the Lutheran understanding. For the Enlightenment, individuals were considered to be isolated units. Each was free and able to decide for oneself what is true and what is right. Missing from the Enlightenment view was the profound disorientation which Luther perceived in human beings, his sense that humans who were "curved in upon themselves" would unconsciously distort everything to make it fit that orientation. Because those influenced by Enlightenment thinking have overlooked this disorientation, "setting free" for them has meant unencumbering instead of transforming. Also absent from this view has been Luther's profound sense of the community. For him the reoriented human was drawn into community not only as the arena of service but also as the arena where decisions could best be made and the truth could best be sought. Christianity, in his view, was profoundly corporate.

We are thus faced with two alternative visions of freedom. The one prevalent in our society grows out of the Enlightenment and emphasizes individual liberty and individual fulfillment. It can be expressed roughly as follows: freedom is the right to do as I please, and the purpose of education is to equip me to get where I want to go. The second vision of freedom grows out of the Reformation. Freedom, as understood here, has to do with how others are treated; it does not pull an individual away from community but instead draws that person into deeper relationships. In order to serve others, one needs to know and understand them, and this becomes the purpose of education. Because humans and human society are disoriented, the freedom to serve involves risk. The second view can be expressed in the following way: freedom is the courage to do what serves justice and serves one's neighbor even in the face of evil. (The word *evil* here refers to those societal forces that make doing what is right more difficult and more risky than choosing to go along with a prevailing pattern of injustice or acquiescing to the denigration of some other person or group.)

During the Holocaust the rescuers exemplified the second kind of freedom. Unlike their neighbors who thought they were free when they were not[22] and were merely following the "script" prescribed by Nazi ideology, the rescuers were genuinely free. They were free *for* the person in need. When asked to help a potential victim, they said "yes," even at great risk to their own lives. In other words, they exhibited courage in the face of evil. Nechama Tec, who herself was hidden by a Polish Christian family, has investigated the rescuers in that country and tried to discern what traits they exhibited.[23] Among the several that she identifies are "independence" (the willingness to take a stand different from the rest of the community), a universal sense of caring (responding to a human in need without regard to the victim's nationality, class, or religion), and a history of caregiving. Those who said "yes" to the victim at their door were not saying "yes" for the first time; they had developed a habit of helping others. Their freedom *for* service was not a random occurrence but part of a pattern which grew out of their ties with others. Because their freedom for service was communal at its root, it could be extended to encompass still others, even total strangers. The goal of the liberal arts should be to elicit this kind of courageous freedom!

When rooted in the Lutheran tradition, the liberal arts do not envision an association of isolated individuals each making up his or her mind, but a community in which humans grow into freedom by leaving prejudice behind and equipping themselves for service. Yes, individuals still do make decisions, but their decision making is not an autonomous pursuit of private goals but deliberations undertaken by individuals-in-community.

It Organizes Itself as a Community of Discourse

If the goal is the kind of freedom discussed in the previous section, then it is not surprising that the liberal arts college is a community. A person can gain new knowledge on one's own, by going to the library, for example, but apart from interaction with others one cannot be set free and cannot gain wisdom. In order to risk freedom one needs to be challenged and encouraged. In order to achieve wisdom, one needs to struggle with diversity in a communal setting where those who are different cannot simply be ignored or dismissed.

A commitment to freedom and wisdom thus gives support to the college as a community of discourse. Two other principles also lend support: an understanding of God's activity and a view of authority.

We have already noted the centrality of Luther's insistence on God's unmerited adoption of humans. Less frequently cited but no less important is the second of two central principles: his view of God as active and present. Let me call it "the incarnational principle" because it asserts that the typical way for God to work is through natural and human means. According to this principle the realm of the finite is not closed off and self-sufficient but open to divine influence. And God is not standing above the world, directing its affairs from afar and controlling what happens, but actively involved and at work right in the thick of things. Luther sees God at work amid ambiguity and conflict, even when God gets bloodied and dirtied in the process. However confused, confusing, and out of control the world may seem, God is nevertheless at work "in, with, and under" human agency to create justice and make room for human dignity. God is not restricted to the religious sphere but involved in every aspect of life—albeit often in a (seemingly) "hidden" way.

If one takes seriously this portrait of God, then one never knows where insights may arise. If, as Luther believed, God could be present in the womb of a poor, young Jewish girl and in a baby born in a stable, then one cannot predict where God will be found, nor can one predict where truth will be found. There is no pipeline that offers privileged access. For this reason the search for truth must be open, and it must be communal. Insight can come from the student as well as the professor, from literature as well as from biology.

Closely related to the portrait of God is another dimension of the Lutheran tradition—namely, its principle of authority. Authority belongs to the Word of God, but the Word is not merely a proposition or set of propositions; it is a living embodiment of the divine being in a person, Jesus, and it is the living voice, the spoken good news of what God has done. The Word is something present, something *happening*, happening *between* God and human beings and *among* human beings. How then can it be discerned? However helpful and important the Bible may be, that collection of authoritative writings cannot be equated with the Word of God.[24] However much an individual person may be able to discern, the individual cannot in isolation decide what is or is not the Word—if for no other reason than that the very character of a person's "world" may be challenged by the Word. However helpful a past experience may be, it is inadequate as a criterion, because the Word draws persons forward into something new. The authority turns out to be the community, but not the community in the debased democratic sense of mere majority opinion; rather the community *interacting*—interacting with each other, with the Scriptures, and with the traces of God's activity in creation as a whole. Amid that interacting the ordinary can occasionally be broken open and in its midst the transcendent glimpsed. Every person is a potential agent of that breaking open and is to be accorded the dignity befitting that role.

By analogy, the standard of authority in a college that affirms this tradition is also the community. No individual in isolation can know the truth, but the truth emerges amid the engaged deliberations of people. In order for this to be true, the members of the community cannot simply be engaged with each other, however; they also need to be engaged with something transcendent. The members of the community all wrestle with something beyond their knowing.

In a little book entitled *What Is God? How to Think about the Divine,*[25] John Haught calls this dimension "mystery." As Haught points out, mystery is not simply an unsolved problem or a question to which one does not know the answer. A not-yet-answered question is a "problem," not a "mystery." Problems (understood in this way) disappear once their answers are discovered; they decrease in number as knowledge increases. "Mystery," however, does not disappear; it grows along with knowledge. It is like the perimeter of a circle that gets larger as knowledge expands. Mystery is what a parent may feel at the birth of a child. All of a sudden, in amazement, one senses that this child who did not previously exist is now alive and is a distinctive person with identifiable features and a personality. If the newborn's parents were to know all the biology and gynecology and genetics and physiology in the world, they would still wonder at the mystery of what is occurring. Knowledge does not cause mystery to disappear. If we allow the scene to change, mystery is also what one experiences at the death of a friend or family member: what was a life is no more; a distinctive person with identifiable features and personality is gone. John Haught himself discerns mystery in the inexhaustibility of knowledge. Atoms were once thought to be the smallest of particles, but the more scientists learned, the more numerous the subatomic particles became. Similarly, the more they continue to learn about the universe, the more expansive it seems. Human beings are also inexhaustible. No matter how long and how hard one tries, one can never claim to have fathomed all there is to know about another person.

In a word, the principle of authority within a college is that community's interacting with mystery, with the great questions of "why?" and its endeavor to identify aspects of that mystery. Nothing external to that interaction imposes its authority on the search. The community itself needs to discover depth and beauty and truth and freedom and mystery[26] in such a way as to gain perspective and thereby be enabled to serve human beings and steward the world. The college is a community of discourse, a community whose members are interacting simultaneously with each other and with mystery/transcendence.

The college is a community *of discourse*, not only because interaction automatically involves words but also because its task is to educate leaders. If a person is to lead, normally that person must be able to articulate, to explain, and to persuade others regarding a course of action that benefits the community. And the wisdom to discern what actually does benefit the community needs to be discovered in dialogue, where the subtleties of evaluating complex human issues can be learned. Information can be uncovered by individuals, but wisdom needs to be sought together, and to be beneficial it has to be expressed in proposals which reflect thoughtfully nuanced principles and carefully crafted ideas.

The Lutheran tradition's understanding of freedom, its incarnational principle, and its principle of authority, considered together, suggest that a college founded in that tradition must be a community, a community whose members are engaged with each other and with transcendence. Such mutual engagement involves them in discourse, and such discourse equips them to lead. Participation in the search for truth is open to all members of the community, and no external authority determines in advance the outcome of its engagement with the truth.

The Colleges Today

We are now prepared to suggest an answer to a question voiced earlier: why have colleges related to the Lutheran tradition retained that connection? One answer is that this tradition so very profoundly undergirds the best aspirations of a liberal arts college. Instead of being at odds with those aspirations, instead of limiting or stifling them, it affirms, enhances, and deepens them. In other words, the Lutheran tradition challenges a college to become more deeply and more profoundly what it already aspires to be. For a college aspiring to advance the liberal arts, this tradition offers an understanding of freedom more profound than the one ordinarily found in American society. For a college aspiring to embody freedom of inquiry, this tradition offers a grounding more deeply rooted than affirmations of "freedom of speech" (however important such freedom may be). For a college aspiring to academic excellence, this tradition offers a rationale more worthwhile than institutional prestige. For a college professing to serve the community, this tradition offers a more profound understanding of what such service entails than can be found in dance marathons or other less self-involving charitable projects (as beneficial as they may also be).

In the college where I teach, I sense no inclination to abandon the church relationship. At root, I think the reasons are those mentioned in the previous paragraph, but they have come to the surface in interesting ways. In 1957, the college, previously all male, admitted women. It did so because the Lutheran church agreed to bail it out of financial trouble, *if* it went coed. (In this regard the college was, of course, well behind Luther's thinking and well behind some other Lutheran colleges in the United States.)[27] No one in the college today regrets *that* kind of church influence. In the late 1960s and early 1970s freedom of speech was a big issue. The church representatives on the Board of Trustees rose to its defense, endorsing the college's right to invite a series of controversial speakers. No one today regrets *that* kind of church influence. In the 1970s one of the supporting synods pressed the college to increase its minority enrollment. No one today regrets *that* kind of church influence. Why should one object to a church connection if it has the effect of nudging the college to become in actuality what, at its best, it aspires to be?

However, this is not to say that things are what they should be. At one time a college affiliated with the Lutheran church could coast along, safely assuming that the presence of faculty, staff, and students raised in the Lutheran tradition would be enough to keep its identity alive. Now, however, larger and larger numbers of faculty, administrators, and students have had no experience with the Lutheran tradition and do not understand what it has to offer. In order for these colleges to retain the advantages of a tradition that challenges them to become more deeply and more profoundly what they already aspire to be, the tradition needs to be articulated more clearly and affirmed more intentionally.

Does the loss of a shared experience mean that the colleges should abandon inclusivity and give priority to persons socialized in the Lutheran tradition? Under some circumstances, as a limited strategy, seeking Lutherans may be helpful, but I do not regard it to be the preferred response, because persons without such a socialization can and do catch the vision and embody it enthusiastically. What is more important is that the college's theological underpinnings be studied and understood and even celebrated so that its tradition and core identity can be reclaimed.[28] To move to the other end of the spectrum, does inclusivity then imply that faculty and staff of absolutely any persuasion be invited to join the community? No, because the identity of the college provides some limits. For example, a materialist who believes that all human actions are predetermined would have no reason (at least if he/she actually lives the philosophy) to teach in a liberal arts college, because for that person the ideal of freedom for which the college stands would be nonsense. Likewise, a person who was so ideologically committed to a particular political or religious position as to be closed to criticism and further inquiry would not normally find a place on its faculty.

In other ways also, not everything is as it should be. Societal pressures (individualism, specialization, and incivility) are undermining appreciative involvement in a community of discourse. Consumerism and careerism are undermining the ideals of the liberal arts. As fewer and fewer Americans participate in "secondary communities" where people meet face-to-face and as trust declines,[29] a sense of vocation and a dedication to the larger community are more difficult to inspire. In this setting, reaffirming the Lutheran tradition is not an endorsement of the status quo; it is a commitment to revitalize college education—to revitalize its resolve to educate community leaders, strive for academic excellence, honor academic freedom, embrace the ideal of the liberal arts, and organize itself as a community of discourse and to seek innovative ways to accomplish these goals. Amid the pressures of our society, reaffirming the tradition is a creative and a forward-looking task.

The Lutheran tradition lives with paradoxes and unresolved tensions. For a college related to the Lutheran tradition, one such tension is that between rootedness and engagement with the world. Things would be clearer if the college could simply endorse the assumptions of the academy (be they modernist or postmodernist) or could disregard the surrounding society and focus on preserving its own tradition, but the Lutheran tradition precludes either of those simple alternatives. It does so because accommodation leaves contemporary cultural fads and social assumptions uncritiqued, while isolation leaves the religious tradition unchallenged. The Lutheran heritage summons the college to work out the tensions inherent in a "both . . . and," *both* an affirmation of its own tradition *and* an engagement with today's world. Its underlying conviction is that the tension is a productive one—productive of insights that actually serve society, of insights that help foster social justice and produce free/courageous individuals, and of the kind of discernment that differentiates between what is humane in religion and in society and what is not.

Two features of contemporary American society affect the tension under discussion here. One is the tendency toward homogenization: the strip malls sprouting in the cornfields west of Chicago are indistinguishable from those being carved out of the mountains of West Virginia. Identical fast food can be found in restaurants along the interstate highways of the West and the South and the Northeast. Colleges contend with this pressure. In the face of homogenization, they must affirm their roots and their distinctive heritage, not for reasons of nostalgia but for reasons of serving the community with a more independent and critical voice. The other feature of contemporary society is a "culture of disbelief"[30] which so marginalizes religion as to create the impression that it is unimportant. Such marginalization occurs also in colleges.[31] Colleges can best resist this cultural trend by exploring a "third option" between the imposition of religion and its marginalization—one that reclaims its importance through careful, discriminating assessments. For much of the twentieth century Lutheran colleges, in some cases while emerging from an ethnic enclave, have stressed engagement with the world. In its day, that emphasis was appropriate, but in the face of the two tendencies under discussion, the task has shifted. The priority at this moment is a critical reappropriation of the tradition so that the distinctive voice of a college related to the Lutheran church can once again be heard. In order to preserve the productive tension, the tradition and core identity of the college need to be reclaimed.

Epilogue

The Lutheran vision was such that training would not do. Indoctrination would not do. Education was needed—education that would strip away whatever was false and whatever distorted human dignity, education that would edify, education that would free people from prejudice and ignorance and from taking too seriously anything that was penultimate, education that would free people *for* service and *for* doing justice, education that would not just serve the church but, even more importantly, serve the community.

And so, as Lutherans came to this country, they established schools and colleges. And the institutions of higher learning they founded were from the beginning (or soon became) liberal arts colleges dedicated to the pursuit of wisdom and intent upon developing, not docile followers, but community leaders in every avenue of community life. Each college related to the Evangelical Lutheran Church in America is an heir of this tradition. I can think of no better goal for these colleges than to reclaim the tradition and become more fully what that tradition calls them to be.

NOTES

1. On four separate occasions between 1995 and 1997, earlier formulations of the ideas in this essay were presented to various gatherings of faculty, staff, and guests at Muhlenberg College, Gettysburg College, and Susquehanna University. I want to thank those in attendance for the benefit of their questions, criticisms, and affirmations and gratefully acknowledge the hospitality of Chaplains Nadine Lehr and Christopher Thomforde. In addition, a special word of thanks to my colleague, Professor Nelvin Vos, for his initial invitation to discuss these issues and for his ongoing encouragement and counsel.

2. Donald R. Kraybill, *The Riddle of Amish Culture* (Baltimore: Johns Hopkins, 1989) esp. 119–140.

3. This "sending" contributed to his sense of vocation; he felt he had been called to become a teacher of the church and thus had an ecclesiastically endorsed responsibility to speak out.

4. Heiko Oberman, *The Harvest of Medieval Theology: Gabriel Biel and Late Medieval Nominalism* (Cambridge: Harvard, 1963) esp. 131–134.

5. The famous passage in which Luther describes this insight can be found in

his "Preface to the Complete Edition of Luther's Latin Writings," *Luther's Works*, eds. Jaroslav Pelikan and Helmut Lehman (St. Louis: Concordia; Philadelphia: Fortress, 1955–1986) 34: 337.

6. Martin Luther, "To the Councilmen of all Cities in Germany that They Establish and Maintain Christian Schools," in *Martin Luther's Basic Theological Writings*, ed. Timothy Lull (Minneapolis: Fortress, 1989) 704–735. The quotation is from 712–713. This open letter can also be found in *Luther's Works* 45: 347–378.

7. *Martin Luther's Basic Theological Writings* 725, emphasis added.

8. *Martin Luther's Basic Theological Writings* 725–726.

9. Luther, "Temporal Authority: To What Extent It Should Be Obeyed," *Luther's Works* 45: 91–93.

10. They did so in the Madison Agreement in 1912.

11. Luther, "Preface to Latin Writings" 337.

12. Martin Luther, "Table Talk," No. 4964, *Luther's Works* 54: 373, and Heinrich Bornkamm, *Luther and the Old Testament* (Philadelphia: Fortress, 1969) 193–194.

13. Luther, "Preface to the New Testament," *Luther's Works* 35: 362.

14. John Updike, *Self-Consciousness: Memoirs* (New York: Fawcett Crest, 1989) 243.

15. Particularly noteworthy in this regard are the words frequently uttered by the director of Hillel at the college where I teach, who tells Jewish parents that "this is a good place for your (son or daughter) to be Jewish, not *despite* its being a Lutheran college, but *because* it is a Lutheran college."

16. Luther, "The Bondage of the Will," *Luther's Works* 33: 15–295.

17. Luther, Letter "To Wolfgang Capito, July 9, 1537," *Luther's Works* 50: 172–173.

18. Luther, "The Freedom of a Christian" [also referred to as "The Treatise on Christian Liberty"], *Luther's Works* 31: 333–377. The reference here is specifically to 356–359.

19. *Luther's Works* 31: 344.

20. Luther, "Temporal Authority" 95–96.

21. Although Luther opposed some of the religious practices of the Muslims—practices which he sought to verify by examining the Qur'an—Luther refused to denigrate the Turks who at the time were threatening to overrun Europe. "Anyone favoring a military struggle against them," writes Luther, "must begin with prayer and repentance for Christian behavior worse even than that of the Turks" (171). "On War Against the Turk, 1529," *Luther's Works* 46: 161–205.

22. Cf. the words regarding freedom from the small-town lawyer, George Hanson, played by Jack Nicholson in the movie, *Easy Rider:* "talking about it and being it is two different things. I mean, it's real hard to be free when you are bought and sold in the marketplace. Of course, don't ever tell anybody that they are not free, because then they are going to get real busy killing and maiming to prove to you that they are. Oh, yeah, they're going to talk to you and talk to you and talk to you about individual freedom, but if they see a free individual, it's going to scare 'em. . . . it makes 'em dangerous."

23. Nechama Tec, *When Light Pierced the Darkness: Christian Rescue of Jews in Nazi-Occupied Poland* (New York: Oxford, 1986) 150–183. A summary can be found on 154.

24. "And the gospel should really not be something written, but a spoken word which brought forth the Scriptures, as Christ and the apostles have done. This is why Christ himself did not write anything but only spoke. He called his teaching not Scripture but gospel, meaning good news or a proclamation that is spread not by pen but by word of mouth." Luther, "A Brief Instruction on What to Look for and Expect in the Gospels," *Luther's Works* 35: 123.

25. John Haught, *What Is God? How to Think about the Divine* (New York: Paulist Press, 1986).

26. Cf. Haught's discussion of these concepts, each of which functions for him as a symbol of the divine.

27. According to Richard W. Solberg, Thiel College in 1870 was "the first Lutheran college to open as a coeducational institution and to maintain itself as such throughout its history." *Lutheran Higher Education in North America* (Minneapolis: Augsburg, 1985) 93.

28. In my experience these ideas can be understood and affirmed by persons who are not themselves Lutherans. I have in mind a colleague who is a Reform Jew, another who is an "ex-Roman Catholic," and a third who is a "lapsed Unitarian," all of whom have voiced such affirmations.

29. For an excellent analysis of the declining participation by Americans in social groups (from parent-teacher associations to bowling leagues) and the resulting decline in social trust (or "social capital"), see Robert D. Putnam, "Bowling Alone: America's Declining Social Capital," *Journal of Democracy* 6 (January 1995): 65–78.

30. Stephen L. Carter, *The Culture of Disbelief: How American Law and Politics Trivialize Religious Devotion* (New York: Basic Books, 1993).

31. One place where this point is discussed is in George M. Marsden, *The Soul of an American University: From Protestant Establishment to Established Nonbelief* (New York: Oxford, 1994) e.g., 433–434.

3.
"BOTH SIDES OF THE HYPHEN"? THE CHURCHLY AND ETHNIC HERITAGE OF ST. OLAF COLLEGE

Michael B. Aune

After a full day at school and immersion in an "American" world of children his own age, of learning, and of the English language, Peder Victorious Holm returns home to his other world of family, tradition, and the Norwegian language. This son of immigrants—the title character of the middle volume of the trilogy by the great Norwegian-American novelist (and 1905 graduate of St. Olaf) Ole Edvart Rølvaag—finds himself facing the conundrum of the hyphen.

> "I'll feed the pigs," [Peder] said quietly. This was his first utterance in Norwegian since he had left home early this morning; the sound of the words, the sight of his sister and his mother going about doing the work—as they had every day of his life—the sight of this room with all its secrets, obliterated in an instant the whole world in which he had lived so intensely during the day. Here was another world altogether. He had had the same feeling before, but tonight it brought with it such wonder that he had to stop to collect himself. Was it here he belonged, or was it out there in the other world?[1]

These restless and brooding questions concerning in which world an immigrant belongs were also faced by the founders of St. Olaf College. Unlike Peder Victorious Holm, however, who thought that the only way he could become an "American" was by discarding his cultural and religious heritage, those Norwegian immigrants who established an academy in Northfield, Minnesota, envisioned a form of education that could combine faithfulness to an ethnic/religious heritage and aggressive engagement with the American context. By serving the young people of the Norwegian-American churches in this way, they made a choice to be attentive to "both sides of the hyphen."[2]

Yet only a few short years after the founding of St. Olaf, someone observed that the school had become so "Americanized" that special prompting was needed to maintain a proper consciousness of its Norwegian roots. And just before the outbreak of World War I, Rølvaag himself wrote in exasperation that his work of teaching Norwegian language and literature seemed to be fruitless.

> I might as well haul manure. If nothing else, it would at least stink. I can scarcely see any difference between St. Olaf College and any other Protestant American college. What then do I have to do here? If we have no special mission, why do we exist at all?[3]

In this 125th anniversary year of the founding of St. Olaf, the questions asked by Peder Victorious and Rølvaag are as pertinent as ever. The present essay, therefore, addresses itself to the following questions: What might it mean to remember that St. Olaf College was established by Norwegian immigrants who sought to be both loyal to a particular ethnic and religious heritage and committed to an educational mission in America, especially in the current life of the college when, for a variety of reasons, it seems there is less and less connection to this history? What difference did St. Olaf's intentionally hyphenated self-definition make in its ongoing considerations of its aims and objectives as an American liberal arts college? And, finally, how is this distinctive heritage at all usable 125 years later for thinking about identity processes in which selves and communities can be reinvigorated and renewed?

Enabling the Stranger

Changes in both the composition of the student population and of faculty, administration, and staff make St. Olaf's ethnic and religious origins and heritage particularly puzzling, if not problematic for "newcomers." That it was established by Norwegian Lutheran immigrants is perhaps known to some. That it sought to provide an alternative model of education attentive to both sides of the hyphen—judiciously loyal to a Norwegian and Lutheran heritage and committed to an educational mission in America[4]—is not widely known, much less understood, even by alumni or donors.

The story of the founding of St. Olaf College, why and by whom, has been told on several occasions. These accounts are interesting, not so much because of their details but because of how they reflect evolving perceptions of the significance of the college's Norwegian origins and heritage. Historians point out that St. Olaf was established as an alternative both to the American "common school" and to an education that was concerned primarily with preparing clergy for immigrant Norwegian Lutheran churches.

On the surface, these details seem simple and straightforward enough. In the seventy-fifth anniversary history of St. Olaf, *High on Manitou*, William C. Benson wrote that the founding of the college "was a distinct venture by an immigrant group only recently settled on the frontier in south-central Minnesota . . . that would enable the stranger to find the kind of opportunity in America that he had hoped for prior to his coming."[5] More than three-quarters of a million of these "strangers" left Norway for the United States during the nineteenth and early twentieth centuries. And what attracted them were not only the prospects of economic improvement but also "the beckoning excitement of a new way of life, free from old institutions and class distinctions. . . ."[6]

Not long after these strangers began arriving in the Upper Middle West in the 1830s and 1840s, they, like others in the nineteenth-century United States, began to recognize the importance of education and the free public school as the key to opportunity and progress, both culturally and structurally. A vexing issue for any stranger who comes to the United States is that of becoming culturally and linguistically fluent "in . . . the skills required to succeed in the majority group's formal institutions and informal social situations."[7] At the same time, however, there was a concern for what scholars these days term "structural assimilation" as well.[8] A general and practical education was seen as offering equal opportunity to immigrants so that they could enter any available position in society. Depending on talent and education, they could, in principle, become anything, "from president to streetsweeper."[9]

Although these first strangers from Norway sent their children to American schools, a controversy developed in the 1850s over the kind of education that the young should receive. The Norwegian Lutheran clergy in particular questioned the adequacy and suitability of these public schools. They were regarded as "godless and ineffective."[10] Hence, congregational schools were organized "to safeguard the influence of the church, the Lutheran faith, and a Norwegian-American group identity."[11]

The "common school controversy" of the 1860s and 1870s indicated that there were a variety of attitudes toward Americanization in general. Some argued that the common school provided the young with a broad education that would make possible full participation in American society. Others objected to these schools, fearing the loss of both influence on the coming generation and of the mother tongue as "the language of the heart."[12]

Animating these controversies over education was the larger question of how to preserve and develop a living cultural heritage while at the same time adjusting to a different and changing context in the United States. In Rølvaag's *Peder Victorious*, cultural preservation is the task of the immigrant group while the mission of the public school, with its melting-pot ideology, is to make complete and full-fledged "Americans." Yet as we saw at the outset of this essay, Peder Victorious Holm experiences considerable confusion over living in such disparate worlds. Exacerbating the confusion is the fact that he receives basically no instruction about his own heritage and history. Peder is forbidden to speak Norwegian at school and is encouraged by his teacher to stop speaking it at home. Rølvaag poses the dilemma which subsequent immigrant generations confront—can an ethnic heritage be preserved or must it be relinquished for the sake of participating fully in American society?

On the one hand, it seemed necessary to provide a grounding in a churchly and ethnic community—its values, its religious commitments, its way of life. For some of the immigrants, this meant a kind of education geared more to the development of leadership for such communities. On the other hand, schools established by the immigrants needed also to include "a general Christian education, stressing the meaning of American citizenship and the importance of taking one's place as a Lutheran Christian in the social and economic community."[13] More radical was the realization "that the future depended not only on pastors but also on well-trained and consecrated laymen and laywomen."[14]

What emerged from these arguments over the purposes of church-supported educational institutions was known as the academy movement. In this context, an academy "is any school that goes beyond the elementary level."[15] With the reluctant recognition that a system of parochial elementary education would not carry the day, attention was turned instead toward the promotion of secondary schools in which religious and cultural instruction could take place within a curriculum of general studies. Here was an alternative to both the common school which lacked a religious/cultural emphasis and the parochial school which seemed intent on keeping the offspring of Norwegian immigrants in a churchly and ethnically homogeneous community.

The immediate origins of St.Olaf can be traced to this academy movement, as exemplified by the efforts of Pastor Bernt Julius Muus (1832–1900) to offer the daughters and sons of Norwegian settlers "a higher education than the schools of their home communities could give them."[16] In 1869, he established Holden Academy in the parsonage of the Holden church, which was located about thirty miles from Northfield.

The curriculum included religion, English, Norwegian, geography, arithmetic, and penmanship.

Though financial difficulties eventually brought the Holden educational venture to an end, Muus organized a similar school in nearby Northfield in 1874. Known as St. Olaf's School (named for Norway's patron saint, King Olaf Haraldsson, 995–1030), it opened on January 8, 1875, with thirty-seven students. St. Olaf's School was a radical departure from prevailing educational patterns that had existed among Norwegian-Americans. Its stated purpose was to equip and empower women and men for service and leadership in American society, making concrete the belief that Christian education was not something only for theologians.

From the addresses delivered on the occasion of the dedication of St. Olaf's School and other documents, we see how the distinctive aims of this educational institution were envisioned. First of all, St. Olaf was "to give the Christian confirmed youth of both sexes a higher education for the practical life than the schools at home are capable of giving" and "to exercise care for the pupils' moral conduct."[17] Unlike other schools established by Norwegian immigrants, therefore, St. Olaf was coeducational from the first day.

St. Olaf's was not simply a transplantation of what had been known in Norway, particularly the Latin school with its program of education based on the study of the classical languages and of the Latin and Greek writings of antiquity,[18] designed for the few who would go on to receive a university education. Rather, it explicitly emphasized the egalitarian development of moral character within the context of a Christian view of life.

Another distinctive aim to be mentioned (one which will be explored further in the last section of this essay) was the determination to preserve a valued Norwegian heritage and to offer it to a diversified American culture. At the outset, the intention of the founders was to regard this ethnocultural heritage as an opportunity rather than as an embarrassment. Norwegian heritage had something important to offer to the shaping of American society. Moreover, those students who had come from particularly "backward" and "provincial" backgrounds could be provided with what was regarded as a "refining influence" of Norwegian literature and culture.[19]

A final aim of St. Olaf's School, founded "for the sake of religion," as its first president Thorbjørn Nelson Mohn stated, was "to give young men and women a practical education on the foundation of Christianity."[20] Such a foundation, according to the Articles of Incorporation, while Christian, was also a specific Lutheran confessional form of the faith, to preserve them

> in the true Christian faith as taught by the Evangelical Lutheran Church and nothing taught in contravention with the Symbolum Apostolicum, Nicenum & Athanasianum; the Unaltered Confession delivered to the Emperor Charles the Fifth at Augsburg in Germany in the year of our Lord 1530 and the small Catechism of Luther.[21]

This assertive confessional stance, from our vantage point 125 years later, could be easily interpreted as the product of an insulated, unreflective, immigrant culture. Yet it is important to note that St. Olaf's purpose was not to specialize in the teaching of religion as much as it was to provide a place where faith and learning could be practiced together. Moreover, if St. Olaf could be a setting for a lively conversation between the arts and sciences and the traditions of Lutheran theology and practice, then both Christ and culture would be engaged. What made St. Olaf different from other schools "was the guiding conviction that what is good and true and beautiful, what the arts pursue and the sciences search out, is intimately bound up with the gospel of Jesus Christ."[22] Or, as President Mohn himself stated, "It is a noble work to lead man to truth, but it is more noble to lead him beyond to its source—the God of truth; for God is love, and man is blessed only when in communion with his creator."[23]

Not everyone, of course, was convinced. In the early years criticism was leveled at St. Olaf for departing from a prevailing educational pattern that had focused on the preparation of would-be pastors. While there was indeed interest in developing and promoting schools for equipping the children of Norwegian immigrants to become good Americans and educated citizens, the greater need was perceived to be preparation for theological education. Even on this point, however, there was conflict, rooted in the distinctive pieties, religious sensibilities, and theological orientations which first had existed in Norway.

Simply stated, this conflict was between those who desired a historic academic Lutheran tradition known as a Latin school education in the *studia humanitatis*—for example, the languages and sources of classical and Christian antiquity as a point of entry into biblical study, theology, and the ongoing experience of human history and culture—and others who desired what they called "the practical preparation of pastors" for the sake of free, living congregations in the United States. Previous educational experience in Norway prompted this latter group, led by Georg Sverdrup of Augsburg Seminary in Minneapolis, to associate a traditional course of theological study with an aristocratic class system and an intellectual authoritarianism which, in turn, tended to perpetuate the separation of clergy and congregations as well as to undermine the religious life. Sverdrup had arrived in the United States from Norway in 1874 and for the next thirty-three years, until his death in 1907, served as both a theological professor and president of Augsburg Seminary.

Interestingly and ironically, both groups had been decisively influenced by awakening movements in Norway which had emphasized the crucial importance of an "experienced Christianity" in the place of perfunctory adherence to a state church. Beginning with the activity of a young Norwegian named Hans Nielsen Hauge (1771–1824) who had experienced a watershed conversion event as a young man, a pietistic lay movement emerged that sought to renew Norwegian ecclesiastical, political, and cultural life. By the middle of the nineteenth century, this awakening movement had received an institutional sanction from a theological professor at the University of Christiania, Gisle Johnson (1822–1894). Many of the pastors who had come under his tutelage and then migrated to America to serve frontier congregations brought the Johnsonian emphasis which combined Lutheran orthodox theology "with a heartfelt religious sincerity, a penetrating logic, and a gift for the psychological analysis of the soul's religious life. . . ."[24]

The consequences of these awakening movements for how secondary and higher education should be approached are difficult to sort out, but a common thread seems clear. It was the desire to balance delicately objective doctrinal truth with subjective religious experience where life and intellect, head and heart, faith and belief were one. How that was to be worked out in actual educational practice on American soil ranged from Luther College's "classical" curriculum based on the Latin school of the Norwegian homeland to Augsburg College's basic philosophy of education which combined beginning preparatory, college, and theological studies into a single nine-year program of ministerial preparation. The view exemplified by the founders of St. Olaf envisioned hospitality to learning, creative engagement with the American context, stewardship of a Norwegian ethnocultural tradition, and a Lutheranism which refused to separate head from heart, faith from life. Such an educational institution was "unlike any then existing among Norwegian-Americans."[25]

Yet, it seems that the older associations of Norway where social class was connected with an educational emphasis in general culture prevented Sverdrup and the supporters of the Augsburg approach from understanding fully what St. Olaf's commitment to the higher education of both men and women for the "practical life" actually meant. Also, the political-ecclesial reality of the newly formed United Norwegian Lutheran Church in the early 1890s with its decision to make St. Olaf its college directly threatened Augsburg's preparatory program and its basic philosophy of theological education.

The form which the controversy took between St. Olaf and Augsburg supporters, however, was over educational quality and the place of what we would call the humanities in a more inclusive course of collegiate study. There was lively debate in the religious press over the nature of what constituted a proper ministerial and lay education. Georg Sverdrup of Augsburg stigmatized the St. Olaf curriculum as "humanist" and "secular." In a series of articles entitled "The Malaise of Humanism" which appeared in 1891 and 1892, he expressed his strong distaste for the Norwegian pattern of educating pastors.[26] He sensed that a college such as St. Olaf with its more general approach to education for consecrated laymen and laywomen somehow seemed to be repeating the mistakes of the Norwegian church whose ministerial training was ill-suited, if not irrelevant, to actual congregational needs.

One might be tempted to conclude that since Sverdrup and his colleagues did not get their way—that is, the opportunity to preserve a kind of theological education which trained future pastors from high school through seminary and made them ready and able to meet the peculiar challenges of the American scene—St. Olaf became the target of bitter criticism. Its "humanism" made of St. Olaf "a common secular college" unfit to prepare Christian pastors, or laypeople for that matter. Indeed, an education in this "humanistic spirit," Sverdrup argued, "led to aristocracy of spirit and to rationalism."[27] It also destroyed the spiritual life and created feelings of superiority. Sverdrup and his friends attacked St. Olaf for "its luxurious facilities, its doctors of philosophy, its masters of arts, and [its] deficits."[28] The retort of St. Olaf supporters to such allegations was to brand Augsburg as a "humbug" institution where piety substituted for intellectual rigor and scholarship.[29]

Lost in such rancorous exchanges was an educational conviction common to both sides in this controversy, the necessity of paying attention to a new and broader context of mission and citizenship. Yet Sverdrup and others seemed to advocate an either/or approach—either a school with a specific religious orientation or none at all; either a school for the preparation of future clergy or a school for the education of Christian individuals to participate as faithful persons in an American manner. St. Olaf, however, embraced a "both/and" approach. It did not preclude preparation for the ministry or teaching, but it also had an eye on a new and broader context where Christian faith could be put to work. This decision, as we shall now see, contributed significantly to St. Olaf's development as a modern American liberal arts college in the twentieth century.

An Unconventional Identity

A significant feature of the identity of St. Olaf College from the beginning has been its "unconventionality."[30] Although founded as an academy, St. Olaf would develop into a four-year church-related liberal arts college by the end of the nineteenth century. Surprisingly, however, it had no "official" church affiliation during the first fifteen years of its existence, though its founders had desired full recognition from the Norwegian Synod. When such support was not forthcoming, principally for financial reasons, the college went its own way. This lack of an official church connection fostered the development of St. Olaf's own educational identity as a "plain and simple" liberal arts college where the young people of the Norwegian-American Lutheran churches would be prepared for worldly occupations while nurtured in Lutheran faith. Finally, in 1899, the United Norwegian Lutheran Church decided on St. Olaf as its college. Thus began a period of transition in which the way was paved "for its significant contribution to the development of the modern American liberal arts college."[31]

The presidency of John Nathan Kildahl from 1899 until 1914 coincided with this period of transition. He saw as one of his principal tasks the enhancement of the liberal arts character of the college, even though there were still those who wanted its primary purpose to be for the preparation of future pastors. Kildahl, however, was committed to continuing and enriching the purposes for which St. Olaf had been founded—"championship of the liberal arts, the English language, coeducation, and religion."[32] The college was to remain an institution engaged with context and culture and offering an education "with which graduates could profitably enter many diverse walks of life, including the ministry."[33] It was the work of Kildahl and others that finally convinced the United Church that a good liberal arts education was of greater benefit than a more restricted mission of pre-theological training.

Evidence of St. Olaf's renewed commitment to providing an American liberal arts education can be seen in the gradual shift from a "classical curriculum" toward wider course offerings and the provision for an elective system. While similar shifts had been under way in other American colleges and universities since 1869, St. Olaf's curricular changes and expansion began occurring in the early 1900s. From a listing of thirty courses in the catalog at the close of the nineteenth century, by 1914 there were around 114. Departments which were added included Biology, Economics, Political Science, Sociology, Education, Public Speaking, Astronomy, and Domestic Science. The college's offerings were grouped into what we would today regard as a precursor of a divisional arrangement. One group consisted of language, science, and social sciences; another included music, religion, and philosophy. Requirements included physical education, Norwegian language, and religion. These curricular changes helped to make St. Olaf a modern liberal arts college.[34] And, at the same time, Kildahl "encouraged the faculty to become more professional, develop their own competence, and build their respective departments in their own way."[35]

It would take time for the college to establish academic standards, win status from accrediting associations, attract qualified instructors, and gain broader recognition. The clear intention of the school's founders to provide a place where a young person could be nurtured in both the traditions of the Lutheran church and all else that went with a liberal arts education also needed to be reiterated, especially in response to those critics who now thought that such an education would undermine Christian certainty. After all, the explicit identification of St. Olaf as a Lutheran college could not mean that Christian teachings were merely appended to a program which was virtually the same at schools with no explicit religious commitment. Christian faith was not simply some godly accoutrement tacked on to a secular enterprise. Rather, the aspiration of St. Olaf presidents and many of its teachers down through the years has been to articulate the relationship between faith and learning in such a way that the two have nothing to lose and everything to gain by being practiced together. All academic disciplines have their own integrity and value and are to be honored as such. These disciplines are seen, however, as integrally related to the goal of practicing Christian faith. That is, these disciplines, in concert, actively participate in the developing of a particular kind of person, one who pursues and searches out what is good and true and beautiful because God has made such things to be so.

Yet at various times during the college's history, it has been necessary to reexamine the faith–learning relationship, precisely for the purpose of articulating a more persuasive philosophy of Christian higher education. In the 1930s, the observation was made that Lutherans in this country had failed to develop such a philosophy appropriate to a Lutheran ethos. In 1950, Conrad Bergendoff, president of Augustana College at Rock Island, Illinois, raised this "disturbing question" once again at a meeting of the Association of Lutheran College Faculties. Why was it, he asked, given the number of Lutheran colleges in this country, that there was no clear or conscious statement of their nature and purpose? In addition, he raised questions about why Lutherans were engaged in higher education and what was the relationship between faith and this educational venture? A committee was assembled to consider these questions and thus began a ten-year study which included several teachers and administrators from St. Olaf. The outcome was published as *Christian Faith and the Liberal Arts* in 1960.

This book's response to the question of whether there was such a thing as a Christian philosophy of liberal arts education was both bold and confident. Professor William H. K. Narum, one of the St. Olaf faculty participants in these considerations, asserted that the study of the Christian religion, more specifically Christian systematic theology (church doctrine) and ethics, provided the integrative center of the liberal arts.[36] As "the basic human learnings," the liberal arts are "core studies" designed to teach one how to think and make judgments and to bring the mind into relationship with knowledge. These "core studies" guided the learner to "communicate clearly, to inquire accurately, to evaluate wisely, to understand synoptically, and to reason validly."[37] It is Christian theology, Narum concluded, that holds together this entire educational enterprise which is engaged in the study of all areas of culture, because theology

> is man's ultimate attempt to relate time and eternity, the profane and the holy, fact and value, etc. to each other in terms of the Christian Revelation. Theology deals with the philosophical questions of the origin and destiny of man and the universe, and answers them in terms of divine revelation. In this manner it trains the mind to see all things and all knowledge from a theological perspective, and prepares the way for that personal integration (the self and God in fellowship) which is superior to intellectual integration alone.[38]

This claim that Christian theology provided the "glue" not only to understanding the created order but also to understanding what the liberal arts seek to illumine was remarkable for its time. Four decades later, as the twentieth century gives way to the twenty-first, however, the landscape of Christian theology is much more contentious and contested. Many kinds of theologies call for our attention—revisionist, liberation, ecumenical, contextual, feminist, womanist, neoorthodox, gay, philosophical, to name but a few. There is also a good deal of suspicion about theology because of the stubborn pretense, still valued by some, to be as omniscient as the God who is the purported subject matter of the whole enterprise. Yet the importance of Narum's insight that theology addresses the whole of human experience dare not be forgotten. Whether it is recognized or not, the reality of Christian grace has already touched our experience of our world and of ourselves.[39]

Such a conception of theology, which both insisted that Christian identity is primary and so inquired how that identity was instantiated in the practices of a particular community,[40] emerged during a major review of what it meant for St. Olaf to be "a college of the church" undertaken in the 1980s. Harold H. Ditmanson noted that to begin with the proposition that St. Olaf is a college of the church means that one begins the discussion with a focus on the sort of community that it is and aspires to be. The shift in emphasis from the assertion of fifteen or so years earlier is noteworthy, for in the *Christian Faith and the Liberal Arts* volume the focus was more on the self (albeit a self and God in relationship). Now, however, the church, which Ditmanson defined as "a congregation of Christian believers or a social institution defined by certain religious convictions and practices," is the point of departure.[41] Accordingly, one of the functions of St. Olaf as a college of the church, he said, is that it "recommends the convictions and engages in the practices of the church."[42] These include making the faith of the church visible and attractive, providing for the public worship of God, and promoting moral action that serves human well-being.

With the addition of the term "Lutheran" to these considerations, the question of what it means for St. Olaf to be a college of the Lutheran church becomes both more simple and more complex. As Ditmanson observed, at one level, the term Lutheran added nothing to the college's identity because essentials of faith are shared with other Christian believers. Yet at another level, what the term Lutheran added to the discussion was a concern or, better, a conviction that there is a center to it all—namely, the presence of Christ in Word and sacrament. Ditmanson emphasized firmness at this point and flexibility on the periphery. Noting that Lutheranism is a very composite tradition, not like a set of instructions or a philosophical essay, he writes, "It is really *anethos*, a combination of factors with its own peculiar character."[43] This tradition exists, moreover, only where there are Lutherans to embody, express, and reform it. Because this is the case, Lutheran tradition is always in motion.

Echoing these concerns, Constance Gengenbach, then senior tutor of the Paracollege, interpreted what it meant to be a college of the church as primarily a concern for the renewal of identity.[44] She persuasively reasserts a vision of Christian faith in relationship to learning where nothing is limited or excluded from the curriculum. Most significant, according to Gengenbach, is that the renewal of church college identity necessarily involves an ongoing commitment to discussion of what it might mean.

The direction signaled in these discussions of the 1980s toward a concern with an expression and embodiment of identity marked by distinctive practices prefigures a significant scholarly emphasis of more recent years and provides a fresh way to reassess the religious heritage/tradition of St. Olaf College. Ditmanson's and Gengenbach's reintroduction of the importance of practices brings with it a reconsideration of tradition and how it shapes both personal identity and meaningful human action. In other words, since human beings are historical, they bear a tradition in the sense that "each of [their] own lives is generally and characteristically embedded in and made intelligible in terms of the larger and longer histories of a number of traditions."[45]

For St. Olaf, these traditions include religion, ethnicity, and liberal arts education. Thus, when St. Olaf is viewed as the bearer of a tradition of practice or practices, its life will be partly, but significantly, characterized by a continuous argument about what Lutheranism is and ought to be or what a Norwegian-American heritage is and ought to be or what a good liberal arts college is and ought to be. When a tradition is living and lively, then it necessarily engenders a historically extended, socially embodied argument, and an argument precisely in part about the goods which constitute that tradition. Thus far, we have witnessed some of these arguments as they took place during various periods of the history of St. Olaf—especially those pertaining to Lutheran identity and to what a good liberal arts college is and ought to be. Now we turn our attention to an argument yet to be considered, namely, the one over the college's ethnic heritage and history.

St. Olaf's Ethnic Heritage: Sentimental or Substantive?

A question which confronts those with connections to St. Olaf—alumni, faculty, staff, and, of course, students—is whether the college's ethnic heritage means much anymore. And this question is hardly new. A student entering St. Olaf as early as 1900 was quite surprised "at the emphasis on things Norwegian" and resented it at first. As late as 1949, the editor of the college yearbook, *The Viking*, a dark-haired, black-bearded student of Greek lineage, dryly observed: "The Norwegian Department has as one of its specific goals the observance and continuance of Norse customs, in order that these customs do not become extinct here in the new world as they have in Norway."[46] Moreover, as college historian Joseph M. Shaw has commented, "The average St. Olaf student, whether of Norwegian ancestry or not, indulges in a ritualistic chafing under the allegedly omnipresent campus reminders that the College has historical and cultural ties with Norway and things Norwegian."[47] Should we conclude, therefore, that this ethnocultural heritage is more sentimental than substantive after all?

Our answer would be "yes" if our operative notion of ethnicity is something static or essential. That is, it would be simply a matter of passing something on from generation to generation—a "something" loosely called "culture" or "values." Following this perspective, we might argue that there exists some kind of static, essential "Norwegianness" that St. Olaf has sought to preserve, cultivate, and transmit these past 125 years. Moreover, it would be easy to find the precise nature of the religious culture in the various churches or denominational cultures which have borne the name "Norwegian."

But if ethnicity is something radically different—"something reinvented and reinterpreted in each generation by each individual . . . something dynamic . . . something that emerges only through struggle . . . a deeply rooted emotional component of identity"[48]—then there is no such thing as a precise Norwegian ethos to which St. Olaf has been connected or which is waiting to be retrieved. The very history of the college itself makes clear that its ethnicity and ethnic identity are reinvented and reinterpreted in and by each generation and in the context of its particular needs and desires.

For example, as the fiction and cultural writings of Ole Edvart Rølvaag make clear, the ongoing appreciation of a Norwegian cultural heritage is more than lutefisk and lefse sentimentality. His collection of essays on immigration, culture, and heritage entitled *Omkring Fædrearven* (*Concerning Our Heritage*) addresses concerns which sound surprisingly contemporary. The fostering and nourishing of an ethnic identity, he said, were for the purposes of empowering feelings of human worth and enabling persons to become true human beings. For Rølvaag, an "ancestral heritage" consisted of particular values and predispositions. He noted that Norwegians, for example, are deeply rooted to a place while possessing at the same time a restless desire for adventure. They have a love of home and of the memories and traditions which belong to it. They value equality and hospitality. They have a keen desire for knowledge and a particular feeling for art and beauty. They also possess a deep religious feeling manifested in a personal relationship to God. Most important, according to Rølvaag, is the love of freedom.[49]

In addition, for Rølvaag, a cultural heritage was composed of language and literature, another kind of self-knowledge, as well as the good and bad characteristics of a people. His insistence on the retention of such a heritage was *not* in order to sneak some "little Norway" into the United States but "to make ourselves and our children into more competent and better people. If we succeed, we are so innocent that we believe it will benefit our country."[50]

We know that in Rølvaag's time as now, a dominant cultural mandate for both citizen and immigrant alike is somehow to forget or to suppress an ethnic heritage. Immigrants were and are to undergo a "conversion" which would "make" them into Americans—a miracle that replaced spiritual conversion. They were to cease being hyphenated Americans. Rølvaag saw this kind of mandate as leading to the loss of values and to spiritual impoverishment. He sought to provide a different answer to the question of what it is to be, or to become, a Norwegian-American, and so a certain kind of person. Such a person, renewed by an ethnic vision that embraces values like equality, hospitality, a keen desire for knowledge, and a particular feeling for art and beauty, Rølvaag argues, will contribute to a richer, powerfully dynamic pluralist society. Here was also an incisive critique of an Anglo-American assimilationist ideology.

This "something more" for Rølvaag was what might be termed today a "moral vision" which can serve as fertile ground for the renewal of humane values. Hence, a Norwegian ethnic, cultural identity, in his mind, has significant historical and ethical consequences. It exists, in large part, in order to contribute to the making of a citizen of a certain kind. Rølvaag once noted in this regard,

> But here we are approaching the Sancta sanctorum, our emotional attachment to the country we have become citizens of, and where our children will live and build after us. The anxious heart will ask with serious and deep concern: How can a person with a distinctly Norwegian view of life—with a "Norwegian soul"!—be a good American citizen?
>
> Well, what makes a good citizen? What is a bad citizen? If the anxious person would look for clarity on this issue instead of climbing up on the rooftop to see which way the wind is blowing, his worry would soon disappear. For me the answer is quite simple. Let us promote the Norwegian ancestral heritage, and our emotional attachment to America will be just fine. For it is human beings this country needs; not just things.[51]

Rølvaag's conviction was that love and need for "the old ways" can and must be blended with an optimistic hope for the future in a multicultural society to which immigrants from all nations contribute their deepest souls and their richest nuances of thought and feeling. In a letter written by President Lars Wilhelm Boe to a faculty colleague shortly after Rølvaag's death, he noted, "It is up to us to make it possible to save those cultural and religious values which our fathers brought with them. Rølvaag had an abiding faith that it would be done. . . ."[52]

When Rølvaag's ideas about ethnic and cultural identity are viewed from the recent theoretical perspectives provided by anthropologists, literary critics, and social historians, we should be struck by similarities of emphasis and theme. For example, scholars like Michael M. J. Fischer remind us that the search or struggle for an ethnic identity is for the purpose of discovering an ethical and future-oriented vision. This was also Rølvaag's concern. While there is an initial focus on the past (recall Rølvaag's immigrant trilogy of novels), the goal of such a connection is to find "an ethic workable for the future."[53] This ethic, like the ethic articulated in newer immigrant/migrant writing and theorizing, is one oriented to responsible "cultural citizenship."[54] Moreover, in the celebration of memory, word, and imagination, the emotional and intellectual force of a culture is reclaimed in the face of homogenization, the erosion of the public elements of tradition, and the loss of historical rootedness.

And so, as we return to the question posed at the outset of this section—does St. Olaf's ethnic heritage mean much anymore?—we see that it is necessary to shift our focus. No longer is our concern with the quaint and nostalgic, with an ethnicity that is something to be commodified and consumed. Rather, we would attend to the emotional and intellectual force of the religion, language, literature, customs, and values of those Norwegian women and men who have gone before. In learning that what they honored most, for example—"warmth and an authentic religious experience in which one's life, work and religion have a kind of integrity"[55]—we could then ask whether such a self-understanding can renew us as well as "contribute to a richer, powerfully dynamic pluralist society."[56]

At the same time, as we expand a focus on a Norwegian-American heritage as a dynamic amalgam, including not only what the immigrants brought with them and what they adapted in this American setting, but what is now available in contemporary Norway as well, we could ask whether these cultural resources can be reworked into enriching tools for the present. For instance, in listening closely to the various voices in contemporary Norwegian literature—their emphases and ranges of expression—we encounter with a particular intensity the emotions and longings that shape us and are challenged to innovative responses to issues that ultimately affect us all.

To read ethnicity in this fashion enables us to move beyond an understanding of Norwegian identity as timeless and fixed. Similarly, it enables us to avoid the pitfalls of the merely nostalgic. It allows us to consider instead, as Rølvaag did, the dynamic identity-forming and ethical functions of a reinvented ethnicity. So for my generation—one which grew up in the 1950s with the mandate to be "American"; one which was educated in the 1960s when everything was sharply challenged; and one which now, at the close of this century, is seeking a revitalized personal and collective identity—St. Olaf's dynamic ethnic-religious heritage offers a living resource for intellectual, spiritual, and cultural reinvigoration.[57] In what might such reinvigoration consist?

Intellectually, we would endeavor to move beyond sentimental, nostalgic evocations of an ethnic heritage in order to see how it was in continual conversation with basic human questions of personhood and how it was committed to the creation of the kind of society that contributes to its wholeness and health. Reading and rereading Rølvaag's fiction and cultural writings, for example, can teach us a great deal about how to address the concerns of our own day, especially those of how to construct individual and collective identity for the sake of active participation in a social world.

Spiritually, we could explore a way of thinking and a way of living which allow the objective and subjective elements of Christian faith "to meet and mingle." As we steer once again a "happy middle course" between the extremes of exaggerated objectivity and arbitrary subjectivity, we encounter a theological option in which communities and individuals are instructed in authentic speaking and acting. A fundamental appeal to human experience takes place because we are intended to respond to God's call as persons.

Culturally, we might learn something of what it is to live with multiple identities—on both sides of the hyphen—thereby becoming acutely aware that a monocultural erasure of difference and a multicultural view of only difference are equally bankrupt. A critical reappropriation of the sort of identity in which two cultural legacies are retained, as Ole Rølvaag and Lars Wilhelm Boe argued nearly three-quarters of a century ago, can—in deepening our thinking about identity and meaning, experience and definition—enable and empower us to participate fully in the ongoing mix that America represents.

Some Concluding Thoughts

Throughout its history, St. Olaf College has lived between a "recollected past and a projected future"[58] for the purpose of maintaining "both continuity of purpose and mobility of approach to new circumstances and opportunities."[59] What I have presented in this essay is, first of all, an interpretation of St. Olaf's past—remembering that it was established by Norwegian immigrants who sought to be both loyal to a particular ethnic and religious heritage, on the one hand, and committed to an educational mission in America on the other. In addition, I have tried to understand the difference St. Olaf's intentionally hyphenated self-definition makes in its ongoing development as an American liberal arts college. Finally, I have suggested that St. Olaf's distinctive heritage is still usable—even 125 years after its founding—for thinking about how to reinvigorate selves and entire communities. Unlike Peder Victorious Holm, who eventually concluded that his life was to be lived solely "in the other world," I have argued instead for a rich and dynamic existence—one that can be lived on "both sides of the hyphen." Standing there, I find St. Olaf's particular churchly and ethnic heritage still contributing worthwhile possibilities for the present as well as the future.

NOTES

1. O. E. Rølvaag, *Peder Victorious: A Tale of the Pioneers Twenty Years Later* (New York: Harper & Row, 1966 [1929]) 97.

2. Todd W. Nichol, "United Norwegian (1890)—A Church and a College for the World: Can the Church Be United for Mission?" *Church Roots: Stories of Nine Immigrant Groups That Became the American Lutheran Church*, ed. Charles P. Lutz (Minneapolis: Augsburg Publishing House, 1985) 178.

3. Cited in Theodore Jorgenson and Nora O. Solum, *Ole Edvart Rølvaag: A Biography* (New York: Harper & Brothers, 1939) 180.

4. Joseph M. Shaw, *History of St. Olaf College 1874–1974* (Northfield, Minn: St. Olaf College, 1974) 20.

5. William C. Benson, *High on Manitou: A History of St. Olaf College 1874–1949* (Northfield, Minn: St. Olaf, 1949) xvi–xvii; emphasis added.

6. Shaw 29.

7. Renato Rosaldo, "Assimilation Revisited," Working Paper Series No. 9, Stanford Center for Chicano Research (Stanford University, July 1985) 1.

8. Rosaldo 1.

9. Rosaldo 1.

10. Odd Lovoll, *The Promise of America: A History of the Norwegian-American People* (Minneapolis & London: University of Minnesota Press in cooperation with the Norwegian American Historical Association, 1984) 67.

11. Lovoll 67.

12. Lovoll 67.

13. E. Clifford Nelson, *The Lutheran Church among Norwegian-Americans: A History of the Evangelical Lutheran Church*, vol. 2, *1890–1959* (Minneapolis: Augsburg, 1960) 42–43.

14. Nelson 43.

15. Lovoll 108.

16. Cited in Peter A. Munch, "Norwegians," in *Harvard Encyclopedia of American Ethnic Groups*, ed. Stephan Thernstrom et al. (Cambridge: Belknap Press of Harvard University Press, 1980) 756.

17. Here I depend on Shaw's 1974 *History of St. Olaf College* 15ff; emphasis added.

18. Todd W. Nichol, "The Tradition Supporting Us: Reflections on an Education" (unpublished paper dated 5 Nov. 1993) 15.

19. Shaw 244.

20. Shaw 244.

21. Shaw 244.

22. Nichol, "United Norwegian (1890)" 179.

23. Shaw 81; cited in Nichol, "United Norwegian" 179.

24. Einar Molland, *Church Life in Norway 1800–1950*, tr. Harris Kaasa (Minneapolis: Augsburg Publishing House, 1957) 41.

25. Nelson 42.

26. Portions of these articles are in *The Heritage of Faith: Selections from the Writings of Georg Sverdrup*, tr. Melvin A. Helland (Minneapolis: Augsburg Publishing House, 1969) 104–115.

27. James S. Hamre, *Georg Sverdrup: Educator, Theologian, Churchman* (Northfield, MN: The Norwegian American Historical Association, 1986) 118. I recall a conversation between my father and his relatives as I was about to leave home to attend St. Olaf. They were "Augsburg people" and they could not understand why he would let his son go to this "den of free thinkers."

28. Richard W. Solberg, *Lutheran Higher Education in North America* (Minneapolis: Augsburg, 1985) 232.

29. Solberg 232.

30. Shaw 17ff.

31. Solberg 234.

32. Shaw 121.

33. Shaw 133.

34. Shaw 139.

35. Shaw 169.

36. William H. K. Narum, "The Role of the Liberal Arts in Christian Higher Education," *Christian Faith and the Liberal Arts*, ed. Harold H. Ditmanson, Howard V. Hong, and Warren A. Quanbeck (Minneapolis: Augsburg, 1960) 11.

37. Narum 9.

38. Narum 11–12.

39. See Anne E. Carr, "Starting with the Human," *A World of Grace: An Introduction to the Themes and Foundations of Karl Rahner's Theology*, ed. Leo J. O'Donovan (New York: Seabury, 1980) 17–30.

40. Sheila Greeve Davaney and Delwin Brown, "Postliberalism," *The Blackwell Encyclopedia of Modern Christian Thought*, ed. Alister E. McGrath (Cambridge: Blackwell Publishers Ltd., 1993) 454.

41. Harold Ditmanson, "St. Olaf: A College of the Church," *Saint Olaf* 35.2 (March 1987): 2. Emphasis added.

42. Ditmanson 2.

43. Ditmanson 2.

44. Constance Gengenbach, "St. Olaf: A College of the Church," *Saint Olaf* 35.2 (March 1987): 3–4.

45. Alasdair MacIntyre, *After Virtue: A Study in Moral Theory*, 2nd ed. (Notre Dame: University of Notre Dame Press, 1984) 222.

46. Shaw 25.

47. Shaw 25.

48. Michael M. J. Fischer, "Ethnicity and the Post-Modern Arts of Memory," *Writing Culture: The Poetics and Politics of Ethnography*, ed. James Clifford and George E. Marcus (Berkeley: University of California Press, 1986) 195.

49. Solveig Zempel, "Rølvaag's Views on Immigration, Culture, and Heritage," *...etter Rølvaag har problema han stridde med, vorte til verdsproblem...*, Rapport fra Rølvaag-konferansen i Sandnessjøen 7.–8. August 1995, ed. Ole Karlsen and Renee Waara (Nesna, Norway: Høgskolen i Nesna, 1995) 31–32.

50. O. E. Rølvaag, *Omkring Fædrearven* (Northfield, Minn.: St. Olaf College Press, 1992) 71.

51. Rølvaag, *Omkring Fædrearven* 107–108.

52. Zempel, "Rølvaag's Views on Immigration, Culture, and Heritage" 40.

53. Fischer 196.

54. See Azade Seyhan, "Ethnic Selves/Ethnic Signs: Invention of Self, Space, and Genealogy in Immigrant Writing," *Culture/Contexture: Explorations in Anthropology and Literary Studies*, ed. E. Valentine Daniel and Jeffrey M. Peck (Berkeley: University of California Press, 1996) 175–194.

55. Gracia Grindal, "Two Tendencies in Tension and Interaction," Remembrance and Renewal: Una Sancta section of *Lutheran Forum* (Reformation, 1981) 16.

56. Fischer 197.

57. So argues Fischer 231.

58. *Identity and Mission in a Changing Context: A Centennial Publication of St. Olaf College* (Northfield, Minn.: St. Olaf, 1974) 1.

59. *Identity and Mission* 1.

4. ST. OLAF COLLEGE, 1972–1998: A PERSONAL REFLECTION

Robert L. Nichols

Journey to Northfield

In late August 1972, my family and I arrived in Northfield from Seattle, where I had just completed my doctoral degree in Russian history at the University of Washington. Teaching history at St. Olaf became my first regular, full-time job after several temporary positions in state universities and a community college. My new prospects seemed doubly daunting because I had now to teach a set of courses at a level that would be challenging yet interesting to capable and hardworking students and because the small church-related college differed greatly from my own educational upbringing and experience. St. Olaf was largely unknown territory for this newly minted Ph.D. who was not Norwegian Lutheran.

Largely unknown, but not entirely unfamiliar. I had heard of St. Olaf as a boy growing up in Poulsbo, Washington, a Norwegian Lutheran small town in the Pacific Northwest, whose Lutheran pastor was a St. Olaf graduate; his children attended St. Olaf. My childhood Luther League friends visited the college during summers and reported back to me about milkshakes so thick you could hold the cup upside down and the contents would not come out (at that time the college still operated its own dairy, I believe). But this knowledge hardly prepared me for the new job that awaited. I had very little idea about a "church-related" liberal arts college.

For one thing, my college and graduate school days were spent at large state universities such as the University of Washington with its forty thousand students. The "UW" housed a College of Liberal Arts, a large division of the university that offered thousands of courses by hundreds of faculty. By its nature, the educational program was, from the student standpoint, incoherent, although, of course, each major had its own specifications and a broad range of courses could satisfy general graduation requirements. By comparison, the students, faculty, and staff at

St. Olaf amounted to about one-half of the number in my graduating college senior class. Thus, I had to adjust for scale: classes were not taught in large lecture halls, where students overflowed into adjoining rooms to watch the professor on television monitors.

For another thing, at Washington church and religion were held at a careful distance from the curriculum and the classroom. In this respect, public university education had strived to erect a barrier between religion and the state that went well beyond what the country's founders envisioned. Those earlier Americans expected that the churches and civil authority shared overlapping goals. But by the 1960s at my university the only course that explicitly included biblical material was one offered in the English department under the title "The Bible as Literature." At that time there were no courses on the history of Christianity, theology, or even "religious studies," since such programs often came to state universities a decade or more later. Additionally, before the Second World War, Washington had been a politically radical state (the forty-seven states of America and the Soviet of Washington, as it was sometimes called). Many of the older faculty thought it inappropriate to teach and study the history and life of Christianity (superstition, really) in an age of scientific discovery and progressive thought. Still, the picture was not completely uniform, and a few of my teachers were actually deeply engaged in research and some teaching on the subject.

Finally, of course, my educational background contained no direct church connection, since I was wholly the product of public schools. The idea that college might be in the service of the church was one with which I was intellectually, but not personally, familiar. I had no idea what it might mean in practice. St. Olaf hired me, not because I could be recognized immediately as one of its tribe, but because it was seeking to attract professionally trained faculty from leading graduate schools. The vetting in would have to be done on the job. As a church college St. Olaf belonged to a large organization, the American Lutheran Church (now subsumed into the Evangelical Lutheran Church in America), that attracted many leaders who were good administrators as well as pastors and theologians. President Sidney Rand, who was president of St. Olaf during my first years at the college, serves as a fine example of this combination; no doubt such leaders thought they could successfully manage to teach faculty like me who were arriving in growing numbers.

Luckily, as one who had grown up in Poulsbo, I had a direct feel for Norwegian ethnicity, not just for all the superficial signs of identity such as lefse, lutefisk, rosemaling, and troll dolls, but for the carryovers from Norway into American life: language, social organizations, class differences, church-centered community (with all of its internal tensions between those who sought a religion of the heart in contrast to what they deemed the stone-cold Christianity of their neighbors), and personal reticence. These things helped me to grasp more quickly the nature of St. Olaf and relate more easily to its students. After all, I had gone to school with such students all my life; I could read their names on my class lists without stumbling. In some odd way, I was an insider outsider at the college.

Looking back at 1972 when I arrived, it somehow seems to me that this ethnic element in the life of the school was then more pronounced and palpable than it is today. The faculty had a lively sense that they were serving an immigrant or not-too-far-from immigrant constituency. Most took for granted the confessional and service aspects of the college's work. The Norwegian Lutherans who founded the college expected that it would not only prepare young men and women for professional life and public service (ministry and education, in particular), but also confessionally nurture them to grow intellectually and spiritually in the Christian faith. Perhaps there is a closer connection between the college's ethnic heritage and its theological purpose than is nowadays acknowledged. Certainly the Norwegian Lutheran legacy is deeply embedded in the continuing structure of the college: in its foundational liberal arts program as the gateway to the professions; in its campus ministry; and in its many programs that have focused on service, such as secondary education, nursing, and social work.

Today, the college's older Norwegian Lutheran animating spirit seems largely eroded. As in America at large, the college's Norwegian ethnicity has become a voluntary identification with the commercialized stereotype of Ole and Lena jokes. Largely eroded, but not quite gone because American Norwegian ethnic identity is also rooted in the Lutheran church in its several synods. Todd Nichol recounts the story of a young couple driving by an unfamiliar Lutheran church and seeing the youth of the congregation having a car wash. One of the couple shouted from the car window, "What synod are you?" "What's the difference?" the youths replied, "We wash all cars the same!"[1] It took me some time to realize that, although our students went through the same educational program at the college, our Lutheran students did not all come from the same synod (St. Olaf was never affiliated with any specific synod). The old battles among the Scandinavian Lutherans of the nineteenth century—the "Hauge Synod," as these American disciples of the great Norwegian Lutheran preacher of evangelical awakening Hans Nielsen Hauge were called, and their several offshoots; the Norwegian Augustana Synod; the Missouri

Synod; and others—still resonated to varying degrees in the families and faith of our students. The American Lutheran Church (St. Olaf's sponsoring church), formed from a variety of these synods and churches, after all, was only twelve years old in 1972.

To learn something of the Norwegian Lutheran story, as I gradually did in my first years at St. Olaf, was a help because it provided a perspective on the questions and problems which our students posed for themselves. Some students had a strong confessional background with a substantial knowledge of the Bible and catechism. To teach them often meant to encourage their encounter with a diverse world of ideas and high intellectual standards. Others, those of a more liberal Norwegian Lutheran background, sometimes lacked the most basic knowledge of the Christian story or how a Christian worldview might provide the key to the question of what it means to be an educated man or woman: what meaning our lives might have for ourselves and for our common pilgrim journey with the rest of humanity. (Curiously, I remember one of my colleagues at the college once expressed her exasperation at the persisting Norwegian Lutheran diversity among the students. "Who cares about all those synods?" she said. "It's all in the past, anyway.")

College Structure and Culture

As a college of the American Lutheran Church, St. Olaf shared the new church's sometime belief in itself as a big, if somewhat quarrelsome, family, suspicious of bureaucracy and structure, but nonetheless confident in authority exercised in a personal way by its leaders. This helps to explain something that I poorly understood in my first years at the college: why so many faculty regarded the administration with a deep suspicion that it was running the college simply for the benefit of a secretly growing number of bureaucrats, when in fact the college had one of the lowest ratios of administrators to faculty and students among the consortium of colleges to which it belonged. At the same time, the president exercised considerable authority and did so in a manner that commanded genuine respect. The president was paterfamilias of the church college family. As family, or community, St. Olaf offered intimacy and sense of belonging; but family, while personal, could also be arbitrary, unpredictable, and often paternal: not the ideal combination perhaps for guiding Lutheran higher education through the civil, women's, and personal liberation movements that have dominated the second half of the twentieth century in America.

Still, I felt a warm sense of acceptance in the college's history department. Kenneth Bjork, who was the acting chair of the department the year

I was hired and a distinguished historian of American immigration history, served as our avuncular and wise elder statesman. Henry Fritz, the regular chair of the department, held a large view of the department's role in the college's growing international studies: global coverage that avoided superficial amateurism by offering professionally taught courses of high quality. Other members of the department worked hard at their teaching and regularly produced scholarly publications. I rejoiced in entering a department of friendly and purposeful scholar-teachers, who sufficiently tolerated a beginner's mistakes and gropings toward an effective teaching style.

The department's professionalism did not always find favor in the wider college, where the suspicion lurked that its professional allegiance transcended its dedication to students, the college as a whole, and the college's relationship to the Lutheran church. Certainly, the college did not trust the history department to tell the institution's own story in various officially sponsored narratives published over the years. But in another way, the department served very well the college's aim to provide a strong undergraduate education for students who regularly sought to enter the professions or business. Large numbers of history majors went on to pursue law, academic degrees, banking, seminary training, government service, and even medicine.

Coincidentally with my first years at the college, women history students began in large numbers to attend law school after graduation. By the end of the decade I was writing significantly more letters of recommendation to law schools for women than for men. Our women students were, for the first time, considering nontraditional occupations and going beyond the educational levels of their mothers. Perhaps this reflected larger changes in the college, where more attention was being paid to the structural and attitudinal ways the school had heretofore reinforced traditional roles. In 1972, the history department itself hired its first woman historian since the retirement of Agnes Larson in 1960 and made several more such appointments in subsequent years. The changed perspectives and behavior of our women students certainly mirrored growing national trends.

Even though my early vantage point in the large state university made the college seem small, I gradually came to appreciate that among liberal arts colleges St. Olaf was large, often nearly twice as large as the other private liberal arts colleges in the Midwest. This is important to understand because too often we are misled by our own rhetoric about liberal arts into believing that we are (or ought to be) a college similar to such Midwestern liberal arts colleges as Carleton, Macalaster, or Grinnell.

Several factors explain St. Olaf's larger size. One is found in the hopes of the college founders that St. Olaf would provide a comprehensive education for students entering a variety of fields, but especially those connected with service. More particularly, later growth derived from the school's early development under President Kildahl (1899–1914), when the original classical course was supplemented by a new scientific and literary course and when new departments in biology, economics, political science, sociology, and education were established. These developments set the college on the path to a more extensive college program than is usual for liberal arts institutions; the college eventually grew to be a small undergraduate university with strongly delineated departments and substantial applied and performance programs such as nursing, music, education, home economics (later called "family studies"), and social work. The post-Second World War generation filled out these larger contours with two spurts of growth: the first in the immediate post-Second World War years under President Clemens Granskou (1942–1963), and the second during the presidency of Sidney Rand (1963–1980). From 1964 to 1984 the student body increased from 2000 to 3000 and the faculty grew from 175 to 355.[2]

It took me some time to understand the significance of this feature of the college's life and its role in serving the Norwegian Lutheran constituency. For one thing, it meant that although religion for many years was seemingly privileged in the curriculum through a three-course graduation requirement (more on this later), neither theology nor the humanities was ever able to define the educational life of the school. The college, until very recently, did not offer an integrated general education. Instead, it merely required that students take a specified number of courses in each division of the college. Some faculty tried to counter this development by proposing alternatives (the Paracollege, for example, the "alternative route to the B.A."; the January Interim, and the on-going Great Conversation, or Integrated Core Curriculum, that for a time combined study in science with that of religion, humanities, and applied arts). More recent efforts to create a program of general education have largely foundered on this same rock of institutional intentionality that first took shape at the beginning of the century.

Of course, faculty complaints about a lack of curricular integration are perennial and not confined to St. Olaf. In the 1930s, Robert Hutchins asked, "Why is it that the chief characteristic of higher learning is disorder? It is because there is no ordering principle in it.... [I]t must be clear that if each person has the right to make and achieve his own choices the result is anarchy and the dissolution of the whole."[3] Felix Frankfurter later added: "That our universities have grave shortcomings for the intellectual life of this nation is by now a commonplace. The chief source of their inadequacy is probably the curse of departmentalization."[4] Echoes of these same complaints resound in the college's own past studies such as *Integration in the Christian Liberal Arts College* written by the St. Olaf College Self-Study Committee in 1956 and in the later *Identity and Mission in a Changing Context*, the centennial self-study of 1973. Thus the criticisms are not new. They are the familiar refrain of reformers in American higher education.

Still, for a college of the church one might have expected a stronger assertion of the Christian faith that we are, in all our diverse parts, actors in the meaningful story of God's continuing efforts on behalf of our salvation, and that this assertion would provide a steady force for greater coherence and integration in the advancement of knowledge and in the teaching about it. The character of higher education at St. Olaf should differ from that of other liberal arts colleges because its educational mission is rooted in the conviction that the triune God actively strives for the perfection of a fallen humanity: God's great never-ending love story that unfolds in an intelligible and meaningful universe.

Somehow the religious and liberal arts activities of the college were often simply assumed to be the normative ones in fulfilling the original aim to educate students "in the true Christian faith."[5] Imperceptibly, the animating Christian activity common among students took place through the varied musical programs, especially the choirs, more than in the intellectual dialogue of the classroom or in daily chapel. In the course of the past twenty-five years the religion department lost its older pastoral and confessional character and its close relationship to daily chapel. It became a more strictly academic department, with some seeking to make it exclusively a department of theology. Such a change had several implications, including a more pronounced search by the general student body for answers to questions about their personal faith outside the religion department in nontraditional gatherings and prayer groups, sometimes on campus, sometimes in nondenominational churches pursuing active outreach to the college. Additionally, since the college generally favored the department's more academic approach, it logically followed that the three-course religion requirement for graduation should be curtailed. Some thought that religion should not be allowed a greater claim on the student's time and attention than that accorded to any other academic department. Others argued that since religion was not a subject for which students had any preparation in the public schools, adequate academic study of the Bible, church history, and theology still required three courses. The outcome of the debate was a modest step away from the older requirement.

Meanwhile, the college put great energy into developing high-quality mathematics and science programs—chemistry, biology, and physics—which it widely advertised in newspapers around Minnesota and the neighboring states. The endeavor matched the interests of prospective students, who enrolled in large numbers in science and math courses as preparation for careers in the growing fields of medicine, computers, and environmental study. (The percentage of entering St. Olaf students aspiring for a professional degree, primarily medicine and law, reached its highest point, 30 percent, in 1981, and then fell to around 17 percent in the mid-1980s, from which it rose to slightly over 20 percent in 1996.) These developments derived logically, if not inevitably, from the college's attempts to provide a fairly comprehensive and professionally strong program for its Norwegian-American constituency and for others who might be attracted to the college, while still affirming its Lutheran church connection.

However, any attempts to define more explicitly the relationship of faith to learning or church to college, if that meant a more focused attention on theology and humanities as a central endeavor of the curriculum, could not under these circumstances succeed. In this respect, little has changed since the 1950s, when the college first began consciously to consider issues of academic excellence and religious vision. According to Joseph Shaw, a historian of the college, the recommendations of a faculty study committee proposing to alter the existing academic configuration found little faculty support. His words still merit quoting as a barometric reading of current faculty attitudes:

> Some thought that the entire endeavor was too heavily weighted on the side of philosophy and theology . . . some feared that integration would mean a reduction of departmental autonomy, or remained unconvinced that fragmentation was any problem.[6]

In any case, the long-existing pattern of comprehensive education structured through departments continues to define the college's approach to liberal arts. In recent years some faculty have seen the erosion of the college's older character as an opportunity to advance toward a better future by making St. Olaf into a national liberal arts school. The model might be Carleton College (albeit a "warmer" Carleton because of the college's church relatedness) or the private New England and eastern liberal arts colleges that long ago discontinued their connections to the church. By contrast, those who see attempts at a stronger role for religion and the humanities as an infringement on departmental autonomy and on the large presence of the natural sciences in the curriculum continue to resist the liberal arts integrationists or the new national vision. The result is an impasse and ambivalence about change, particularly at present, when the college's financial resources are strained to the utmost.

International Education

My first years at St. Olaf coincided with the last reverberations of the student upheaval of the 1960s. By 1972 the earlier earthquake now gave out only minor shock waves that virtually disappeared by the end of the decade. Yet the 1960s and early 1970s left their mark in a variety of ways: through creation of the Paracollege, formation of interdisciplinary studies (for example, Women's Studies, American Studies, American Minority Studies, Environmental Studies, and Computer Science), the organization of area programs (Asian Studies, Russian Studies, Medieval Studies, and so forth), and the expansion of international study. In this, St. Olaf took part in the great transformation in American higher education in the second half of the twentieth century, when enrollments expanded, American universities became world-class institutions, faculties and student bodies became more ethnically and gender diverse, and new fields of research and instruction opened up at breathtaking speed. The college recognized that American understanding, and the understanding of our students in particular, of other parts of the world should grow not only because other peoples were interesting and important, but also because our students could play a sensible and effective role in a shrinking world only if they understood other parts of the world and the changes that were sweeping the globe.

Here the college particularly drew on its older missionary heritage and its Christian identity as the point of departure for new programs such as Asian Studies and the abroad Term in the Middle East. These quiet and peaceful innovations produced profound changes that not only deeply affected the nature of the curriculum, but began to expand St. Olaf's higher education in an international direction. The world, not only Minnesota or the United States or the Western world, is now the campus for St. Olaf students.

These changes, of course, did not come without strains and stresses of various sorts. They certainly added new financial burdens, and some faculty openly complained about our "Cadillac" study abroad programs that favored those students whose checkbooks provided greater qualification for foreign study than did the academic preparation of less wealthy students. Others felt that these study abroad programs lacked intellectual rigor and amounted to little more than academic tourism, particularly since language study was often omitted either as a prerequisite or as a component of the programs. In a way, the tension represented a variation on the continuing underlying conflict between professional and general educational goals, between departmental and integrational ways of organizing knowledge. As in an uneasy marriage, the arguments of both sides had merits and defects, but on the whole the college emerged from the changes with strong programs that continue to attract a substantial portion of the student body to participate in the new endeavor. A March 1997 study by the college's Office of Educational and Institutional Research confirms this observation with respect to the expectations of newly entering students. More than a fourth of the students who answered a questionnaire on the subject cited international studies opportunities as a "key factor" in deciding to attend the college.

Did the church-relatedness of the college make a difference in all of this? I think the answer must be "yes." The college's older Norwegian Lutheran character naturally encouraged the school to look to Europe and to remember external ties that went beyond American borders. Moreover, Lutheran evangelicalism fostered in our students a strong sense of service in the world. With some exceptions, such an outlook at the college rarely took on a pietist missionary fervor. St. Olaf's historical experience with mission, particularly in China, coincided with the rise of Christian modernism in the late nineteenth and early twentieth centuries. Sometime about 1890 the theological leadership of America's chief denominations broke with the earlier Evangelical Awakening in Protestantism under the impact of new scientific ideas and discoveries, especially those of Darwin, the findings of the new biblical archaeology and higher biblical criticism, the rise of pragmatism in philosophy under the impress of Schleiermacher's theory of experience as the heart of religion, Rudolf Euken's philosophy of activism (culminating in the work of William James), and the growth of modern nationalism. American Protestant modernists preached the Social Gospel to realize the kingdom of God in this world by crusading against economic injustice through such organizations as the YMCA/YWCA under the dynamic leadership of George Sherwood Eddy. Modernists, unlike the earlier generations of Protestant missionaries, were not interested in tallying baptisms.

Christian modernism found expression at St. Olaf through such figures as President Clemens Granskou, who once told me about the deep impression Eddy had made upon him as a young man. Eddy convinced him that earlier missionaries in China had been mistaken in their approach, which amounted to little more than forcing an alien creed down the throats of a resisting Chinese people, whereas they should be taking part in building a whole new social order in the East. Modernists advanced the Social Gospel as the means to fight against the evils of oppression and tyranny; Jesus was a revolutionary. Such an approach, of course, did not require any deep or careful study of Chinese culture and civilization, since they were to give way to the ideals of freedom and liberty.

President Granskou had already been retired for a decade when I first met him. At that time, I taught modern Chinese and East Asian history, and he was pleased to be invited to speak in my classes about his earlier experiences in China. Students found Granskou's approach puzzling because in the aftermath of the 1960s on American campuses, they were too accustomed to equating missionaries with imperialism; Granskou seemed to be speaking to them from another world. I mention this feature of the college's past because it is part of the impetus for our international programs. St. Olaf shared in a larger international enterprise, and naturally St. Olaf faculty felt our educational program should reflect that role. Moreover, the modernist approach, with its stress on the need for change abroad, did not place on students an unusual burden of language acquisition or preparatory study of a different civilization and culture in its own terms.

This point should not be overstressed. Just as St. Olaf earlier avoided too deep an engagement with Lutheran pietism, so it also shared with Lutheran theologians generally a reticence to embrace such progress-oriented movements as the Social Gospel.[7] Nonetheless, Christian modernism did in some measure contribute to a context at the college in which the more professionally trained faculty of the 1970s and 1980s could find acceptance for courses on the governments, histories, economics, and cultures of the world. Students could still resonate to the modernist message. I vividly recall the deep and profound response students gave to Paul Wee of the Lutheran World Federation when, in the early 1980s, he spoke brilliantly and passionately to students on campus about their Christian calling to take part in the political (and even military) struggle to end apartheid in South Africa.

From Small Town to Sprawling Suburb

Although the change had already long been under way by the time I came to St. Olaf, I have certainly observed the disappearance of students coming from rural America. When I first began teaching, I could still count on a few students from farm families in each class I taught. Today, I rarely have a single one. But more importantly, perhaps, the shift from small town to suburb has provided the greatest change in the students I teach. Historically, the college taught the children of small-town elites: the doctors, lawyers, schoolteachers, pastors, merchants, and others. When the students graduated, they often went home to take up the professional and business roles of their parents. St. Olaf's reputation was exceptionally high in small-town Minnesota. I remember one Fourth of July in the early 1970s, when my car's water pump decided to give out in Brainerd, Minnesota. The GMC dealership luckily was open that day, but when I read the large sign "No Checks" over the service window, my heart fell, since that was the only way I was going to be able to pay for the repairs. When the dealer learned that I was from St. Olaf, he immediately reassured me that my check was good. After all, both his son and his daughter attended St. Olaf!

Yet it is likely that the dealer's son and daughter left St. Olaf for careers and lives in the suburbs, and their children are the ones who now turn up with increasing frequency as our students. They are probably on the whole better prepared for college than their small-town predecessors. But it may also be true that their postgraduation influence and impact on Minnesota and Upper Midwestern life is more diluted than in earlier generations. I am not certain what to make of this trend, but it should at least make us pause to consider the ways the past model of church-related St. Olaf education might need to be amended. Here, perhaps, the implications are greatest for our residential life program.

The college I first encountered in 1972 seemed better suited to small-town Minnesota than to the impersonal and homogenized suburban America from which we now largely draw our students. Over the past quarter century, without always realizing or fully articulating it, the college seems to have been seeking a new approach and structure suitable to the changed environment. At least some of the heat and emotion generated in our current time of difficult change (the late 1990s) under President Mark U. Edwards Jr. is connected with the strains entailed in moving the college away from some of its traditional moorings and practices.

Are we now further from the world of the Norwegian American Lutheran college than we were twenty-five years ago when I first arrived in Northfield? The question might seem paradoxical in an America that in the past quarter-century has more strongly than ever before emphasized and rejoiced in its ethnic and religious diversity. At the moment St. Olaf is not certain how to answer the question, and we have not been certain for quite some time. Perhaps this is why the college with ever greater frequency has formulated and reformulated its "vision" statement (I am told a college committee is now drafting still another one); why it has needed to make explicit its policies on "values in the workplace"; why it has organized committees and task forces to reexamine and articulate its identity as a church-related college; and why comprehensive curricular changes have dragged on for a decade with no end yet in sight.

For the outside observer the college's continuity with the past seems self-evident. St. Olaf students still seek an education suited for service in society and for successful careers; they still value the Christian connection to their educational pursuits. The college still strives for a strong diverse academic program rather than for a purely theological one. Study abroad continues to attract large numbers of new students to the college. The list can easily be extended.

At the same time, some older features of the college are now less evident. Norwegian Lutheranism, as distinct from some other more abstract Lutheranism, has clearly receded as a defining element in the college's ongoing daily life. Along with it, the college's foundational goal to "preserve the pupils in the true Christian faith as taught by the Evangelical Lutheran Church" has lost much of its earlier nurturing confessional purpose. Finally, for better or for worse, the college's older familialism is rapidly vanishing, as we move toward more rationalized forms of organization and activity.

For historians, change over time is their stock-in-trade. No person and no human institution is exempt from it. Yet, how we manage change depends on the college's ability to balance the new and the old, on its ability to promote change within tradition. In this, the college is best served by remaining mindful of the gospel admonition to discover what is new and valuable in the treasury of the old.

NOTES

1. Todd Nichol, *All These Lutherans* (Minneapolis: Augsburg Publishing House, 1986) 11.

2. Mark Granquist, "Religious Vision and Academic Quest at St. Olaf College," *Models for Christian Higher Education*, ed. Richard T. Hughes and William B. Adrian (Grand Rapids, Mich.: William B. Eerdmans, 1997) 90.

3. Robert Hutchinson, *The Higher Learning in America* (New Haven: Yale, 1936).

4. Letter to Alfred North Whitehead, in Alfred North Whitehead, *The Aims of Education* (New York: Free Press, 1967).

5. From the college's 1874 Articles of Incorporation, as cited in Granquist 83.

6. Quoted in Granquist 89.

7. See Sydney E. Ahlstrom, *A Religious History of the American People* (New Haven: Yale University Press, 1972) 518–522.

PART II:

Biography: Who has shaped St. Olaf?

Lars W. Boe

St. Olaf Archives

5.
LARS W. BOE
1875–1942

William H. K. Narum

Lars Boe was the most colorful president St. Olaf had up to his time, and arguably is to the present day. The first alumnus to become president, Boe was a person of dominating character. His presence was immediately noted if he walked into a crowded room. Of medium height, and of more imposing girth as he grew older, he was without doubt the person in command. He could be abrupt, unpredictable, aggressive, then turn around and be tender, sympathetic, and reassuring. Gruff of speech, he encouraged people to differ with him, and cheerfully acknowledged adverse opinions. Faculty meetings could bring lively discussions. Before taking office he hinted that, with him in charge, the Board of Trustees would have little to do. Despite his hard-nosed demeanor, students affectionately referred to him as "Prexy Boe." As his friend and colleague, physics professor Erik Hetle, wrote of him, Boe was "equally successful, one might say spectacular, as pastor or politician, as educator and church statesman."[1] He affected anyone he met, even to the point of projecting himself into a person's private affairs. Howard Hong, now Professor Emeritus of Philosophy, recalls that early on in his career Boe called him into his office, criticized his clothes and shoes (Hong had just returned from Europe, where he had picked up both), and complained that to boot Hong had no telephone. What surprised Hong was Boe's "personal interest" in him. Aware of the young couple's monetary plight, Boe gave them a settee from his own house of such good quality that they still have it.

Boe was born December 27, 1875, in Calumet, Michigan, son of Pastor Nils Boe and Anna Reque Boe. When he was three, the family moved to Leland, Illinois, where Boe did not attend English school but stayed at home to learn Norwegian. At eleven he entered first grade; "but it took only three months to catch up with my age," he wrote years later in a letter to author Louis Adamic.[2] In 1887 his mother and infant brother died, and his father was left with five children to bring up alone, the youngest three years old. Pastor Boe accepted a call to Silver Lake, Iowa, and there he maintained an ordered and disciplined home life, with family devotions morning and night and duties for each child. There Lars was obliged to work on his father's farmland. Despite the frugality and the discipline, the home was "filled with reading, music, and a good deal of joking and pranks within the family circle." The father himself, according to accounts, was an inveterate prankster.[3] Lars never forgot the lessons he learned in Iowa, and would often reminisce fondly of *Den Gamle Prestegaard* ("the old priest's yard") as the place where he had learned to demand the most from himself, and as a result to demand the same from others. Many a time he was ordered to the woodshed by his father, once for presuming to complain that his father was underpaid and the children had to suffer.

> His answer was to take me out to the woodshed and give me what I had coming. He said to me that I must always look upon the opportunity to do God's work as being so big that it would not make much difference what kind of pay I got.[4]

From age sixteen on Boe was educated away from home, although he spent vacations at home—first at a Lutheran high school in St. Ansgar, Iowa, from 1890 to 1893, and then for one year at the preparatory department of the United Norwegian Lutheran Seminary in Minneapolis. At the latter he met a fellow student who became a friend for life, Johan A. Aasgaard. President M. O. Bockman of the seminary, noting the high abilities of both young men, urged them both to go to St. Olaf. They did, roomed together, and perpetrated many pranks as residents in Old Main. In winter they would hold the classroom thermometer outside the window before the professor entered. He would always check the thermometer first thing and, seeing the low reading, would throw more wood on the fire. Everyone sweltered including the puzzled professor. Both Boe and Aasgaard graduated with high honors in 1898, and both entered the United Church Seminary as roommates again, graduating in 1901. Both were ordained, but both were ultimately destined for service in the church other than being parish pastors. Both became college presidents, Boe at Waldorf from 1903 to 1914 and at St. Olaf from 1918 to 1942, and Aasgaard at Concordia in Moorhead from 1911 on, helping it to become a college in 1917. In 1925 Aasgaard was elected the president of both colleges' parent church body, the Norwegian Lutheran Church of America.

Boe spent only two years in an Iowa parish before being called to become the first president of Waldorf College, Forest City, Iowa. Sponsored by the church, it was a high school until 1920 when it became a junior college. When Boe arrived, there were thirteen students, and when he left eleven years later, more than three hundred. During his stay, he found time to court and eventually marry an instructor at Waldorf, Helga Jacobson; two daughters were born to them, Esther and Margaret. Waldorf proved to be a good preparation for heading St. Olaf later, as Boe acted not only as president, but as registrar, carpenter, janitor, and teacher—all besides being pastor of the local Lutheran church. Boe's successor as president of St. Olaf, Clemens Granskou, who attended Waldorf, remarked that Boe was the best teacher he had ever had.[5] Boe grew disturbed at how political discord was "tearing my church to pieces," and encouraged by friends, he decided to run for the Iowa legislature, to "find out what it was about and whether it was worth the trouble it caused." He was nominated by the Republicans and handily elected, serving both in the House and in the Senate from 1911 to 1915. Urged by some to run for governor, Boe declined. He said that for clean politics and good government what was needed was "intelligent, independent, and informed public opinion" and that he had decided to go back to his job "of helping to create it."[6]

In 1915 Boe accepted an appointment by the United Church to be head of its board of trustees, and in 1917 after three Norwegian Lutheran synods merged, he took the same position and also headed the board of education of the successor church, the Norwegian Lutheran Church of America. St. Olaf and Luther (the latter from the former Norwegian Synod) became colleges at large of the new church; other colleges belonged to distinct districts of the new church. In 1918 Boe was elected by the NLCA convention to become president of St. Olaf.

It should be said here that after accepting that position, Boe continued to play an important role in the broader Lutheran church. Because of his experience in the merger negotiations, Boe was named to the organizing committee of the Lutheran World Convention (later Federation) in the early 1920s. Later he was one of two Americans named to its executive committee, where he had a strong voice in its operations and major meetings. After 1935 he continued to serve as a consultant. As a result, Boe became a well-known figure in world Lutheranism. Joseph Shaw, in his history of the college, comments, "If Boe was instrumental in building a greater St. Olaf, full recognition must be give to the remarkable confidence which he secured for the College through his service as a leader in the Church."[7]

When Boe arrived at St. Olaf in September 1918, the college had been struggling for over a year to adjust to war conditions; also among faculty and students there had been much dissatisfaction with the previous president, Lauritz A. Vigness, who finally resigned to accept an executive position in the NLCA. When Vigness had been elected president of St. Olaf in 1914, Boe had been one of the candidates, and many faculty wished he had been elected at that time (Boe had also been disappointed then). Almost immediately upon Boe's assumption of office there was an influenza epidemic, which Boe handled with dispatch. His biographer Hetle says of him: "He was a full-blown president in a day and took charge without hesitation."[8] He was inaugurated on September 27 with two former St. Olaf presidents in attendance, Dr. J. N. Kildahl and Vigness.

Boe's achievements at St. Olaf were many—building up the faculty (he personally sought out and appointed faculty), strengthening the academic program, creating such monumental buildings as Holland Hall and Rølvaag Library. When he came, the college had a faculty of 38 members, 500 students; when he died in office there were 85 faculty and 1,125 students. He worked hard, and he expected his faculty to work hard, as he had learned to do growing up as a teenager in Iowa.

Boe spoke almost weekly in chapel, held then in the old gymnasium. There was no college pastor in his day, so that he acted as that too; a faculty chapel committee assisted him in selecting speakers when the president did not take charge. Sometimes it seemed to Boe's hearers that he spoke on a text "off the cuff," drawing on his knowledge and experience.[9] Chapel was not required under Boe as it had been under Vigness, but Boe made it clear that going to chapel was "expected" of all students and faculty. In fact almost everyone was at chapel—during these years the vast majority of students were Lutheran, 85 percent or more— and students who skipped did so as unobtrusively as possible to avoid antagonistic stares. Mondays were famous as Boe's time for "hanging out the wash"; after a short devotional talk he would take up some campus issue that

ST. OLAF ARCHIVES

Lars W. Boe reading *Lutheraneren*

concerned him. For example, he was proud of the appearance of the campus grounds: students and faculty were to walk on the sidewalk, not on the grass. The campus during his day was remarkably free of unsightly dirt paths. On one Monday he reminded his audience that they were to walk on the grass only to pick up stray paper or other objects, and he commended that student who had shouted from his Ytterboe window to Boe: "Get off the grass!" Boe had held up a candy wrapper to show he was practicing what he preached.

One of his favorite statements was "St. Olaf is not a college. It is a crusade!"[10] By that he meant the college was to turn out crusaders for the kingdom of God. In no way did he ever put the college ahead of the church. But the church was not an end in itself; it was the chief means given by God for the promotion of the kingdom. Another favorite statement about the college was that it was "dedicated to God without apologies to men." Boe expressed his philosophy of the college in a brief essay published in 1927 in the *Viking* yearbook, "What of the Future?":

> St. Olaf is a Liberal Arts College, frankly denominational, Lutheran, positively Christian, with a background reaching into the history and culture of the peoples of northern Europe, especially Norway, and still American in the fullest sense of the word.[11]

Boe said that it was important "to be abreast of the day," but still to appreciate the "factors from the past which have proven their worth." He said that "St. Olaf has a real contribution to make along these lines, none as a colorless, Liberal Arts institution. We dare to be different. We must be." Boe was not unaware of the difference between his ideal and reality. In November 1932, he gave a chapel address and later sent it out as a Christmas message to parents and alumni. In it he lamented his inability to inspire faculty and students to his ideal. He wanted to lift them out of their lethargy "in relation to the finest things St. Olaf has to offer, to the heights of idealism where you become Crusaders for Christ and His Kingdom."[12]

Boe insisted on this philosophy all of his years as president. Toward the end of his presidency, he wrote a Foreword to the Faculty Manual of 1941, which was reproduced in an issue of the student newspaper, the *Manitou Messenger*. In it he stated three objectives: the Christian objective, the cultural objective, and the scholastic objective. The first, the Christian objective, was the reason for St. Olaf's existence, without which it had no reason to exist. As for the cultural objective, Boe argued that St. Olaf wants to "keep in contact with the cultural heritages of all the peoples that are in harmony with the true genius of America." He treasured the Norwegian heritage of the college, but he insisted that St. Olaf was "eager to see these [other] heritages nursed and amplified so as to insure the finest cultural texture and growth in the college community." Last Boe pointed to the achievements of "significant individuals" at St. Olaf who had given scholastic recognition to the college. He was probably thinking of people like F. Melius Christiansen in music, E. O. Ellingson in chemistry, Julius Boraas in education, and O. E. Rølvaag in literature. He had all along urged faculty to "go the second mile" in producing articles or books, or engaging in other activities that benefit the general public. He looked ahead to the completion of the new library, which would make it possible for St. Olaf "to present itself with increasing definiteness and certainty as an American liberal arts college of high rank." He closed his statement with these words:

> In an institution like St. Olaf, no amount of piety will make up for poor scholarship, and no amount of scholarship and culture will make up for lack of real Christian life and faith.[13]

Boe never dictated any religious stance for his faculty. In a letter to a St. Olaf graduate studying at Harvard, Boe defended the conservative religious nature of St. Olaf but said that it was his desire to create there "an atmosphere in which men can think freely and act freely."[14] Faculty and students during Boe's time agreed that he exerted no pressure on them to conform to his own religious ideals and practices. Professor Theodore Jorgenson of the Norwegian Department wrote of Boe, "He was not a fanatical Lutheran," and never laid down any hard-and-fast rule about what his faculty should believe and do: "except to be a thorough teacher in one's own area."[15]

Throughout his years at St. Olaf, Boe consistently upheld a standard for his college, a sturdy combination of Christian faith and intellectual excellence, but at times he wondered whether this ideal was unreachable. In the late 1930s he expressed his doubts in a letter to James Baird, then dean of Berea College, saying that he would like to visit Berea to see what it means to conduct an institution with an idea behind it. He continued:

> In many respects St. Olaf is like Berea, but our people have been more affected by the sophistication of the day and the age in which we live, which . . . makes it difficult to continue being a college with an idea back of it. The tendency is to level down and become just another college.[16]

He cautioned the Berea president that what his college was doing was "undermining the very thing you want," because higher education gives people more sophistication. Boe knew the tension between spiritual and intellectual nurture and how the latter could eat away at the former.

Boe died on his sixty-seventh birthday in December 1942. Donald J.

Cowling of Carleton, another of the era's "take-charge" college presidents, had attended Boe's inauguration in 1918; and in January 1943, as one of the speakers at Boe's memorial service, President Cowling suggested that a new chapel, of which Boe had dreamed, be named after him. The cornerstone for Boe Chapel was laid ten years later, in 1953. O. G. Malmin, editor of the church's weekly magazine, the *Lutheran Herald*, titled his memorial: "L. W. Boe—Man of Vision."[17] That he had been, and it could be said of L. W. Boe that St. Olaf College was the lengthening shadow of his achievements and vision.

NOTES

1. Erik Hetle, *Lars Wilhelm Boe: A Biography* (Minneapolis: Augsburg, 1949) 1.
2. Hetle 14. Adamic had recently spoken at the college.
3. Hetle 14ff.
4. Hetle 15.
5. Hetle 37.
6. Hetle 46–50. The quotation about his decision to run was from an interview in the *Minneapolis Star-Tribune*, January 15, 1940.
7. *History of St. Olaf College, 1874–1974* (Northfield, Minn.: St. Olaf College Press, 1974) 350.
8. Hetle 58.
9. Ansgar Sövik, Professor Emeritus of Religion, confirms that suspicion. He related that once, when he was also assistant dean of men, Boe joined him as both walked to morning chapel. Pulling his New Testament from his pocket, Boe asked Sövik, "What would be a good text for chapel today?"
10. Quoted by Dr. C. A. Mellby in "Biographical Sketch of President Lars W. Boe," *St. Olaf College Bulletin* 39 (February 1943): 2. The full text of the letter went this way [Boe is speaking of the death of business manager and treasurer P. O. Holland]: "We are going right on even though one who has filled a large place has to drop out. We simply close up the ranks and march steadily on. St. Olaf is not a College. It is a Crusade." The words were often used in other contexts by Boe.
11. *The Viking* for 1928–29, published in 1927.
12. His chapel talk was reproduced in *St. Olaf College Bulletin* 28 (December 1932): 8, and sent as a Christmas letter to parents.
13. The *Manitou Messenger* 28 (November 1941): 2.
14. Letter to George Hartwig, 15 October 1924, in the St. Olaf archives.
15. *Nordmans Forbundet* (March 3, 1943): 4. Found in the L. W. Boe Papers in the Norwegian American Historical Association Archives at St. Olaf College, D 460, where there is a translation from the Norwegian by Charlotte Jacobson dated June 17, 1987. Mary Aasgaard Hinderlie is also quoted in this issue, p. 5, as saying that Boe had shown students a living witness as to how an honest man looked and acted.
16. Letter to James Baird, November 29, 1939, in the St. Olaf archives.
17. January 12, 1943.

F. Melius Christiansen

St. Olaf Archives

6.
F. MELIUS CHRISTIANSEN 1871–1955

Joseph M. Shaw

On a Sunday afternoon in March of 1943, the St. Olaf Choir gave its annual joint concert with the Minneapolis Symphony Orchestra. A review by John K. Sherman, music critic of the *Minneapolis Star-Journal*, began with these sentences:

> Occupancy of Northrop's stage by the Northwest's two premier musical organizations—the Minneapolis Symphony Orchestra and the St. Olaf Choir of Northfield—always gives University ushers their biggest assignment of the season. The auditorium, as usual, was packed to the doors.
>
> The choir now operates under dual control, a kind of king-and-crown prince partnership—Dr. F. Melius Christiansen, and his son, Olaf Christiansen. The latter conducted the program proper, and the father, hailed by stormy applause when his stocky, snow-thatched figure appeared from the wings, led three numbers.

The adulation directed at F. Melius Christiansen on this occasion was typical of the enthusiasm he and the St. Olaf Choir aroused during thirty years of performing in concert halls throughout the United States and abroad. Having founded the St. Olaf Choir in 1912, F. Melius Christiansen was its sole director until 1941 when Olaf, "the crown prince," joined him as associate director. During his retirement years Dr. Christiansen was a familiar and respected patriarchal presence on the campus of St. Olaf College. Recognized as a leader in American choral music and possessed of a singular, fascinating personality, he was undoubtedly the most famous member of the St. Olaf faculty for half a century.

F. Melius Christiansen was brought to St. Olaf College in 1903 to establish a department of music. He retained a keen interest in his first love, the St. Olaf Band, and from time to time led the St. Olaf Orchestra. But for the most part, he is remembered as founder and longtime chairman of the music department and the founder and first director of the St. Olaf Choir. And for those who sang under his inspired direction, the mere mention of "Christy" evokes memories of a unique, beloved mentor who left a permanent impress on their lives.

Fredrik Melius Christiansen was born April 1, 1871, in Berger, Norway, a small community some three miles from Eidsvold, where Norway's Constitution was signed on May 17, 1814. With such a birth date and the esteem and affection he enjoyed during his decades in the St. Olaf community, it was inevitable that his birthday was always recognized. On one particular April 1, P. G. Schmidt, manager of the St. Olaf Choir, had the Choir members all primed to surprise F. Melius by singing "Happy Birthday" for him at rehearsal. Willis H. Miller, Class of 1940, tells what happened:

> Precisely at the starting time, the revered and beloved maestro entered the rehearsal room and walked briskly to the conductor's stand. There he bowed ceremoniously to the members of the choir and sat down at the piano.
>
> With two thundering chords, Christy started to play the piano. The tune reverberated through the room. It was "Happy Birthday to you. . . ." The choir gasped and then broke into a hearty applause. Christy had pulled an April fool's joke on them!

As a young man growing up in Norway, Christiansen received his first musical education while the family lived in Larvik, a seacoast town on the west side of the Oslo Fjord. Encouraged by his father, mother, grandfather, and an able local musician, Oscar Hansen, Melius played clarinet, violin, piano, and organ. Prospects for a career in music were limited in Larvik, so he emigrated to America in 1888, aspiring to be a concert violinist.

At the age of nineteen, F. Melius Christiansen was hired as director of the Scandinavian Band in Marinette, Wisconsin. He also gave private lessons in violin, piano, and organ, and served as organist and choir director at Our Savior's Lutheran Church. In Marinette he met Edith Lindem, whom he would later marry. When a male quartet from Augsburg Seminary in Minneapolis gave a concert in Our Savior's, one of its members, recognizing that the young musician should develop his talents with further education, urged him to come to Augsburg.

At Augsburg, Christiansen made friends, took some courses, and pursued his music. He was in demand as a violin soloist, directed the Augsburg Seminary Chorus, and taught a class in singing and theory. He also played the organ and directed the choir at Trinity Lutheran Church. After a year he enrolled in Northwestern Conservatory of Music in Minneapolis to study violin, piano, harmony, and counterpoint. After marrying Edith Lindem in 1897, he spent two years in Germany at the Leipzig

Conservatory where he studied theory and composition under Gustav Schreck.

Returning to Minneapolis, Christiansen joined the violin faculty at Northwestern Conservatory, played violin in the predecessor of the Minneapolis Symphony Orchestra, performed violin solos, played the organ and led church choirs, composed music, and directed a male chorus called the Kjerulf Club. It was largely through a member of the Kjerulf Club, a young mathematician named Paul G. Schmidt, that Christiansen went to St. Olaf College.

Schmidt joined the faculty of St. Olaf College in 1902. When the president of the college, the Reverend John Nathan Kildahl, asked if he knew anyone who might be suitable as director of music, Schmidt told him about F. Melius Christiansen. The president of the United Norwegian Lutheran Church, the Reverend T. H. Dahl, interviewed Christiansen and recommended him to President Kildahl, who engaged his services as music director at St. Olaf, beginning part-time in the fall of 1903 at a salary of $600 per year.

At St. Olaf Christiansen was to be in charge of the music department, direct the band and the chorus, and teach violin and music theory. After a successful first year, he was named full professor and his salary increased to $1,000 per year. He moved his family to Northfield in the summer of 1904. For the rest of his long career, St. Olaf College in Northfield, Minnesota, was the base of his operations as music teacher, composer, conductor, and pioneer in American choral music.

While the reputation of F. Melius Christiansen is bound up with that of the St. Olaf Choir, his first task as "Director of Music" was to bring order and academic standing to the music activity. As founder and chairman of the music department, listed in the catalog as "School of Music" in 1904, he established a sound and broad base for musical development at the college. He persuaded the faculty to give full academic credit for elective courses in music. The catalog for 1904–1905 carried this statement: "In a college of general education, and especially of Christian education and co-education, is the place for a school of music." Courses offered that year were Musical Theory, Harmony, Counterpoint, Canon and Fugue, Musical Composition, Analysis and History of Music, and an advanced course in piano, violin, or voice. Later, the School of Music offered a two-year course in public school music.

Christiansen was expected to train and direct the St. Olaf Band. He quickly transformed it from a casual, fun-loving group that played marches and waltzes for its own entertainment to a disciplined musical organization that learned to perform at a much higher level, and to enjoy it. By 1906 the Band's competence was such that Professor Christiansen took the aggregation, with P. G. Schmidt as drum major, on an unprecedented performing tour to Norway.

Between 1907 and 1914, Christiansen collaborated with President Kildahl in working up an effective "Song Service" format featuring choral anthems by student singers interspersed with comments on the texts by Kildahl. Such well-known Christiansen choral arrangements as "Built on a Rock," "O Bread of Life," "Wake, Awake," "Praise to the Lord," and "Beautiful Savior" were developed for these song services. As the meditations dropped out of the program, the result was a pioneering form, the sacred concert. When the Choir made its memorable tour to New York and other eastern cities in 1920, critics and other listeners were impressed by the entirely sacred nature of the program as well as by the uncommonly high quality of the a cappella concert, sung entirely from memory.

It took some time and experimentation for Christiansen to develop the choral ensemble that came to be known as the St. Olaf Choir. Steps along the way included his working with the Choral Union, dividing it into ladies' and men's choruses, touring with a mixed octet, creating a favorable impact with the "song services," and directing the choir at St. John's Lutheran Church in Northfield. The St. Olaf Choir began in 1912 when the choir of St. John's church, consisting mostly of St. Olaf College students and a number of adult members of the congregation, made an Easter tour into Wisconsin and Illinois as "The St. Olaf Choir."

Many have been fascinated that a violinist and band director should switch his interest to a cappella choral music and create a world-famous choir. When a reporter asked how this happened, F. Melius gave this disarming reply: "The choir just grew. Most of the children were too poor to buy band instruments. The voices were there, and singing didn't cost anything."

Could Christiansen have achieved similar results elsewhere? Without a doubt, as far as his talent as a musician was concerned, but the St. Olaf setting itself offered a conducive atmosphere, acknowledged by F. Melius when the Choir returned from the East Coast in 1920. "The choir and the band are a natural outgrowth of the culture here," he said. "They have grown naturally from a little seed way back in history and like flowers in the woods, grew under favorable conditions. That we were successful was only that the *flavor of St. Olaf* was given to the world and they seemed to like it."

A lively musical life prevailed at the college before Christiansen came. Students were accustomed to singing the great Lutheran chorales in their home churches and at the college. Vocal groups went out from the college to sing in churches and in Choral Union gatherings. F. Melius himself, both before and after he came to St. Olaf, helped create a musical culture within the whole Norwegian Lutheran Church body to which he belonged, serving as its musical tutor through his leadership in the Choral Union, his compositions and arrangements. "He taught our Church to sing," wrote the editor of a church paper.

His energetic plunge into choral work was illustrated primarily by his work with the St. Olaf Choir but also supported by compositions in *The St. Olaf Choir Series* that began in 1919. These initiatives had the educational aims of demonstrating the riches of sacred choral literature, inspiring congregations to improve the quality of their choirs, and elevating tastes in church music. "Bad taste is sin," he once remarked.

F. Melius Christiansen's musical genius only begins to account for his contributions to St. Olaf College and to choral music throughout the world. He was a highly gifted man with a sure instinct for an approach that transformed choral music. He once summed up in two sentences how he trained the St. Olaf Choir: "We revived and practiced a certain principle of ensemble singing that the world had forgotten. This consisted of dispensing with the tremolo voice and singing straight tones for the purpose of good intonation." Some have called this the Northern European style of choral singing.

Although a cappella singing dated back to sixteenth- and seventeenth-century Europe, it was not common in this country. Christiansen's choral work made it much more familiar. A reporter quoted him as saying, "Always they sang in this country with organ accompaniment. Then if the voices were bad the organ could drown them out." In his unpretentious way, Christiansen commented once about the "luck" of the St. Olaf Choir in coming on the scene when it did. He told a reporter in 1937: "This country had too much flimsy Church music. We came along at the psychological moment with the right kind of Church music sung in the right way. If the time had not been particularly right we should not have been so lucky."

Christiansen was a churchman who affirmed the Christian tradition in his own free-spirited way, disdaining too much formality in worship. A friend referred to him as "a believer, deeply and devoutly, without fuss and feathers." Religion was important to his personality and to his sense of vocation. He wrote to St. Olaf President Lars Boe, "I am not sentimental when I say that the spiritual condition is very important in this work." As a person of faith he viewed talents as gifts from God meant to be developed through disciplined work and put to use for the glory of God's kingdom. In a 1929 chapel talk he told the students, "Let no one stop you from making the best possible use of your talents. You owe it to yourselves and to your Creator."

A journalist who visited a rehearsal observed: "Work is the very essence of Dr. Christiansen's philosophy of singing sacred music." When asked how he achieved such stunning results, Christiansen himself would say, "We work! and again we work!" In a 1930 article he wrote, "We must learn to like our work and we must be willing to work hard on the perfection of our means of expression in order that the spirit may be set free and given the fullest liberty and power." One Choir member familiar with the exacting, repetitive polishing of every note and phrase at rehearsals wrote of Christiansen's "vast technical patience, an inexhaustible interest in the analytical side of his work."

All of this concentrated effort was aimed at creating beauty. Wrote F. Melius in 1929, "The better equipped a person is technically, the easier he is able to bring out the beauties of the art." In his view, the art of music required that the feeling expressed be genuine and that it be expressed beautifully. One of his Choir members said, "Christy preached that perfection was truth which became beauty and inspiration to the listeners." Beauty was essential for the proper praise of God. In a letter to President Boe, Christy wrote of being true to our calling, true to the Master, and true to art. "The spirit of art is much like the Spirit of Christ."

Dr. Christiansen enjoyed not only admiration but total loyalty and love from Choir members. They were willing to work hard because they saw how unsparingly he devoted himself to their common musical challenges. They were confident that the grueling hours of rehearsal would bear fruit in fulfilling concert performances. They also learned from him that there was more to singing than achieving technical perfection. Once at rehearsal he paused to say this:

> You sing notes as if you are pulling sausages out of a tight hole; as if it is hard work. The value of singing is that which is *more* than the actual singing; you can't sing unless you have the love of singing in your hearts.

And in all their contacts with him, they were charmed by his lovable, puckish personality. "Christy" had the magical touch. He could lighten practices with his droll, spontaneous humor. He could lead his singers to heights of accomplishment they never thought within reach. He could mesmerize audiences by his masterly control of the ensemble.

Beyond the St. Olaf campus, Christiansen was recognized as a leader in conducting and composing. The annual tours made the St. Olaf Choir known throughout the United States and in Europe. Choir directors and other musicians became familiar with the music of F. Melius through more than 250 compositions and arrangements published in *The St. Olaf*

Choir Series. The king of Norway bestowed on him the Order of St. Olaf. Christiansen was awarded honorary doctorates by Oberlin College, Capital University, Muhlenberg College, and the University of Minnesota. For his eightieth birthday, Leopold Stokowski sent warmest greetings with the comment: "The whole world is indebted to you for what you have done for American choral music."

F. M. Christiansen and O. E. Rølvaag. Spring 1926 (Commencement)
St. Olaf Archives

F. Melius Christiansen reached the age of eighty in April of 1951, setting off an entire month of birthday observances. Especially notable was the concert the St. Olaf Choir gave in Northrop Auditorium on April 13, 1951, as a tribute to its founder, who was in the audience. "The big moment came at the end," wrote John K. Sherman, "when the stocky, snow-haired founder of the famous choir rose from his seat . . . made his way to the stage, and took over." Sherman continued:

> Not for many years has Minneapolis seen the grand old man of Minnesota music, the patriarch of American choral singing, mount the platform and assume his old role. The occasion was an affecting and memorable one. The last song was his, the one so long associated with him and the choir—"Beautiful Savior."

Through the St. Olaf Choir, his hundreds of compositions, and his creative leadership in choral conducting, F. Melius Christiansen made an impact on the world that prompted Richard S. Davis to write: "For generations to come the effect of his devoted service will surely be felt."

The truth of that prophecy continues to be confirmed at St. Olaf College. Very few St. Olaf faculty persons have made such a lasting mark on the college as F. Melius Christiansen. He gave music an honored place among the liberal arts as a medium for ennobling the human spirit and as a vehicle for the jubilant worship of God. In a 1929 chapel talk he said, "The student organization known as the St. Olaf Choir is an expression of the spirit of the institution." Because of the extraordinary pioneering work of F. Melius Christiansen, the members and directors of the St. Olaf Choir annually bring the spiritual and cultural values of the College before varied audiences throughout the world. And the listeners seem to like what they hear.

O. E. Rølvaag as a student, c. 1905

St. Olaf Archives

7.
OLE EDVART RØLVAAG
1876–1931

Solveig Zempel

When Ole Edvart Rølvaag immigrated to the United States in 1896 he joined the community of Norwegian Americans, the people Rølvaag came to call "his people." According to his own account, Rølvaag left his beloved home and family in Norway in order to satisfy his ambition to become something great in the world. Already at an early age he had developed a sense of calling and a desire to become more than a fisherman. Writing to his fiancée, Jennie Berdahl, Rølvaag reported that "I spent my entire childhood in a struggle with the Arctic. This struggle has left an indelible impression on me; for the passions of my soul are as powerful as the storms up north." Later he added, "I loved to be alone with my intense longings and dreams of achievement; for I would achieve great things when I grew up; of that I was convinced. Once—I recall it as well as if it were yesterday—mother asked me what I wanted to become. I answered without hesitation; either a poet or a professor. You can just imagine how she laughed; for how could a poor fisherman's boy ever become anything like that."[1]

Rølvaag was born and grew to young adulthood on the North-Norwegian island of Dønna, just below the Arctic Circle. His father, Peder Benjamin Jakobsen Rølvaag, was a fisherman, and his mother, Ellerine Pedersdotter, took care of the home and the family of seven children. In spite of poverty and limited formal education, the family were all voracious readers, making extensive use of the local library and keeping up with the outside world by subscribing to a national newspaper. Ole was especially close to his gifted older brother Johan, who set a high standard for the younger brother to live up to. "As soon as I was old enough to handle an oar, I had to go to sea," he wrote. "I and my oldest brother Johan were constantly together."[2]

The Rølvaag children ended their formal schooling—nine weeks a year for seven years—as soon as they were confirmed. Ole, like the other boys, sailed to the Lofoten fishing banks as a fourteen-year-old and continued working as a fisherman for the next five years. He nearly lost his life in a terrible storm in 1893 and shortly thereafter wrote to an uncle in South Dakota asking for the loan of money for a ticket to America. Rølvaag finally received the precious ticket and set out in 1896 at the age of twenty—knowing not a word of English—to join his uncle in Elk Point, South Dakota. He worked for three years as a farmhand, later describing life as a newcomer with drama and humor in his first published novel, *Amerika breve* (*The Third Life of Per Smevik*).

Farmwork, however, was not the kind of opportunity Rølvaag had dreamed about. Encouraged by a local pastor, he enrolled at Augustana Academy, a Norwegian American Lutheran preparatory school in Canton, South Dakota. It was here that he first became acquainted with the Berdahl family, who had come to South Dakota as pioneer immigrants in the 1870s. Rølvaag became good friends with John Berdahl at Augustana Academy and later married John's sister Jennie, who also attended that school. He got much factual information about the pioneer period from her father and uncles. During his student days at Augustana, Rølvaag was influenced by several important teachers, and he not only began serious study of literature but also made his first attempts at writing—manuscripts of short stories and plot outlines from this time are found in the archives of the Norwegian American Historical Association. Rølvaag graduated with honors in 1901, and in his commencement address he spoke to the issues that would occupy him for the rest of his life: the notion that immigrants can become good citizens and contribute to their adopted country only by drawing on their own language, culture, and national heritage.

Following graduation from Augustana Academy, Rølvaag continued his education at St. Olaf College. Again, he chose a school with strong Norwegian American and Lutheran ties where he could acquire a well-rounded, classical education. Here too, he was fortunate to meet excellent teachers who encouraged his love and understanding of Norwegian language and literature. He took a heavy academic load, wishing to make the most of this opportunity and also to make up for lost time. Among other subjects, he studied Latin, Greek, German, English, history, church history, mathematics, and psychology. In addition to course work and co-curricular activities he continued writing, and a number of short pieces—inspirational essays, poems, and short stories—appeared in the college newspaper, the *Manitou Messenger*. He also found time to write his first novel ("Nils and Astri: Fragments of Norwegian-American Folk Life"—a love story in a rural immigrant setting), which, though never published, shows where his ambitions lay. In 1927, Rølvaag reminisced about his student days at St. Olaf in an article in the *Manitou Messenger*. There he described the restricted curriculum (only two prescribed course plans to choose from), the fixed study hours, and the even more restricted personal life: "Doors bolted tight and all lights out at ten. No student using tobacco was allowed quarters in the dormitory; smoking on the streets or on the campus absolutely forbidden, with a death penalty for cigarette smoking."[3]

Already older than most of his fellow students when he graduated in 1905, Rølvaag was eager to begin a career, get married and settle in a home of his own. When President J. N. Kildahl offered him a teaching post at St. Olaf, contingent on doing a year of graduate work at the university in Norway, he eagerly seized the opportunity. He borrowed money from Kildahl, and in 1905, less than ten years after he had left as a poor fisherman, he returned to Norway as a graduate student.

While at the University in Kristiania (Oslo), Rølvaag found that he had been changed by his American experiences, that he was no longer a Norwegian but had become a Norwegian American. He was not only older, but bolder. His professors, all important scholars of the time, influenced Rølvaag's views on Norwegian history, literature, and culture. In addition to his concentration on Norwegian literature and history, Rølvaag was especially interested in the study of psychology. Rølvaag continued writing, revising the manuscript of his unpublished novel, and sending frequent letters home to Jennie. In one of these letters, sent on Christmas Eve, he included a sentimental short story he had written as a Christmas gift, as he could afford no other.

Even though hampered by frequent bouts of pleurisy, Rølvaag passed his M.A. examinations with flying colors, and finally was able to visit his home on Dønna before returning to St. Olaf in the fall of 1906 to take up his teaching duties. Rølvaag married Jennie Berdahl in the summer of 1908, and they established a home in Northfield. Four children were born to the family, but the eldest and the youngest died in early childhood. Both the surviving children graduated from St. Olaf College and both attended the University of Oslo. Ella Valborg completed a master's degree in Scandinavian languages and literature and taught Norwegian and English at St. Olaf, Luther, and the Universities of Minnesota and Wisconsin. Karl Fritjof, who died in 1990, had a distinguished career in Minnesota politics, having served as lieutenant governor, governor, and ambassador to Iceland.

Rølvaag started teaching at St. Olaf in both the academy and the college. In addition to Norwegian, which was his main subject, he taught geometry, physiology, geography, Greek, and Bible history. He was also head resident in the dormitory. As time went on, he gradually came to concentrate on Norwegian language and literature. He became chairman of the Department of Norwegian in 1916, a post he held until shortly before his death. In 1920 he added his two favorite courses, The Dramas of Ibsen and The History of Norwegian Immigration, both taught in English. Rølvaag felt strongly the importance of teaching Norwegian American youth about the culture from which they came, and about the history of their own people in America. The course on immigration history gave him the opportunity to convey to students his ideas on the importance of preserving one's culture and to inculcate a sense of pride in their Norwegian heritage. Clarence Kilde, a former student of Rølvaag, reminisces about him: "He entered the classroom with a firm step and with the manner of one with a mission. There is work to be done here. . . .Rølvaag's lectures were not just information and interpretation, . . . but also enthusiasm. . . . There were such very important considerations as standards in morality, loyalty to family and cultural ancestors, and disciplined standards of work."[4] Einar Haugen, one of Rølvaag's protégés and himself a distinguished professor with a long career at the University of Wisconsin and Harvard, agrees with that assessment and adds, "Rølvaag saw in his students the bearers of his own mission, to whom he wished to impart some of his enthusiasm. He took endless pains with his students, giving them time that his children sometimes begrudged. . . . Rølvaag's alternation between severity and facetiousness, seriousness and jollity, was an important aspect of his temperament. Students crowded into his classes, especially after 1920 when he initiated two courses in English: one on Ibsen's plays, another on Norwegian immigration."[5]

Rølvaag was a strict disciplinarian with a great concern for his students' lives as well as their academic success. Early in his teaching career he wrote to his friend Reverend O. C. Farseth, "When I think of my position here at St. Olaf, I would rather sail a small craft from Fleinvær to Værø on a stormy January night. . . . [How] to guide so many young people? I have to stop every now and then and ask myself, 'Is this the right course? Am I steering straight?'"[6] Personal letters and reminiscences indicate that Rølvaag was a gifted and beloved teacher. Former students corresponded with him (and with his wife) for years after graduation. They told about their lives and careers, asked for advice, and discussed ideas about life. His extensive course notes (found in the NAHA archives) indicate that he was a dedicated teacher who prepared his lectures thoroughly. He carefully commented on student papers and essays, and spent much time counseling and guiding the young people he loved to work with. Rølvaag encouraged the best students to study for a year after graduation in Norway and worked toward setting up a scholarship for that purpose. St. Olaf President J. N. Kildahl publicly praised Rølvaag as a teacher, stating that he was not only excellently trained in his subject but that he was also a born teacher capable of arousing young people to idealistic enthusiasm.[7]

Though Rølvaag loved teaching and working with youth, and was intensely loyal to St. Olaf College, his position was burdensome at times, especially when he felt that his real calling was to be a writer. Personal letters reveal that he thought of resigning on several occasions but was held back both by economic considerations and by his love of teaching and loyalty to the college. On occasion he had to defend the teaching of Norwegian against attack from colleagues in other departments and from church leaders. Rølvaag was very close to President Lars Boe, and became part of an inner circle of advisers. Shortly after Rølvaag's death, Boe wrote, "I had selected him from among the members of the faculty as the one with whom and to whom I could speak freely. I had very few plans that I did not discuss with him and I believe that was the case with him too, as far as I was concerned." Rølvaag willingly stepped in to help whenever necessary, even serving briefly as college registrar. He went on fund-raising missions, and himself donated regularly to college fund drives. Perhaps his biggest sacrifice on behalf of the college was to give up part of his first sabbatical in order to travel around the Midwest raising funds to replace the chapel which burned down in 1923.

Even with this interruption, he had completed nearly half the manuscript for *I de dage* (*Giants in the Earth*) before sailing for Norway in the spring of 1924. There he finished the manuscript, and it was accepted for publication by Aschehoug Publishing Company. It was a tremendous coup for Rølvaag, as an obscure Norwegian American writer, to have a novel published by one of the leading Norwegian publishers. *I de dage* and *Riket grundlægges*, published as two separate novels in 1924 and 1925, were enthusiastically received by the Norwegian public and critics. When the English translation appeared as *Giants in the Earth* in 1927, it was selected by the Book of the Month Club and immediately sold thirty thousand copies. Rølvaag went from being an obscure professor to a famous writer overnight. *Giants in the Earth* was both a popular and a critical success. It has been in print continuously to this day, and has been translated into numerous languages.

However, Rølvaag was not so obscure within his own group, and by the time *I de dage* came out in Norway, he had published four novels (in Norwegian) in America. He had also published several textbooks and a book of essays. He wrote constantly in newspapers and journals, he gave

O. E. Rølvaag seated

ELLA VALBORG TWEET

speeches throughout the Midwest, he was active in Norwegian American organizations, and his novels, poems, and short stories were known to the Norwegian American reading public.

Rølvaag interrupted his stream of fiction briefly to gather together his thoughts in a volume of polemical essays on the issues of immigration, culture, and heritage. The resulting book, *Omkring Fædrearven* (*Concerning Our Heritage*) was published in 1922 under the imprint of the St. Olaf College Press. Rølvaag's friends worried that President Boe and the college would be criticized for the book, as indeed was the case. Boe, however, wrote that

> it may be that I am getting myself into trouble by doing what I have done with Prof. Rølvaag's book. However, it is done, and so far, at least, I do not have any regrets. Prof. Rølvaag has been doing excellent work at St. Olaf College in maintaining an interest in everything that pertains to our ancestral heritage. He is entitled to every bit of encouragement that we can give. In addition, I disagree with him in so many of the things he says, that it affords me a good opportunity to do something to establish the spirit of 'free thinking' which is needed so much among our people. In the third place, he has expressed far better than I can many things wherein I agree with him. Undoubtedly we shall be attacked . . . however, it may be fate that has started us out on Rølvaag's book. It concerns a matter which has been, is, and will be of importance to us at St. Olaf.

Rølvaag helped organize and was an officer for many years of Nordlandslag (Society of People from North-Norway) in 1909. In 1910, he was elected secretary of the Samfundet for Norsk Sprog og Kultur (Society for Norwegian Language and Culture). This group of Norwegian American educators was devoted to the promotion of the teaching of Norwegian and to providing adequate textbooks and teaching materials. During the height of the antiforeign hysteria during and after World War I Rølvaag helped found the society *For Fædrearven* (For the Ancestral Heritage). He was secretary in this organization and wrote many of the columns that appeared under the masthead of the society in the weekly paper *Visergutten.*

In 1925, Rølvaag helped found the Norwegian American Historical Association (NAHA) and was its first secretary. The mission of the NAHA is "to locate, collect, preserve and interpret the Norwegian American part of the whole of American history, and to do so with accuracy, integrity, and liveliness." Rølvaag devoted countless hours to correspondence, organizing meetings, and collecting books, pamphlets, and other materials for the NAHA archives. In addition to his novels, the NAHA, which is today one of the leading immigrant historical associations, may well prove to be Rølvaag's most enduring legacy.

Rølvaag was a man with many irons in the fire all his life, combining teaching, organizational work, support for the college, and writing. He was often plagued by ill health, suffering from angina pectoris which sapped his energy, and he was sometimes discouraged because he could not accomplish all that he wanted to do. His heart finally failed him, and he died in his home in Northfield at the age of fifty-five in November of 1931.

During the last years of his life, Rølvaag found himself catapulted into literary fame on two continents. He was courted by Norwegian authors who solicited his help in finding translators and publishers in America, and he gained new friends among the literary and intellectual establishment in the United States. The poor fisherman from Norway had fulfilled his calling and been faithful to his mission in life, and it had led him down a remarkable path.

NOTES

1. Letter from Rølvaag to Jennie Berdahl, September 22, 1904.
2. Rølvaag, "Romance of a Life" fragmentary unpublished autobiography. Norwegian American Historical Association archives.
3. *Manitou Messenger,* December 13, 1927.
4. Clarence Kilde, "My Memories of O. E. Rølvaag as a Teacher," unpublished MS, NAHA archives.
5. Einar Haugen, *Ole Edvart Rølvaag* (Boston: Twayne, 1983) 20.
6. Letter from Rølvaag to Reverend O. C. Farseth, January 8, 1908. NAHA archives.
7. *Lutheraneren*, November 12, 1913.

E. O. Ellingson, May 1957

St. Olaf Archives

8.
EMIL OSCAR ELLINGSON
1877–1968

Albert E. Finholt

Emil Ellingson was an alumnus who was brought back to teach at St. Olaf College by President Lars Boe with a clear injunction to develop an outstanding chemistry department. This was a stroke of administrative genius. Ellingson was not only a brilliant chemistry teacher but he built a department that became a model for his college and his country. He knew exactly what he wanted to achieve and he lived to see his goals fulfilled.

During my first years at St. Olaf in the 1950s I was fortunate to share an office with this man whose name now appears on one of our dormitories. Dr. Ellingson had stepped down from his position as chair of the chemistry department but he was still actively teaching. It was my privilege to enjoy his wit, good humor, and his many stories of the college. He gave a young professor an unforgettable introduction to his college.

Ellingson grew up on a farm in southern Minnesota and in his youth he had to work on the farm for many months out of the year, delaying his schooling. His family chose him as their most academically promising child and sent him to Lutheran Normal School in Madison, Minnesota. He graduated at age twenty-two after finishing with a certificate to teach rural schools in the Midwest. He taught parochial and public school for three years. During these first years of teaching Emil found time to visit a young woman, Lena Boraas, who had been a classmate at Lutheran Normal School. He took a train from southern Minnesota to Cannon Falls, with his bicycle in the baggage car. Lena often met him at the station, and they walked across the fields to have a few moments alone before they reached the Boraas farmhouse and its family of thirteen children. This friendship led to marriage when Emil was in his second year of college.

Ellingson came to St. Olaf College as a student in 1902 because several of his normal school classmates were there and his family knew staff at the college. Ellingson was an excellent student. He received one of the four prestigious Talla scholarships, a mark of the esteem in which the faculty held him. After Ellingson graduated with a B.S. degree, President Kildahl invited him to accept a job as a teaching assistant at a salary of $600, provided that he would go to summer school in science. At the end of the 1906–1907 school year Ellingson's mentor and chemistry teacher, Paul Glasoe, left to accept the presidency of Spokane Junior College. Ellingson replaced him as an instructor with full responsibility for all of the teaching in chemistry.

The next few years were perhaps the most difficult of Dr. Ellingson's life. It had been his intention to attend summer school until he attained a master's degree. With a rapidly growing family, he began to feel increasing financial pressure and his salary was minimal. During his first years of teaching at St. Olaf he had considered a position as superintendent of a high school, but he turned down the job after considerable urging from St. Olaf not to leave. He was aware of his lack of advanced training but decided to stay at his alma mater to do the best teaching of which he was capable. He worked long hours in the classroom and laboratory and considered that he had undertaken a "tough job."

At the end of the school year on May 29, 1909, without any previous warning, Ellingson was notified that the Board of Directors had decided to recommend someone else for the chemistry position at St. Olaf for next year and Dr. Glasoe would be that person. At this time President Kildahl was ill and had gone from the campus to Oregon. Ellingson respected and admired President Kildahl, and he wrote to him to try to gain a better perspective as to what had happened. He had been told there were vague questions about his teaching and some thought that the faculty had too many alumni teachers. In considerable agony he wrote, "I am glad for the sake of St. Olaf if Dr. Glasoe could be persuaded to return to St. Olaf, but I am very sorry (and it grows worse the more I think of it) to know that I . . . am not wanted here apparently on account of inability as a teacher . . . . If there is anything I [should] know it would in the long run do me good to . . . be told of it. . . . Please excuse me for writing all this, troubling you with my troubles but I had to tell them to someone besides my God." At this point he thought ruefully of two opportunities that he had rejected. One was the high school superintendent appointment. The other was an offer to teach at the University of Wisconsin while he did advanced studies. In the end, Wisconsin renewed its offer. Ellingson went there in 1909, attained a master's degree in 1910, and a doctorate in 1912. He subsequently taught as a full-time professor at Wisconsin for seven years.

In 1918 at St. Olaf College a new and energetic president, Lars W. Boe, took office. In 1919, with a vision for greater academic attainments, Dr. Boe invited Dr. Ellingson to return to St. Olaf College to work with

Dr. Glasoe to build an outstanding chemistry department. Boe had written a letter of inquiry to the University of Wisconsin asking about Ellingson's teaching ability, adding that he was well aware of his "scholarship." The chairman of the chemistry department, Dr. Kahlenberg, wrote back, "[He] has done very excellent work here as a teacher. He has the respect and goodwill of all of the students who have ever been under his care. He is a thorough and inspiring teacher and works devotedly for his students, not only in the classroom but also at all other times and occasions. I need hardly say that his scholarship is thorough."

Ellingson accepted the St. Olaf appointment despite a cut in salary, but he did write to President Boe, "I have decided to accept the position of professor of chemistry at St. Olaf College . . . with the understanding that . . . a year from now it is the intention to place me on the same salary scale with the professors who draw the maximum salary. Permit me to assure you that the future welfare of St. Olaf College lies close to my heart."

President Boe played a significant role in Ellingson's life. Many years later Emil wrote: "I learned to know President Boe intimately. He was an inspiration to me in my work. At times he was like a father to me. . . . He always gave me the impression that he was more than ordinarily interested in our work in chemistry." In later years Dr. Boe said that Ellingson was an "ideal teacher running an ideal department."

In 1921 Ellingson took over the chairmanship of the chemistry department and held this position without a leave of absence until 1950. In these years he often signed his letters E.O.E. This accounts for his popular nickname EO. The period of his leadership was one of continuous expansion in facilities, course offerings, and enrollments in chemistry. This was an exciting time but it placed a tremendous burden on a small chemistry faculty. Ellingson poured himself into the development of his department, making it the sole focus of his energy apart from his family and his church. Eventually the workload took its toll. In 1929 his good friend Dr. Adolph Hanson of Faribault noticed he had a myocardial condition. By 1937 the ailment had reached the point where Hanson felt it imperative to write to President Boe to ask for relief for this conscientious professor. President Boe replied that he would take immediate steps to see that Dr. Ellingson held down his activities. Fortunately the medical advice worked since EO taught for another fifteen years, until age seventy-five, and lived to be ninety.

Ellingson was a cordial and correct man in his relationships. When he first started teaching he was concerned about the second-class status of science at St. Olaf and he worked all his life to achieve respectability for chemistry in a liberal arts framework. He was "jealous" of maintaining the

E. O. Ellingson ST. OLAF ARCHIVES

attention of his chemistry majors and was unhappy with the hold that music and athletics had on some students. These misgivings did not prevent him from thoroughly enjoying athletic contests on the campus. He shared, with all persons who have ever taught, the conviction that "the administration" of the college was often sadly lacking in perspective and judgment, even his admired leader Boe. A rare glimpse of frustration was shown one day after a visit with the president. EO came back to the chemistry department, threw his papers on his desk and said in exasperation, "To ask for money for the chemistry department is like asking for money for the devil."

Ellingson had little time for recreation and vacation but he enjoyed games and other activities with his children. He also enjoyed eating, "especially baked ham and blueberry pie." The family was musical and liked singing, although most of them had no formal training. His daughter Vivian became a music teacher. EO had a good voice and at one time sang in a church choir. On winter evenings the family sat in a circle in the living room for an hour or two while father read books like Grimm's *Fairy Tales*, *Robinson Crusoe*, or *Tom Sawyer*. He was a concerned and caring parent who saw that all of his children received a college education, but he never tried to influence the choice of a major or a vocation.

Above all, Ellingson was a great teacher. His students recalled him vividly since he shepherded them through all the upper-class courses. His lectures were straightforward with few jokes or anecdotes but with many lecture demonstrations. He was considered to be a stern disciplinarian and his excellent sense of humor came through only to a few students. In the laboratory he allowed great freedom to his upperclass students. They worked on their own but he was always available for help and advice. He regularly ate lunch at his desk. He addressed his students formally as "Mister" or "Miss" but he liked students and enjoyed talking with them. Students considered his recommendation so crucial to further education that they would forgo playing varsity football or singing in the famous St. Olaf Choir in order to merit a good letter of reference.

Ellingson saw that his students got assistantships or fellowships at some of our best universities. He wrote to them in graduate school and afterwards. By 1952, sixty-eight alumni of St. Olaf had achieved the Ph.D. in chemistry. Many students took that path because of Ellingson's guidance and encouragement, and they wrote back to the college to voice their gratitude for what they were given by Dr. Ellingson. In 1957 the Manufacturing Chemists Association selected him as one of the nation's outstanding teachers of undergraduate chemistry. He was in the first group of six teachers to receive the award. The heritage passed on by Dr. Ellingson has enabled St. Olaf to be the only four-year college to be listed by the American Chemical Society among the top twenty-five institutions in production of chemistry majors.

Following retirement Dr. Ellingson continued his letter writing to chemistry alumni. He appeared on the campus on special occasions but he avoided crowds because he seemed to become particularly susceptible to colds and influenza. As he neared ninety he carefully wrote out any talk he had to give in the still firm, flowing penmanship. He died in 1968 after participating in the groundbreaking for the new Science Hall on the campus he loved. He was an inspiring teacher and one of the great academic builders of St. Olaf College.

This essay is adapted from the *History of the Chemistry Department 1889–1986* by Albert Finholt and Allen Hanson.

Gertrude Hilleboe St. Olaf Archives

9.
GERTRUDE MIRANDA HILLEBOE 1888–1976

L. DeAne Lagerquist

"There never was a time within my memory when my life was not in some way linked with St. Olaf." So begins Gertrude Miranda Hilleboe's memoir, *Manitou Analecta* (1970). Her association with the college spanned its presidents from the first, Mohn, to Rand, the sixth. As a child she and her Ytterboe cousins made delighted dashes up and down the staircase in the newly constructed Main, which overlooked the town to the east and the countryside to the south. There the Ytterboes and the Mohns lived on the first floor, beneath the classrooms and male student residence rooms. When Gertrude arrived as a student in 1908, drafty, wooden Ladies' Hall was overflowing; during her senior year it was replaced by "old" Mohn Hall (located on the site of the current science center). In 1915, in response to President Lauritz Vigness's invitation, Miss Hilleboe returned as Dean of Women and took up residence in already too small Mohn. At the midpoint of her career, she broke ground for the new women's residence she had helped to plan; and she encouraged the decision to name it for Agnes Mellby, first woman graduate of the college division. In 1951, seven years before Hilleboe's retirement, the latest women's dormitory was named Gertrude Hilleboe Hall; it sits on the edge of the hill and offers a view toward the southwest.

The length of Hilleboe's connection with St. Olaf—through presidencies, construction of buildings, and growth in size—is impressive. The expansion she witnessed signaled other changes as well. When she came to visit her uncle Halvor Ytterboe, St. Olaf was more or less a family enterprise. Most of its small staff and student body shared a religion, a culture, and an ethnic background, if not direct blood relationships. Soon after her retirement, changes in the rules for the behavior of women students began taking place on the campus. For all of Hilleboe's deanship, they did not officially drink, smoke, dance, entertain men in their rooms, or wear slacks in the classroom, library, or cafeteria. The sixties brought a dramatic shift in most of these rules, except for the prohibition against alcohol. By then most faculty members had long since moved off campus, as Hilleboe did in 1952. St. Olaf had taken its place among American colleges in fulfillment of its founders' aspirations. Dean Hilleboe had fond memories of the old ways and did her part to maintain some of them; she also helped to make way for the new.

In the *Manitou Messenger* for June 1912, she was described by her classmates: "As a student she stands alone and excels not only in one but in all lines. However, she is not satisfied with book learning alone but enters upon everything she undertakes with a vim and enthusiasm nothing can resist." By the time of her commencement in 1912 she had already taught in both public and church schools, and now she intended a career of teaching high school in a church-sponsored academy or on the China mission field. In preparation, she attended the University of Minnesota in St. Paul where she worked in a dormitory; then she taught for a year at Waldorf College in Forest City, Iowa. She also spent a year in Iowa keeping house for her widowed father. Although his need continued, he insisted that she either return to school or seek employment before he would accept that arrangement for the long term. When appointed in 1915 as Dean of Women (a new title for St. Olaf and for higher education), Hilleboe intended to stay only a single year, until someone more qualified could be found. One year lengthened beyond four decades during which she brought such vim and energy to all lines of work that one colleague characterized her as a dynamo.

Her appointment as dean was in keeping with a trend at coeducational colleges. In a manuscript titled "How I Became Dean of Women at St. Olaf College," Hilleboe says, "The title itself was indicative of a new concept of the enlarged scope of the position of the woman who was in a special way to represent the women students and their concerns." The first women students at St. Olaf's School were attended to informally by the wives of faculty members; then by a series of Preceptresses beginning with Agnes Mellby. During Hilleboe's career the field of student services evolved and she matured with her emerging profession. The scope of her work encompassed every aspect of student life from reading admissions files, to matching roommates (as some suspected, she did consider body type), to organizing the World War I Red Cross, to hosting a myriad of social events, to speaking in chapel, to encouraging women's participation in student government, and, of course, to enforcing rules. Throughout her career she was also a classroom teacher, and she continued to meet Latin classes even after her retirement as dean. This range of activity was matched by its duration and intensity. Often Hilleboe was at her desk late in the evening; seldom did she leave the campus and her responsibilities to it completely behind. During a medical leave necessitated by a foot injury in the late 1930s, her correspondence with President Boe includes his reports on enrollment and staffing matters as well on the progress of the new women's dormitory. Indeed, while still on medical leave she traveled to Chicago to help President Lars Boe and Business Manager and Treasurer P. O. Holland select the furniture for Mellby Hall.

At President Vigness's suggestion, she attended the second meeting of the National Association of Deans of Women in 1917. Not yet thirty years old, among the youngest women there and small of stature, she was dubbed "the infant dean" by her colleagues. The next year, after women students listened to Hilleboe's enthusiastic report of the conference, they asked if she intended to return. When they heard that college funds might not be available, the students themselves took up a collection for her expenses. Throughout the next decades the St. Olaf dean continued to be active in the National Association of Deans of Women. Among its membership she made several enduring friendships with women from around the country and at institutions quite unlike St. Olaf. When she traveled to annual meetings she often took time to visit those friends and to see their campuses. These contacts, as well as her work in the American Association of University Women, gave the St. Olaf alumna a broader view of higher education, particularly for women, than would have been available from the perspective of only her own campus, or even within the close-knit group of Lutheran colleges.

"[H]er chief concern," Georgina Dieson Hegland ('04) observed in the *Alumni Magazine* for September 1958, "has always been for the building of strong and beautiful character and the developing of a deep and true spiritual life—more than for the letter of the rules. . . . She even dared to love her girls." By the expansive character of her own involvement with the school and its students, Dean Hilleboe anticipated late-twentieth-century concern for a seamless environment which spans classroom, residence, and social life. She was thoughtful about how religious concerns were addressed. During the late twenties, some church folks criticized St. Olaf faculty members, O. E. Rølvaag in particular; they regarded St. Olaf as less devout in spirit than it should be. A vigorous public defense of the faculty was provided by President Boe; on September 18, 1929, Gertrude Hilleboe sent a long, almost formal letter to her friend Beulah Folkedahl in California, carefully defending the school, her faculty colleagues, and their approach to education. She recalls that on a September morning just before chapel service, "I stood at the east entrance of Mohn Hall . . . and watched the students pass. One cannot help but be almost overwhelmed with the thought of the responsibility that rests on any group or institution charged with the guiding and directing of such youth in our day." As one who accepts this responsibility herself, she also recognizes the limits of what she and her colleagues can do: "Ours is a definite program to plant the seed, to surround our students with all the constructive influences for spiritual growth that we can. We can nurture and cultivate, but we cannot force growth. We may see fruits in some, in many none, but we know that if we are faithful God will give the increase."

Hilleboe's concern for female students included development of character and responsibility as well as close attention to their dress and social behavior (for such attention not all were grateful). This concern extended to their professional lives as well. Shortly after returning to St. Olaf as dean, she urged the Board of Education of the Norwegian Lutheran Church in America (then the college's governing body) to expand physical education for female students. Already in the 1910s she fostered organization of the Girls' Union (later known as the Women's Student Government Association and then in turn the Associated Women Students). An early constitution enumerated several purposes: furthering a spirit of unity, increasing students' sense of responsibility toward each other, setting and maintaining high social standards, and communicating the girls' wishes to the faculty. The Union held meetings, sponsored social and educational events, and sent representatives to regional association conferences.

Similarly Miss Hilleboe was instrumental in the organization of a Northfield chapter of the American Association of University of Women. Her membership had consequences both for St. Olaf students and for the institution itself. Every year she hosted a tea for the women of the graduating class to encourage them to join this organization when they arrived in their new communities. One alumna recalls that in a job interview not long after her graduation she was asked how she would make herself a part of the town life; she found herself repeating Hilleboe's suggestion, and she got the job. On March 17, 1952, Dean Hilleboe composed another long, carefully written letter, this one to President Clemens Granskow; she informed him, firmly, of her concern that "the position of St. Olaf at present is very precarious when it comes to the matter of qualifying for remaining on [AAUW's] approved list." In particular she drew his attention to the absence of women from college policy-making committees and objected to changes in the organization of student services which decreased the official influence of the Dean of Women. AAUW also encouraged a coeducational school to include women on its board as well as among its faculty. Hilleboe asserted: "Regardless of the AAUW requirement, I think we would all be agreed that there should be at least one woman member on the Board at an institution in which almost half of the students are women." Her personal influence and the power of her arguments elicited Granskow's largely favorable reply; in a letter dated April 23, 1952, he requested that she join the President's Cabinet and spoke of ways that the other deficiencies she mentioned might be addressed.

From her first year as dean, Hilleboe was a constant advocate for improved housing for women. Her major project in her Columbia University master's program (completed during a leave in 1922, under President Boe's administration) involved planning a dormitory, and this proved useful when a new women's dormitory for St. Olaf was proposed in the 1930s. Because the female enrollment consistently grew more quickly than residence halls were built, Hilleboe also cultivated interaction between the students who lived on and off campus. With her support a trio of students conducted a study of housing conditions, surveying their classmates about matters such as lighting, access to pressing, homelike atmosphere, and cultivation of college activities. Once the completion of Agnes Mellby Hall expanded the number of women who could live on campus, the dean launched the Junior Counselor system, a program that remains today a part of St. Olaf residence life. She invited a few upperclass women to forgo their housing arrangements in town in order to live in pairs in corridors of first-year women. Women selected for the honor of being Junior Counselors were trained by the dean herself. The program gave first-year students easy access to experienced juniors whose counsel was closer to student life and more intimate than that given by adult staff members.

Miss Hilleboe was initially hired as Dean of Women and is remembered primarily in that capacity; however, that office was a fluid one allowing her participation in areas no longer considered student services. She involved herself directly in student recruitment, sometimes traveling as far as Chicago to visit prospective students in their homes. She taught Latin and attended parties arranged by classics students; in her scrapbook she has preserved photos of a Roman banquet, complete with togas and laurel wreaths. As a member of the faculty she took part in the "Round Table" conclave during the afternoon lunch hours in Mohn Hall cafeteria. She describes these in *Manitou Analecta*: "Best of all was the sociability at the Round Table . . . it was a most expandable table always having room for one more until there would be eight or ten sitting around it. Everything from the last or the next basketball game to problems of world import were subjected to analysis. Jokes and stories added to the fun"

(61–62). She took time to instruct new teachers in the history and culture of the college, reminding them of the standards of proper behavior that they should model for their students. In 1949 the example she set and her own service were acknowledged by an honorary Doctor of Law degree conferred by Augustana College in Sioux Falls.

Hilleboe not only expanded her own view and St. Olaf's by involvement in national educational organizations, but she also nurtured its internal connections through public events and activities. Many women students were invited to her cocoa parties every year. Each spring Hilleboe held a reception for seniors and faculty. The entertainment focused on St. Olaf history and heritage, games to test the guests' knowledge of the alma mater. Thus, at the moment that they were poised to leave the hill, the dean reinforced students' connection to the place and its people. Once they had graduated, many continued to be in touch with St. Olaf through her. Halfway through her career, she sent personal birthday greetings to the 1,300 women who had graduated during her tenure. A similar number of St. Olaf military personnel received a series of long, mimeographed letters during World War II.

From 1915 until 1952 Hilleboe lived in one of the residence halls. For the first twenty years she used two Mohn Hall student rooms—one to live in and one to work in. When she moved into Mellby Hall in 1938, she had a private bath for the first time. After four decades of living on campus, she built a small house on Lincoln Lane and there entertained faculty and staff in a series of Sunday supper parties. Throughout her connection to St. Olaf, she fostered a gracious, rather formal social life, and students and alumni responded in kind. A group of Twin Cities Oles honored her with a dinner and a gift of money. In her thank-you letter to them, written in August of 1959, Hilleboe recalled having admired the "beautiful lines" of a particular silver service—made by a Danish silversmith, with black wooden handles—and announced her intention to purchase one to equip her new home for continued hospitality.

Dean Hilleboe's long service to the college was motivated by deep loyalty to its people and the devotion to the school's mission that she articulated in her letter to Beulah Folkedahl. The financial rewards she received were small in comparison with the wide range of her tasks and the devotion she gave to them. Despite her nonstop engagement with students and others in the campus community, she maintained a professional reserve and her personal interactions were formal. Even colleagues who worked closely with her recall that Miss Hilleboe was a private person, not known intimately by anyone. Nonetheless, her relations with colleagues were warm and marked by small gestures of kindness such as a thoughtful note of appreciation or a gift of flowers. Her sense of humor was expressed in a willingness to tell a story on herself at the Round Table or to play a comic role at the faculty Twelfth Night Party. Commitments in classroom, office, reception room, and beyond the campus did not prevent her from an occasional evening spin on the ice-skating rink in Mellby lawn. Yet, even as she moved over the ice, stocking cap on her head and skirt flying behind her, she was the dean. At St. Olaf College Gertrude Hilleboe discovered that her talents suited the work and that they met real needs within the college. By her words and her actions she urged her students, especially the women, to similar involvement and equally responsible use of their talents and their education.

Gertrude Hilleboe skating, c. 1945
St. Olaf Archives

Conversations with several of Hilleboe's colleagues and with alumni who knew her were most valuable in my effort to resuscitate her from documents in her personnel file and in her personal papers, both located in the St. Olaf College Archives. Together with her published memoir, these conversations and papers provide the basis for this sketch.

John Berntsen St. Olaf Archives

10.
JOHN BERNTSEN
1892–1971

Norman E. Madson

"I don't think St. Olaf could run without John," said a professor in the sixties. He would have echoed the opinion of any number who knew the story of John Berntsen's long and varied services. A dedicated, intelligent, and skillful workman, he served the college for fifty-two years, most of the time as Superintendent of Grounds and Buildings. It wasn't a job but a mission.

John Berntsen was born in Egersund, Norway, on November 12, 1892. Early in life he learned cabinet making in his father's shop: the demands for precision in that trade surely carried on into the demands for superior craftsmanship he made of everyone who worked for him in later years. After his father's death when John was seventeen, he ran the shop for about a year, and then set out for Chicago to study furniture finishing. He had planned to return after a year, but his mother's death changed his plans and he decided to settle in Chicago. A trip to Duluth to visit a brother and to Northfield to visit a boyhood friend named Chris Grastvedt, who was working in the St. Olaf power plant, changed his plans again. Chris persuaded him to stay in Northfield, where he spent the rest of his life.

P. O. Holland, professor and business manager, offered John a job at St. Olaf as a janitor. Not yet twenty years old, he accepted and began his work on March 29, 1912. Two months later he was promoted to the position of cook and shortly after was transferred to the "repair department." From then on he dealt with the maintenance and development of buildings and grounds, working the wide range of crafts from locksmith to forestry; and for twenty-five years he was also the cutter who prepared the meat supplied by college farms for college kitchens. In 1915 Berntsen married Edith Schenstad of Faribault. Their three children, Robert, Gladys, and Harry, grew up near the campus and all of them graduated from St. Olaf and went on to successful careers: Robert became a college chemistry professor, Gladys was a teacher, and Harry had a long career with Eastman Kodak.

Berntsen became a virtuoso: he arrived when the college had less than five hundred students in a few scattered buildings, and he soon found himself involved formally and informally in every aspect of the campus development. With a special interest in and knowledge about lawns, shrubs, trees, and flowers, he developed a campus that was known for its orderliness and beauty, and he protected it from anything or anyone who might damage it. The specimen ginkgo tree, supposedly not an inhabitant of Minnesota, that John started with hope and care south of Holland Hall is big and flourishing sixty years later.

Mr. Berntsen was present on that memorable day in May 1939 when the college was host to the Crown Prince of Norway. As the Crown Prince was speaking, Doc Mellby, sitting at the back of the stage platform in the Old Gym, tilted too far back on his chair and fell backwards into the gray curtain and off the stage. John and a student, Ralph Nitz, caught Mellby before he hit the floor and gently eased him back onto the stage, to the delight of the Crown Prince and the entire audience. Of that experience John said, "People keep adding to that story and taking away the details. It's the one story that I have never told myself but I've heard it often."

Mr. Berntsen was determined to keep all properties in good condition and to use his time and that of his crews efficiently. The careless actions of some students caused him considerable grief. Broken furniture, gouged oak paneling, damaged walls, unauthorized painting, and similar damages brought an unnecessary waste of time and money. He said, "If we could take all the time we spend fixing things that are broken, just think of all the beautiful things we could make." In spite of these experiences he maintained a balanced view of the conduct of the entire student body. On one occasion when he was angered by some deliberate damage to the oak paneling in Thorson Hall he still said, "I tell you, ninety-five percent of these kids are awfully nice people."

He was especially protective of the green lawns, and, as a former staff member said, "If Berntsen caught you walking on the grass, you had better stoop down and pick up something." His son, Robert, spent his summers mowing campus lawns making ten cents per hour though he preferred being on the paint crew where he could have made fifteen cents per hour. His dad kept him and his brother, Harry, on the mowers because "it's the lawns that people see first when they come to the campus."

John's eagerness to learn brought him to America and the learning continued throughout his life. He read continuously about building materials, sweeping compounds, paint, lawn fertilizer, anything that would enable him to do his work better. His personal library included a ten-volume set on all aspects of construction. President Rand once said, "John Berntsen had a fine mind. He could talk about ideas and principles. He was an example of the blending of mind and hands in the work of the world."

Even though his only formal education was three years in a Norwegian furniture finishing school, he was on intimate terms with some of St. Olaf's most distinguished professors. In his carpenter shop in the basement of Hoyme Chapel, John and F. Melius Christiansen traded jokes, and it is said that O. E. Rølvaag stood at John's carpenter bench as he worked on his novels.

It seems possible that their bond of friendship was strengthened by the fact that all three of them were immigrants. After hearing John sing in the shop, Christiansen once said, "John, you've got music in your soul. You should take music lessons or the Lord will punish you for not using your talent." John didn't take the advice but said, "I thought if he really wanted me to, he'd ask again but he never did."

Mr. Berntsen had a special friendship and working relationship with Arne Flaten, who arrived in the early summer of 1932, after two years in Europe, to start a department of art. To provide a place for him to teach, the Art Barn was designed by Flaten and built from the ground up by Berntsen including the high north windows and massive front door. Flaten then supplied the extensive wood carving together with other details, reminiscent but not imitative, that gave the Art Barn its unmistakable Norwegian flavor. Among other joint efforts by Arne and John was the design and construction of the furnishings in the small chapel in Agnes Mellby Hall. The altar and eight simple but elegant benches were designed by Arne and built by John, and all of the items, complete with Arne's carvings, are in place and in use to this day. Flaten and Berntsen were friends, and these joint efforts must have been very satisfying episodes in the careers of both men. It was fitting that when Flaten Hall was dedicated in 1956 Arnold Flaten should set the date stone and he be assisted by John Berntsen.

Some of St. Olaf's most distinguished graduates were at some time members of John's summer crews where they received firm directions for their tasks and knew instinctively that they were expected to work hard and to do their work well: Fredrik Schiotz, American Lutheran Church president, and Randolf Haugen of Augsburg Publishing House were the first custodians in the gym constructed in 1918; Herman Bakken of ALCOA did concrete work on the Ytterboe steps; Minnesota Governor Karl Rølvaag worked for John clearing stumps; and Dr. Herbert Schmidt, of the Mayo Clinic and member of the Board of Regents, was on the summer crew painting college barns in North Dakota. Orville and Cy Running, who became well-known artists and college professors, worked summers for John.

Ed Sövik, who worked on John's painting crew for three summers, graduated from St. Olaf and later returned to Northfield to establish an architectural firm, which, for several decades, designed many of St. Olaf's buildings. He recalls his experiences as a member of John's summer crews:

> I can see John Berntsen making his tours around the campus, straight up (though of medium height), elbows slightly out, not simply walking but going somewhere. Somewhat tight-lipped even when he smiled, sharp eyes alert to pick up in this continual inspection what might need attention: peeling paint, a broken pane, a particularly dark iron stain in the limestone walls that would have to be chiseled out. And I can see a few minutes before seven when all the summer crew gathered at the shop behind Ytterboe, John suddenly appearing and everyone alert to know what the day's assignment would be. We were various, some quasi professionals like Marty Fossum, who ran the bookstore when college was in session, but turned into a plasterer in the summer, some like Bob Berntsen, who walked all day behind a reel lawn mower (no Toros those days), or tending the landscape in other ways, some assigned to a thorough yearly cleaning of the rooms and corridors, and some painters. John, the expert cabinetmaker, said that when something was repaired—a broken chair or window—it must be as good or better than new; no patchwork allowed. With his crews he could be scathing if he found laziness or stupidity; he expected people to behave responsibly, and around him they almost always did. He was scant in praise, but to be hired for another summer was a sort of praise.

Those who know John remember clearly his unusual techniques for hitching up his trousers. Apparently to avoid soiling his clothes with dirty hands, he would use the inside of his wrists to tug repeatedly at the sides of his trousers near the beltline. Old-timers who tell about this technique always accompany the telling with a demonstration of how it was done.

The March 1962 issue of the *St. Olaf Alumnus Magazine* was devoted to John as he was completing fifty years of service to the college. It said of him, "John Berntsen is on intimate terms with every stone, every blade of grass, the teachers, and the students. He can truly be called a builder of St. Olaf from the ground up."

On March 29 of that year, the St. Olaf family honored Mr. Berntsen with a testimonial dinner for his fifty years on the St. Olaf staff. Mrs. Berntsen, their three children, and four grandchildren attended, as well as John's old friend, Chris Grastvedt, who was the one who persuaded him to stay and work in Northfield, and many other guests who had played prominent roles in the last fifty years of the college. More than 325 people attended the dinner presided over by President Granskou. Speakers included Dr. Fredrik A. Schiotz, Dr. Herbert Schmidt, and Peter Fossum, all former members of John's summer crews. President Granskou praised John as a builder of St. Olaf and added that his own experience had been enriched by being "the fourth college president to serve under John."

Mr. and Mrs. Berntsen were given a fund which would allow them to take a five-week trip to his home in Egersund, Norway. Mrs. Berntsen had never before been to Norway and this was the first trip back for John since he came to America.

Mr. Berntsen retired in June of 1964. Dr. Sidney Rand was now president, so John had served under five of the first six presidents of the college. On June 5, 1964, a resolution was adopted by the Board of Regents, "acknowledging John's service to the college and expressing gratitude of the college for the tireless devotion to the development of the St. Olaf Campus."

John Berntsen died on January 18, 1971, at the age of seventy-eight—about seven years after his retirement. Funeral services were at St. John's Lutheran Church in Northfield with interment in Oaklawn Cemetery.

To honor their father, Robert, Gladys, and Harry and their families gave the college a Memorial Garden Classroom, located on the south side of Rølvaag Library. Dr. Harlan F. Foss, President Emeritus of St. Olaf, conducted the dedication of the site on July 23, 1995. A bronze plaque mounted on a large stone contains the following message:

IN MEMORY OF JOHN BERNTSEN WHO SERVED ST. OLAF COLLEGE FROM 1912 THROUGH 1964. WHILE SUPERINTENDENT OF GROUNDS AND BUILDINGS, HE SAID, "I WANT TO MAKE ST. OLAF SO NICE NO STUDENT WILL EVER HAVE TO APOLOGIZE FOR IT." THIS WAS HIS PURPOSE FOR DEDICATED SERVICE AND EXCELLENCE IN HIS WORK.

In 1995 the college established a John Berntsen Endowment for Campus Beautification. It is the only fund at the college where the income is used for this specific purpose. Gifts have come from family and friends to carry on the work that was so important to Mr. Berntsen and to which he devoted his life.

André Gide wrote that "Man's happiness does not depend on his freedom but on his acceptance of a duty." In these terms, John Berntsen was a happy man.

Agnes Larson St. Olaf Archives

11. AGNES M. LARSON 1892–1967

Gary De Krey

Dr. Agnes M. Larson, class of 1916, chose to teach at St. Olaf. She made the choice more than once, influenced both by a strong sense of Norwegian American identity and by Lutheran convictions that not even a Radcliffe Ph.D. could efface. Her professional life contrasts with that of her sister, Henrietta Larson (1894–1983), the only St. Olaf alumna to precede her in obtaining a Ph.D., and a longtime faculty member of the Harvard Business School. Both historians, the two sisters developed different careers that reflected the complementary aspirations of the college in the second third of the twentieth century. Henrietta fulfilled the desire of the college's leadership that its graduates should have an impact upon the broader American professional world. Agnes, on the other hand, worked to improve academic standards at St. Olaf, where she was eventually joined by a third sister, biologist Nora Larson (1901–1988).

The family's Lutheran roots were strong. Agnes and her sisters were born in the Spring Valley Norwegian immigrant community in southeastern Minnesota. They were the daughters of a farmer-businessman with a good education and diverse intellectual interests. Hans O. Larson had been baptized at the Old Muskego Church in Wisconsin, one of the earliest Norwegian American congregations, and a church also known to the family of his wife, Karen M. Norgaarden. For the sake of the education of their daughters, the Larsons eventually moved to Northfield, where Agnes attended high school before matriculating at the college. After graduation, she tried social work in Chicago and high school teaching, eventually in Northfield. The choice of teaching was common for college alumnae at that time; but Agnes Larson was to be an uncommon teacher. She traveled to New York in 1921–1922 to obtain a master's degree in history at Columbia, and she then returned to Minnesota to join the faculty of Mankato State Teachers College. President Lars Boe offered her a position at St. Olaf in 1926. Boe was not able to match her salary at Mankato, but Agnes Larson chose St. Olaf anyway, commenting that the opportunities "of serving my alma mater and my church quite outbid the difference in salary." To her friend Gertrude Hilleboe, Dean of Women, she confided her hopes that "I may be a faithful servant."

Still, Larson's return to Northfield proved short-lived. Boe wanted to create a new generation of college leaders with enhanced academic credentials. In Agnes Larson he saw one of those who would "replace us who are older." In 1929, with Boe's support, Larson left St. Olaf for Cambridge, Massachusetts, to embark upon further graduate training. The next three years were difficult but crucial for her. With inadequate financial support, and with an uncertain future at St. Olaf, she encountered the customary stresses of a rigorous graduate program amid a deepening depression. She turned from European history to American, finding a mentor in Harvard historian Frederick Merk, who had been trained by the frontier specialist, Frederick Jackson Turner. Her appreciation for the founding figures of the republic was deepened by her residence in a state that had bred so many of them. A study she undertook of the vocational patterns of the alumnae of Eastern women's colleges opened another world to her, one from which an attractive job offer would come. In the meantime, messages from Boe about her salary and teaching fields at St. Olaf were not encouraging: she offered to resign in 1931. In response, Boe informed her, and not "as a compliment," that she was "one of the chosen" who were destined to create the college of the future.

In 1932, Larson decided to return to St. Olaf to take on her "life's big work," as Boe put it. She reaccepted a call to the college, believing, like Martin Luther, that the choice of service is an exercise in freedom. She returned "full of enthusiasm," and determined to stimulate "a greater love for learning," in order to make St. Olaf "different" from most educational institutions in the Midwest. Athens had been nice, but Jerusalem would be better.

The details of the career that followed are easily summarized. She taught survey courses in European, U.S., British, and Latin American history and more specialized courses in American immigration and Western history. Continuing to research and write her thesis, she received her Ph.D. in 1938 and eventually published an expanded version of her thesis as the *History of the White Pine Industry in Minnesota* (University of Minnesota Press, 1949). In 1941, when she became acting head of her department, she began two decades as history chair. Some four thousand students encountered her rigorous standards and forthright manner in their history classes. She retired in 1960. Suffering from ill health thereafter, she nevertheless completed, shortly before her death in 1967, a study of the nineteenth-century Wisconsin Norwegian American entrepreneur, John A. Johnson.

The bare facts of this summary fail, however, to reveal the overriding commitments of Dr. Larson's professional life in history. Her first commitment was to St. Olaf College as a liberal arts college of the church. Remembering that "tantalizing" offer from an eastern women's college in a 1960 letter about her retirement, she reaffirmed her preference for giving her "services" at St. Olaf: "These were *my* people and this was *my* church."

This commitment to St. Olaf as a liberal arts institution was apparent from the beginning. It informed the study that Dr. Larson undertook at Radcliffe of the vocational preparation and employment of liberal arts alumnae of selective eastern colleges. She undertook this work for the St. Olaf curriculum committee, some of whom apparently worried that the college's course offerings for women were insufficiently practical and even insufficiently secretarial. To this sentiment, Larson replied, as an alumna and faculty member, that the college must remain a purely liberal arts institution, developing in its students, female and male alike, "those resources that make life rich and full and give the soul immunity from the changes of fortune and the shocks of fate." At Cambridge she observed that "a Radcliffe woman does the same work as a Harvard man." She believed that the same should prevail at St. Olaf if the college were to remain true to its coeducational foundation. Her recommendations for St. Olaf included a "raising of its scholarship and standard[s]" and more attention to informing women students about the variety of occupations actually open to them.

Dr. Larson articulated these sentiments throughout her years at St. Olaf, most notably again in the mid-1950s, when the college undertook a major curricular self-study. She responded at great length to her faculty questionnaire. What she hoped to impart as a teacher, she said then, was a "love for learning, a sense of curiosity that will cause a student to continue the search for truth which has been fostered during the undergraduate days." The merits of a liberal arts education are revealed, she thought, only as each student comes to "maturity—when experience, reflection, suffering, growth *spiritually* and *intellectually* have become a part of that person's possession."

Her commitment to her students as lifelong learners was clearly as important to Dr. Larson as her commitment to the college. She needed no instruction about the potential influence of a liberal arts education upon character: "Teaching must be formative as well as informative," she wrote in 1944. As a teacher of history, in particular, she experienced a "tremendous challenge of instilling into our students a sense of responsibility as national and world citizens; to create in them a sense of social justice which will drive them into action; to create in them a spirit of tolerance . . . so that fair judgment[s] may be given."

Her desire to superintend, intellectually, the development of citizens able to make informed choices was notable. In the midst of the nation's confrontation with Nazi Germany, she wrote about the responsibilities of history teachers in training citizens for their "obligations" in a democracy and in encouraging open "discussion . . . [and] criticism." Looking to the American past, she revered great figures like John Quincy Adams and Abraham Lincoln, who she believed epitomized the republican values she hoped to nurture. At Harvard, Frederick Merk had chided her for romanticizing the past, but she nevertheless presented the early American patriots and pioneers as icons of civic virtue. They leaped from page and podium in her dramatic teaching: "The past was so alive in her classroom," wrote a student from one of her last courses: "I believe that Miss Larson had the Bible, together with all American history, in her very heart."

Particularly interested in how the American environment transformed European ideas and institutions, Larson often assigned exercises in family history to provide her students with personal knowledge about the juxtaposition of the Old World and the New. Proud of the college's ethnic heritage, she helped her largely Norwegian American students to appropriate their own identity or, in favorite words from the prophet Obadiah, to "possess their own possessions." Her own values were, in part, derived from the Middle American main streets and rural routes that provided the college with its students. American civilization, however, she presented as the product of different ethnic and racial groups, as the "work of many races and of no single race." For her, colonial Pennsylvania was a model of tolerance; and George Washington Carver was among the builders of American culture. She was serious also in forming "world citizens" at St. Olaf, rejecting Midwestern isolationism and perceiving patriotism and global interests as complementary. As a teacher, she introduced the study of Latin American history into the St. Olaf curriculum. All this was required if her students were truly to "possess their own possessions."

Students were often daunted by "Aggie" Larson's teaching presence. Swooping back and forth before her class, and vigorously pummeling the air for emphasis, she was always enthusiastic about the substance of history. To her most able students, she imparted her conviction that history is often best learned from primary sources, a perspective that still characterizes the St. Olaf department. Still, in her discourse, the facts sometimes flowed as freely as the "freely flowing trade" that she believed had built the nation. Some students would have preferred more conceptual or interpretive approaches. One presumed to tell her so: "There is only one person who can get along without the facts, young man," she responded, "and that person is God." Students who came to reading conferences in

Dr. Larson's office with notes copied from the notebook of a friend wilted before her detailed questions. But most respected her passionate historical teaching, a commitment that even her colleagues could find overwhelming. A story is still told about the contagious excitement evident on her countenance one morning: the teacher who inquired about what personal good fortune could have produced such radiance was startled to learn instead that "Today we start the Renaissance!"

Agnes Larson's teaching was not restricted to the classroom. She taught in chapel talks and in radio courses offered over WCAL. She gave public lectures, and she wrote for Lutheran publications. But her real teaching legacy was the continuing impact she had upon her students after their graduations. Many kept in touch. A lonely soldier in Inchon, Korea, wrote in 1953 about his memories of the "little talks" she had given her students. A future bishop wrote to thank her for her "positive constructive attitude," one that had assisted him in dealing with campus "cynicism." A high school history teacher in Wyoming said she remembered Dr. Larson's classes as her most "outstanding and unforgettable experiences" at the college. Others attributed their acceptance to do graduate work at Harvard, Columbia, and Chicago to her letters of recommendation. From Harvard, Merk told her in 1948 that an applicant "who has your strong recommendation and that of St. Olaf College, is the sort of graduate student we ought to have." President Boe had worked to build Dr. Larson's generation of teachers at the college; she worked to build the next.

Finally, Agnes Larson was a colleague and historian committed to keeping both faith and learning at the center of the college's intellectual life. "The only thing that can possibly make St. Olaf what it should be is an able *faculty*," she once wrote, explaining that "the most vital people in a faculty are those who do research with an eye to publication." Her lengthy tenure as history department chair was not notable for innovations in the departmental curriculum; but it was notable for the increasing specialization and professional training of new faculty, still largely drawn from Lutheran or Scandinavian backgrounds. They addressed her as *Dr.* Larson, and she was equally formal in response. She was somewhat puzzled by the interest of some junior colleagues in interdisciplinary ventures. For her, historians were, by definition, the great integrators of any college faculty, drawing their methodologies from a variety of other disciplines and seeking always to view particular epochs or areas in "the spirit of universal history." "Complexity and interrelatedness," she suggested, are "the very stuff of history."

Dr. Larson's style as chair of the history department would not be considered consensual today. She occasionally wore a certain red bonnet to signal the approach of issues that might make for a turbulent department meeting. Colleagues outside the department found her awesome. During a faculty meeting, one young scientist—a future faculty dean, as it happened—made a motion to discontinue the long-established policy of reporting individual attendance records to the dean of students. It was soundly defeated. After the meeting, he found himself confronting Dr. Larson's jabbing finger and formidable gaze: "We want to maintain the highest academic standards at St. Olaf College, and we cannot do that unless we have students attending our classes without exception." She could be equally outspoken in responding to junior colleagues who thought the college might safely become a little less Lutheran. But she was also fair and compassionate. She permitted one historian to cancel classes for fall hunting dates. "A man must have his day in the woods," observed the sympathetic forest historian. She grieved with another young colleague upon the unexpected death of his wife.

Wood carving by Arne Flaten to commemorate the publication of Agnes Larson's *The History of the White Pine Industry*, 1949
ST. OLAF ARCHIVES

Dr. Larson's own professional life was a model of coming to possess one's possessions. Shortly after her return to the college in 1932, she assisted in putting the work of the recently founded Norwegian American Historical Association on a more professional footing. Boe had hoped that her dissertation would also be devoted to the history of Norwegian Americans, but she chose instead to work in the broader field of Midwestern regional history, which was just as much a part of her heritage. Her forebears had pioneered in Wisconsin and Minnesota. She provided a pioneering study of the relationship between a once dominant regional industry and the development of upper Midwestern society. Her *History of the White Pine Industry* was written in a characteristically rich Victorian prose, a style that lent lyricism even to statistics about board feet. She saw timber barons like the Weyerhaeusers and the Lairds as regional examples of American entrepreneurial skill, but she was also fascinated by the culture of the camp worker. Her collection of north-woods stories and songs from octogenarian lumberjacks was "history from the bottom up" long before it became a professional rage. Similarly, she was a public historian, writing for numerous local audiences, before the field of public history was developed. A few years after her death, her white pine study was reprinted in a series of works devoted to the "use and abuse of America's natural resources." And today, fifty years after its publication, her words address our own environmental debates. For her, the history of this and of other extractive industries presented a choice that remains before us: "One cannot with impunity rob Mother Nature of her treasures. . . . The price we must pay for the rapid use of our forests is a vast area of wasteland for generations, or else a wise and vigorous policy of reforestation."

This concern for the coming generations was also clearly characteristic of Agnes Larson's work as a teacher-scholar at a college of the church. She seems never to have regretted her choice to return to St. Olaf. The dormitory that bears her name is a towering tribute to a graduate and a professor whose zeal in her vocation made her a refounder of the college in her generation. We name buildings for people like Dr. Larson not to preserve our past but rather in hope of choosing our future.

I am indebted to previous sketches of the Larson sisters by Joan Olson, St. Olaf College Archivist, "The Larson Sisters" (unpublished essay, St. Olaf Archives, 1994), and by Carol Jenson, class of 1961, "The Larson Sisters: Three Careers in Contrast," in *Women of Minnesota: Selected Biographical Essays*, ed. Barbara Stuhler and Gretchen Kreuter (St. Paul: Minnesota Historical Society Press, 1977) 301–324. I am grateful to Joan Olson, Katherine Rottsolk (class of 1942), Joe Shaw (class of 1949), Erling Jorstad (class of 1952), Henry Fritz, and Albert Finholt for sharing recollections and oral traditions about Dr. Larson with me. The other sources used for this essay, all from the St. Olaf Archives, include the Agnes M. Larson Papers, the Larson Sisters Papers, Agnes Larson's Personnel File, and her faculty questionnaire for the College Self-Study Committee of 1952–1956.

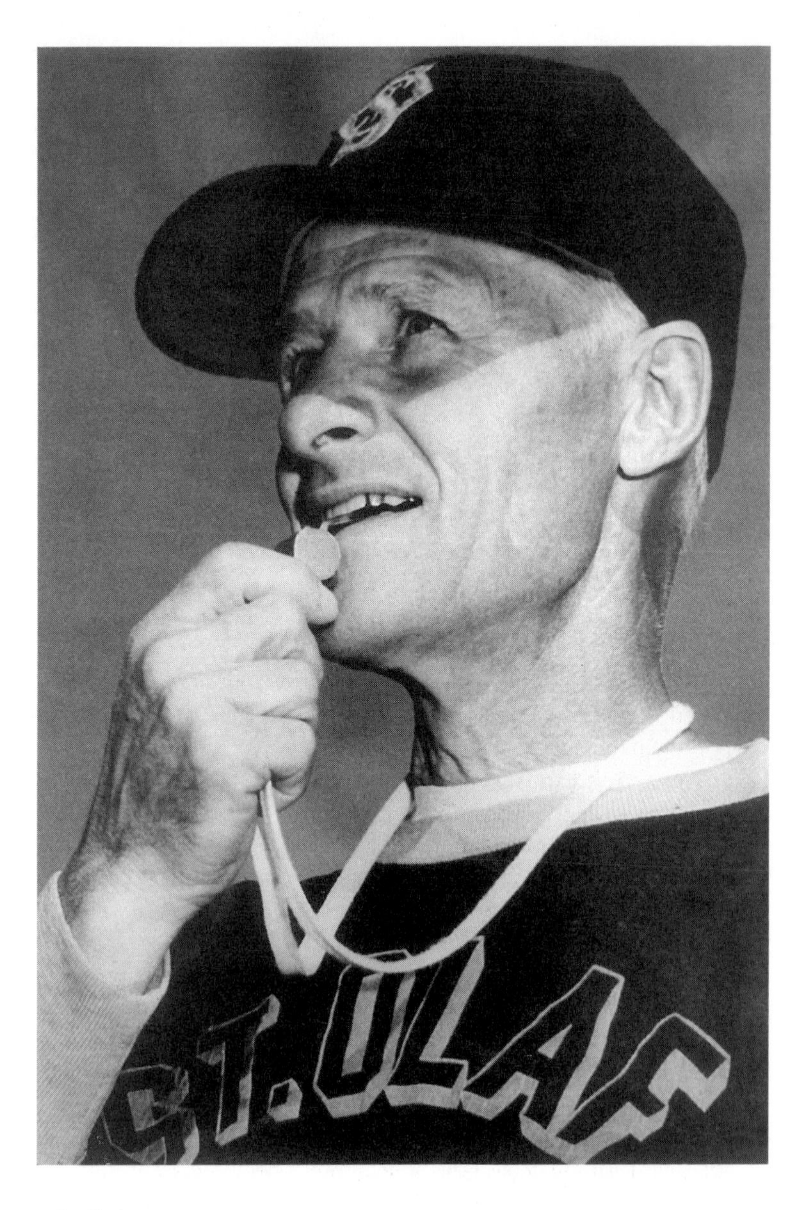

Ade Christenson

St. Olaf Archives

12. ADRIAN LEONARD ("ADE") CHRISTENSON 1900–1993

Tom Porter

Ade Christenson served St. Olaf for thirty-eight years as coach, athletic director, and chairman of the physical education department. His legacy to the college was a program of physical education and intercollegiate athletics based upon the stated goal of the college, "an education committed to the liberal arts and rooted in the Christian gospel." Behind both were the discipline, principle, and faith that fueled Ade's own life. A coach's job, he often said, "is to make athletics important but not too important."

He was born in 1900 in Soldier's Grove, Wisconsin, and lived in Stanley where his father Martin ran an implement dealership. They lost everything in the "Stanley Fire" around 1911. The family moved to Northfield in 1912 so that the three sons might attend St. Olaf. Ade was a star athletic performer at both Northfield High School and St. Olaf: in football, basketball, and track. A number of his teammates became lifelong friends and colleagues. These included Arne Flaten as well as Olaf and Jake Christiansen, sons of St. Olaf's famous choir director who went on to make names for themselves in music and in athletics. Ade graduated from St. Olaf in 1922 as the college's Honor Athlete and an all-state performer in three sports. He was known as "The Little Napoleon" in football because of his brilliant field generalship. As the quarterback, he directed the team during games. Offensive strategy, that is, play selection and formations, were then the responsibility of the quarterback, not the coach.

Ade's undergraduate years included both World War I and the 1918 influenza epidemic. His brother Art went into the army and served in France. Ade joined the Student Army Training Corps at St. Olaf. One day while students were out "policing the grounds," Ade was struck with the flu and he keeled over in a faint. He was put in the college infirmary, where one night the men on each side of him died.

He planned to go to medical school after he graduated from college. One afternoon as he was sitting on the front porch, a friend walked by. Gay Vigeness had graduated a year or two earlier and was on his way to St. Olaf to inform the Placement Office that he was leaving his high school coaching job in Story City, Iowa; that position would be open. "Why don't you take the job?" Gay said. "In a year or two you could save up for medical school." As Ade's son Larry later said, "My father applied for the job . . . and stayed in coaching for the rest of his life. After retirement my father once said to me, 'I didn't realize it at the time, but I believe God put me on the front porch that day. I was supposed to be a coach.'"

He coached at Story City for two years, with two championship football seasons, and then at two Minnesota high schools: a year at Coleraine on the Iron Range, with another undefeated championship football team, and a year as basketball coach at Minneapolis Roosevelt. In 1927 President Lars Boe persuaded Ade to join the physical education faculty at St. Olaf and appointed him head football coach in 1929. He remained at St. Olaf until his retirement in 1965, serving for most of his tenure as teacher, department chair, head coach for various sports, and athletic director.

During World War II, when there was a limited male enrollment at St. Olaf and the football program was discontinued, Ade took other assignments. In 1942 he trained in New York to become a United Service Organization director. On the way home, he was seriously injured in an automobile accident. The resulting nerve damage in his neck forced him eventually to resign from his USO post in Carthage, Missouri. He spent the academic year of 1943–1944 at the University of Southern California studying for a master's degree. With degree work completed and the intercollegiate football program at St. Olaf not yet reinstated, he took a coaching position at Ely, Minnesota, for one year. The high school football team had an outstanding season. The team was undefeated, untied, and unscored upon until the final game of the season. Ade sometimes joked that his record on the Minnesota Iron Range was the best of his career—two undefeated seasons, Coleraine and Ely. In 1945 he returned to St. Olaf as athletic director, chairman of the physical education department, and head coach of football and track.

In Story City Ade had met "Mimi" Donhowe, a nurse, and married her in 1924. Three children were born to them: Adrian, Jr. ("Spud"), in 1925, Larry in 1928, and Joanne in 1932. In Northfield, the family purchased the house where Ade had lived as a boy, 809 St. Olaf Avenue. Later they moved to Lincoln Street. They spent most summers at their other home on Island Lake near Northome, Minnesota. This summer home in the North Woods came to serve not only as a place of recreation and enjoyment, but as a place of therapy. It was here that he and Mimi lived after their retirement.

Ade Christenson was best known as a successful coach. When he retired from active coaching in 1958, his St. Olaf football teams had won six conference championships. The 1953 team led the nation in several offensive categories. He also coached track for thirty-one of his thirty-eight years and basketball for nine years with several championships in each. In 1970 he was inducted into the Minnesota Coaches Hall of Fame.

Ade came on the intercollegiate coaching scene when the "professional coach" was taking on a more prominent role in preparing a team for competition and directing its strategy during contests. This contrasted with his playing days when teams frequently played without "game plans." St. Olaf teams reflected the character and philosophies of Ade. A highly inventive and creative coach, he usually had plays, formations, and strategies that surprised and confused the opponents, such as the fullback spinner series from the double wing and the shovel pass. Offensive football was his forte. To him defense was the period of time between offensive thrusts, and he assigned defensive strategies to assistant coaches. By today's standards, Ade's teams employed a "wide-open" style of play. They relied on quick movements and deception, finesse rather than physical force.

Ade was a firm believer in the personal value of athletic competition, but he never viewed sports as an end in itself. He taught and coached through athletics. Football, basketball, and track were but media through which he conveyed the meanings and lasting qualities of a Christian life. In 1958, Ade published a book, *Verdict of the Scoreboard*, in which he attacked professionalism in college athletics and called for colleges to "restore dignity and honor to competitive sports." College athletics "will never reach its quality of greatness outside the framework of amateurism," he said. "Our pledge to athletics must be written in a deep faith and a selfless love. Throwing touchdown passes is important in the final outcome of a football game, but touchdowns are not a justifiable reason for the establishment of scholarships, grants, free rides, and convertibles as living testimony to what is considered important in American education."

Ade was fond of saying that "victory at any price leads only to professionalism." He often reiterated John Ruskin's statement: "The greatest reward for a man's job is not what he gets for it but what he becomes by it." Ade insisted that his coaches be teachers first and that they resist the temptation to bend the rules to win. A coach "loves to please and the easiest way to do that is by winning. But in victory or defeat, a coach has to put aside his thoughts and remember what the institution stands for."

When Ade retired, editors of the college alumni magazine wrote, "We shall omit his won-lost record, which is impressive, and his championship teams, which are numerous. Instead, we shall hand him a pen and ask him to write about the principles that guided his coaching and the men he coached. For his athletic record is a story of men and principles, rather than wins and losses." A book dedicated to Ade carried this tribute: "Though his players knew him as a superb teacher, and opposing coaches respected him as a brilliant gridiron tactician, it was the force of his own life and personal example that made the deeper impact on those who knew him. When I meet men who played under him, I sense always that note of respect and affection that men reserve for another man whose influence has strengthened the fiber of discipline and integrity in their own lives."

Ade's contribution to St. Olaf went beyond his public success as a coach. He shaped the college's distinctive athletic program and gave his values to it. He considered intramural athletics as important as intercollegiate athletics. He created an innovative program in which 90 percent of the male student body participated. The program was designed on a "club" basis. Men would join a club team, such as Gophers or Badgers or Illini, in their freshman year and remain members for the four years. Student managers directed teams during the year and were responsible for participation in the wide variety of individual and team sports that varied with the season of fall, winter, and spring. The basic purpose of the program was the enjoyment and benefit of physical activity, team camaraderie, and spirit of competition. An elaborate point system granted for individual and club participation and achievement served as an additional motive. At the conclusion of each year awards recognized individual and club leaders. Ade's program became a model for many high schools and colleges in the United States and Canada.

He was a master teacher. He designed and updated the curriculum for department majors who were preparing for teaching and coaching careers, acting as adviser for most men. He enjoyed teaching classes of every kind and level: theory classes in administration, activity classes (his favorite was badminton), classes in adaptive physical education and in camp counseling. The one-credit camp counseling class was a requirement for all St. Olaf physical education majors. It came out of Ade's experience as director of a camp for inner-city youth sponsored by Lutheran Welfare, which he and his wife Mimi ran near Lake Pepin for about ten summers.

He was a lifelong exponent and example of a disciplined lifestyle. He was disciplined in his speech (he never cursed or swore), his habits, his physical fitness. His way of dealing with an injury illustrates this. After a fishing trip in 1939, Ade was opening an ice chest when a steel splinter flew into his right eye. His high school classmate and fellow athlete, Leo Fink, now a surgeon, operated on the eye to remove the splinter, but there was neurological damage. President Boe granted Ade a year's leave of absence to recover his health, and the family moved to their summer home in Northome. Ade spent the year in vigorous physical work, mostly cutting and splitting wood used for heating the house. He recovered in a remarkable way, regaining health and strength, but the sight in the right eye was permanently lost. In hunting and archery he then retrained himself to aim and shoot off his left side, at least well enough to teach his students.

Whatever Ade expected from his students, he expected from himself. When he was in his forties, he taught five hours a day of men's required physical education. Each class began with vigorous calisthenics. With each successive class, Ade led the calisthenics. Leonard Aamot, a freshman at the time, told Ade's son Larry, "Man, your dad is really in shape. He goes through five classes of calisthenics and halfway through our class I was flat out pooped."

He did much of his teaching both in and out of the classroom by example. His daughter Joanne May tells a story about her teenage years, when she and her friends would take advantage of her parents' absence to hole up in her bedroom and smoke. Her father strongly disapproved of smoking. One day as the girls were puffing away, they heard a knock at the closed door. "What are you doing in there?" said the voice of her father. She opened the door and said, "We are smoking." Ade replied, "I am aware that you have been smoking." And walked away. He said no more. Joanne and her friends were so embarrassed that Ade knew they were smoking that none of them ever smoked again while they were teenagers. They respected him and his opinion that much.

He was a person of deep faith, as all who were around him could testify. This faith was tested and deepened by the deaths of those close to him. Shortly before he graduated from college his mother, Rachel, died. After Ade's own death, his daughter Joanne found a volume of poems that he had been writing throughout his life. Several were written during the time of mourning for his mother and they show him trying to reconcile this loss with the Christian faith his mother had taught him. One poem begins with these lines;

When sorrow comes to you and me
Our faith shall meet a test
Can we believe when loved ones pass
God meant it for the best?

Years later Ade and Mimi lost their older son. Spud had served in World War II, then gone back into the military as a jet fighter pilot. In May of 1951, the family received word that Spud had been shot down in Korea. He was seen outside his downed plane, and so the Defense Department listed him as "missing," with the possibility that he may have become a prisoner of war. The night of the wedding of Ade's son Larry to Nordis was the night when Korean POWs were coming across the line at Panmunjom. According to Larry's account, "Ade and Mimi went home from the wedding and sat glued to the radio as the names were announced on national radio. Spud was not among them. He was later listed as 'killed in action.'" There were no poems in the volume written about this death.

Joanne says this of her father: "After retirement, so much of his focus was on developing a deeper relationship with God. He often referred to Jesus as 'the master.' A favorite Bible verse was John 3:30, 'He must increase, I must decrease.'"

It should also be mentioned that Ade had a sense of humor. In 1926 he wrote poems about his high school and college friends, Ole and Jake Christiansen, sons of the St. Olaf Choir director, F. Melius. Of Ole, who in 1941 succeeded his father as Director of the Choir, he wrote:

> A youngster blessed with a musical mind,
> St. Olaf may someday call him a find.
> He's much like his Dad—at least in his looks.
> The rest he'll try and acquire from books.

Of Jake, who ended up becoming Director of Athletics at Concordia College in Moorhead, he wrote:

> Jake that sturdy Viking lad
> Didn't aspire to be like his Dad.
> He wouldn't toot, he wouldn't sing.
> He'd rather be the "knockout king."
>
> He's teaching now but that's a shame
> For such will never bring him fame.
> To make him teach! It isn't right!
> Jake's a fighter! Let him fight!

Ade Christenson died June 18, 1993, at the summer home on Island Lake. He was 93. After he died, one of his former players at Ely High School, Jim Klobuchar, a longtime columnist for the *Minneapolis Star-Tribune*, wrote: "He came to my hometown for one year as a high school football coach in the middle of World War II when the college where he coached temporarily discontinued football. He was directly involved in my life for two months, forty-nine years ago. Yet apart from my father, I know of only two or three men who revealed more to me in all the years that went before or after."

At Ade's funeral those present who had played under or coached with Ade were asked to stand. Several hundred men stood up. An eighty-five-year-old man from Story City, Iowa, who played on the first team Ade coached, was there. Ade's grandson, Arne, who played quarterback on the last team he coached at age seventy-nine, was there.

St. Olaf College was richly blessed by the life of Ade Christenson. As physical educators, we are fortunate that Ade chose this profession. I am sure he would have had as great an influence had he chosen another, although physical education and athletics would be the poorer.

Credits: Son Larry Christenson and daughter Joanne May contributed significantly to this essay with information about their family. Other sources used were: *The Verdict of the Scoreboard* (New York: American Press, 1958); Service of Remembrance for Ade Christenson; *Minneapolis Star-Tribune*, August 15, 1993; *St. Paul Pioneer Press*, June 20, 1993; *Northfield News*, June 1993.

Arnold Flaten carving, c. 1965 St. Olaf Archives

13. ARNOLD W. FLATEN 1900–1976

E. A. Sövik

When the Reverend Arnold Flaten was invited in 1930 to join the St. Olaf College faculty and start a department of art, liberal arts colleges generally did not have classes in the studio arts; painters and sculptors had their own schools. But President Lars Boe was aware of the currents of change, and he proposed to Flaten that he should prepare himself by a couple of years of study in Europe to inaugurate the new department. At the time Flaten had been for two years the associate pastor at a burgeoning urban congregation, Central Lutheran, of Minneapolis. That period had been preceded by three years in a small town named Laurel, in Montana, the first call for the young minister after his three years at Luther Seminary in St. Paul, and his ordination in 1925.

Boe came as president to St. Olaf in 1918, the same year Arnold Flaten began his freshman year. Both had St. Olaf rootage: Boe had graduated in 1898, Arnold was the second son of Professor and Mrs. Nils Flaten. (The elder Flaten spent his long and notable career teaching languages at St. Olaf.) That President Boe was tracking the career of the younger Flaten isn't surprising; he had been a standout collegian, he was bright, he was a track man, state champion tennis player, and captain of the football team (a slight asymmetry in his lower lip was the result of a gridiron injury), and he was a very attractive personality, so that among his classmates everyone, both men and women, knew him and liked him. Furthermore he had showed his exceptional artistic gifts in drawings, calligraphy, and designs he did for the college yearbook and other campus enterprises. One of these other enterprises was a large wall mounting, on which were inscribed the names of all the St. Olaf men and women who had been or were missionaries in foreign lands. Boe, much interested in foreign missions, may have asked for this beautiful and skillfully decorative work, adorned with color, gold leaf, and symbolic devices, the voluntary work of one whose commitment to an evangelical church combined with a talent for the visual arts.

Flaten agreed cautiously to Boe's persuasion and set about finding funds for the studies in Europe, a process that traveled with him through the sojourn. In Florence, his first destination, the self-taught American was admitted by examination to the top level (and tuition-free) painting classes at the Royal Academy of Fine Arts. He painted until the early summer of 1931 and traveled also to the art-rich cities. Then he moved to France.

While Flaten was at Central Lutheran he and a young member of the parish named Evelyn Solberg found themselves in love. Not long after Flaten left Italy Evelyn also traveled to France and they were married in Paris. They had a fine year. Marriage was a great joy; they made pleasant friends; Flaten engaged the broad spectrum of the art world and worked hard under good instructors. He took up sculpture as well as drawing and painting; it was his métier, and his teacher encouraged him to submit two portrait heads he had carved to the annual Grand Salon (one was a beautiful head of Evelyn in Carrara marble). Both were accepted for exhibit, which was something like a walk-on selected for an all-star game. Toward the end of their year they were blessed also with the arrival of their daughter Anne. Now Anne Pixley, she is an artist, living in the land of her birth. A son, Robert, born in 1934, is retired as a former U.S. ambassador. Mary, now living in Northfield, joined the family in 1940, and David, who heads a West Coast college theater department and does freelance stage design, is three years younger. Evelyn continues to live in the rural Northfield home that Arnold designed; there they lived together until his death in 1976.

The arrival in Northfield of the Flaten family from Paris was an occasion of love and faith and hope; but 1932 was the depth of the Depression, faculty salaries had been whittled down, credit was dubious, housing was unsettled, and a proper place for teaching art didn't exist on the St. Olaf campus. Arne and Evelyn ultimately found a home adjacent to the campus, which meant that they could get by without a car, and they found a friend to finance the purchase. That purchase, which was the Flaten home for thirty years, was unremarkable except for the generous hillside site. But it became soon a place of memorable richness due to the variety of changes and imaginative embellishments with which Arnold invested it. Yet it was a rich place primarily because of the warmth of hospitality. Evelyn and Arne had an "open house." Hundreds of students found their way to 1406 Forest Avenue. To some it was like a second home, to many a place where they could find counsel, cheer, wisdom, stimulation, or simply a resting place.

In the course of the summer of 1932 Arne designed, and he and a small crew under John Berntsen built, the "Art Barn." It seems a fitting concurrence that on the remaining foundations of the Hoyme Chapel, which had burned in 1923, the new art department should be built. Its form was functional: one spacious studio with large high north windows, a smaller work space with a small balcony for Arne's office, and a tiered lecture room seating fifteen. This structure is said to have cost about $2,500; it served unchanged for a decade, except that a basement was carved out to be a ceramics studio. Its form was not only functional but also celebrative, not imitative of Norwegian stave churches, but reminiscent of them because of the dark wood exterior, carved ridge pole, decorative porch, and an elaboration of decorated pilasters and panels. Arne worked at the main sculptured elements for a couple of years and then passed the work to students. Arne thought of himself primarily as a sculptor, but he drew and painted in oil and watercolor equally, so the large studio sheltered classes in drawing, painting, and sculpture. And the little lecture room was the site of art history classes that before long became known around the campus and attracted good students from every discipline.

In college Flaten had not prepared himself for theological studies with the customary discipline of the classical languages; the commitment to the ministry came late. He finished his three years at St. Paul, not with a degree in divinity, but with the less respected (among academics) "canditatus." Clearly this was not a detriment for him in accomplishing the real work of a pastor. Similarly the lack of formal academic recognition for the years of intense study in Florence and Paris left him without gown or hood, but didn't detract from his ability to teach. He was, toward the end of his career, given an honorary Doctor of Fine Arts by Concordia College. Until then Flaten disdained academic processions; he considered the colorful insignia of academic achievement unreliable certifiers of real accomplishment.

This minor matter reflects his exceptional commitment to the genuine, the real, the authentic. It reflects his skepticism of public ceremonials, his distrust of tradition, his wariness of institutions, of conventions, of formalisms. This commitment was profound and comprehensive, although he was not overtly a rebel. His students found him exceptional; he could be trusted; he could discern reality; he spoke the truth. This quality clung as close to Arnold Flaten as his name. He wore a wedding ring inscribed with the Greek letters γνήσιος, "sincerity."

What people discovered about Arne was not academic erudition. He never wrote a book or an article for a professional journal; his history classes were far from being a serial catalog of artwork. And when he presided over any studio class it was not to give a thorough instruction in tools and techniques; students got the essentials about materials and

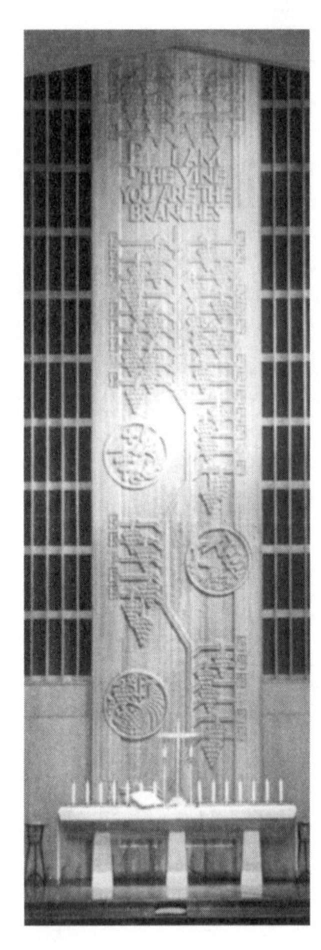

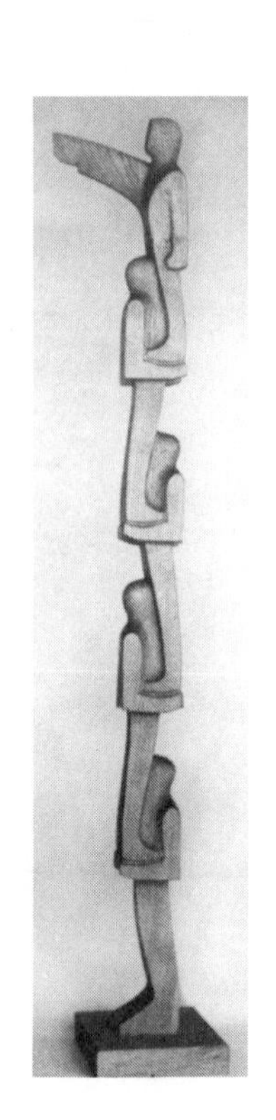

"The Vines and Branches" The image of the Christian community. One of several large-scale church projects. Trinity Lutheran, Moorhead, Minnesota.

"Teacher" Visual reflection on the nature of the profession.

"Jacob's Ladder" A metaphor of the artistic vision.

"King Olav" Not the saintly hero, but a tough warrior.

Carrara marble portrait head of Evelyn Flaten done in Paris and exhibited in the 1932 Grand Salon.

"I am the Way . . ." A pew-end carving, one of a series of many at First Lutheran, Williston, N.D.

"Esthete" Arne made several other witty comments on human affectations and aberrations.

"He shall be like . . ." The initial carving of the sequence illustrating Psalm 1 on the ten stone spandrels of the south wall of Rølvaag Library. (Photo by John Gorder, St. Olaf Church Relations.)

I AM THE WAY
THE TRUTH AND
THE LIFE

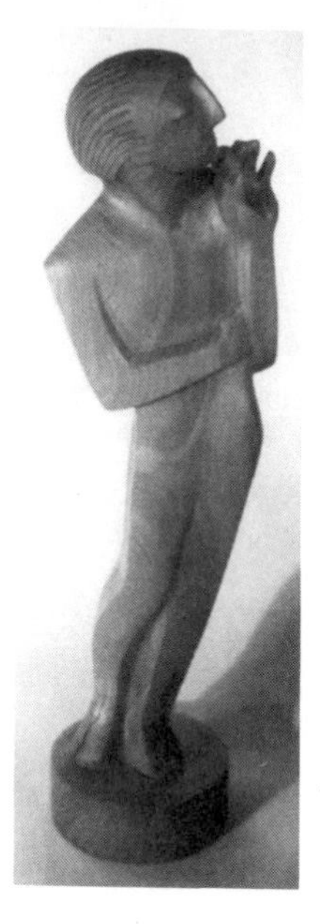

methods and then were encouraged to find their way along. What students discovered was that their eyes and minds were being opened. They found that art was connected to everything, that they were being set free to develop their sensibilities and curiosity, to apply their intelligence and energy, and learn with and from each other. The camaraderie was lively; Arne was an adventurer also, the leader of the crew, and the sense of companionship between professor and students gravitated to the use of his given name, even though such informality was very rare elsewhere on the campus.

Arne entered with relentless energy into his career as a teacher. The burdens of being a one-man art department, participating in his share of other faculty responsibilities (he was for some years also the tennis coach), and being paterfamilias could have used all the time and energy of most people; Arne had the sense that he had been given an enviable life and he filled it. In 1937, not content with nine months of teaching, he and Evelyn offered the first of a series of "art camps," a summer month in which about a dozen students assembled for an intensive time of making art, doing physical work, and engaging in intellectual and religious conversation and study. The first was sited at the Flaten home, with housing partly in tents; subsequently Hovland, a hamlet on the north shore of Lake Superior, was the locus, and the building of a small church one of the goals. Evelyn was a gracious hostess, counselor, and expert manager of the kitchen; Arne was leader, teacher, and pastor. For the campers the times were intense, happy, illuminating, and unforgettable.

Once in those early years he said his idea of his life would be to teach a third of the time, produce art a third of the time, and study a third of the time. His art production was continuous and voluminous. The work of painting, design, and especially carving was a serious calling, and it was also work in which he had great joy. He was a superb craftsman as anyone who sees his portrait heads in stone, marble, or bronze can tell, and the hundreds of wood carvings he made at his home workshop are full of surprise, charm, humor, and power (most were photographed and appear in the book *Arnold Flaten, Sculptor*, published in 1974 by Augsburg Publishing House). But it was not skill that is most memorable in his work. Nor is it the capacity for self-expression or the happy pleasure of the decorative. Arne was a communicator; the work of art was a way of saying something, in ways that can be more memorable than speech or text. It might be simply an expression of his love for the created world or for geometric or nonrepresentational form, it might be commentary on human personality, it might be illustration, or it might be symbolic figure.

Arne belonged to no school or tradition, accepted no limits to the concept or practice of art. He looked at the currents and fashions in the art world with interest but had no eagerness to swim in the public stream. For one thing he was too busy to involve himself in competitions, exhibits, and museums. For another he had his own agenda. The agenda was distinctive for several reasons: first, it was soaked in the biblical story; second, he liked to combine words with images like an illuminator; and finally, compared to making autonomous art objects, he preferred to make art in context. On the St. Olaf campus is evidence: there are stone carvings on Holland Hall, the Rølvaag Library, and the old gym; there are carved wood and polychrome in the Organ Studio, the College Center, and the Agnes Mellby Hall chapel. They are invitations to contemplation, sequels to the work at the Art Barn.

Three fine portrait heads, one of Nils Flaten in the Old Main, one of F. M. Christiansen in the Music Hall, and one of Erik Hetle in the Science Library, are also site-related. One head in pure Carrara marble and one in local gray limestone illustrate also how the sculptor's sensibility and imagination responded to the nature of the material and to the subject. The musician's portrait is elegant, beautiful craft, almost academic. In contrast, tool marks remain on the squared limestone head of the elder Flaten; shape and detail depict the stern, noble, and disciplined scholar who was sometimes referred to as the great stone face. Hetle's portrait is a bronze casting; Arne carved and he also worked in clay. That Arne's range of style and expression was much greater yet is shown in the large images of three kings of ancient Norway that gave the name to the Kings' Room in the St. Olaf Center. Massive sculptured wood, but quite surprisingly smooth, painted polychrome and gold leaf, they tell tersely and with humor the mythic stories of the warlike heroes in a way fit for a dining room. The sculptor searches for truth.

These pieces could be called secular art, but most of the work Arne left on the campus is Scripture-inspired and is often matched to citations from the Psalms or the New Testament. Work similarly referential and reverential appears and reverberates at a dozen church buildings in the Midwest, sometimes in very large panels, and representing almost innumerable themes in unique treatments. A visit to Trinity Lutheran in Moorhead, Minnesota, and First Lutheran in Williston, North Dakota, will exemplify. At Trinity Church is a magnificent reredos approaching forty feet tall carved large and deep on the theme of the Vine and Branches. In Williston Arne undertook many works, including a score of carved pew ends that tell in picture and symbol stories from the Bible, the church, and the pioneer heritage.

In addition to the sculpture, Arne had a direct responsibility for the architecture itself of those churches and dozens of others. The depth of his interest in architecture, his loyalty to the church, and his impatience with anything inauthentic propelled him to do something to interrupt the procession of imitation gothic and imitation colonial churches that betrayed the authenticity of the gospel. He had mounted a carved adage in the Art Barn: "History is for inspiration not imitation." Thus when a former student entered the study of architecture after World War II, he proposed that the new architect join him on the art faculty. There he would add an introduction to architectural studies in the art curriculum, and join in establishing an architectural practice that would aim to bring the architecture of churches into the twentieth century. The new firm, begun in 1949, was busy very soon in the design of a series of new church buildings; the quick success was due in large part to Arne's broad acquaintance among the clergy and church people, and to the faith they had in his person and his understanding of the arts of the church.

When one considers Flaten's work, especially in comparison to that of most twentieth-century artists, words like *rich, nourishing, inventive, thoughtful, warm,* and other adjectives that imply both admiration and affection come easily. The work welcomes, it is accessible and communicates in the language of common intuition. But Flaten was also a person of admirable sophistication. The books in his library were evidence of a serious and wide-ranging scholarship. Along with the works on art history and art biography that one would expect of any teacher of art would be found general history, philosophy, theology—Berdyayev, Spengler, Coomarswami, Maritain, and a great range of things in disciplines other than art. Blake and Dostoyevsky were favorites, and one year he led a voluntary seminar series on the latter. For thirty years he and Evelyn were lively participants in a reading group made up of bright professors from several disciplines, with their spouses. He was always reading, and his students were aware of it because he read critically, and made connections between the life of the mind and the work in the studios.

Much of that part of his career that he wanted to devote to study was spent in the concerns that were closest to the focus of his thought, namely, the implications of the life of faith. He didn't set aside, when he left the parish ministry, the conscious commitment to be a servant of the Word. Even when the obligations of being a heavily loaded teacher, a productive artist, and the father in a growing family were crowding his days he instituted a weekly open Bible class. It was an intimate and happy group; attendance was irregular but it attracted people from across the campus. The discussion could move to any kind of personal or public issue; people learned that everything was faith-related; Arne read the Bible with such freshness that the grace of the gospel seemed to illumine everything.

Arnold Flaten '22 and Tom Peinovich '70, Homecoming 1969 during the reunion of the 1919 football team
St. Olaf Archives

Arne continued to be the preacher in churches also, variously as a guest, and for a few seasons during World War II as a regular at a Methodist church in a nearby village. He had volunteered and been rejected for a military chaplaincy and undertook this extra duty. At the college he frequently spoke at the daily chapel service. He gave the impression of being an adventurer into new ideas, always footloose. In a milieu of Lutheranism he was a willing liberal, with a strong sense of the social gospel, an ecumenical openness, and an aversion to the legalistic and to imperative orthodoxy. And there was clearly a profound personal faith, abundant good cheer, an attractive candor, deep loyalty to the church.

Arnold retired from teaching in 1970, his department staff being then five, and many of its graduates having become artists of various sorts. He sojourned subsequently as a guest teacher at other colleges and traveled to remote places. When at home his workshop output was continuous.

It has been said by some of his close friends that if there were to be one word that would attach most fundamentally to Arnold Flaten, the word would be *Grace.* He was anointed and empowered by grace, and was himself its agent. When he was at last terminally ill and housebound, and the strength to wield chisel and mallet left him, he again took up water colors and made a series of devotional sheets. Each of them has a lettered stanza from George MacDonald's nineteenth-century devotional *Diary of an Old Soul*, and each of them is illustrated with Arne's evocative and expressive brush and colors. One stanza is an appropriate epilogue, being lines that Arnold himself might have written.

> We make, but thou art the creating core.
> Whatever things I dream, invent or feel,
> Thou art the heart of it, the atmosphere.
> Thou art inside all love man ever bore;
> Yea, the love itself, whatever thing be dear . . .
> Because thou first art love, self-caused, essential, mere.

Edna and Howard Hong, 1997 JUDITH HONG

Wedding party, June 8, 1938. JUDITH HONG
Theodore Hong '40, Howard Hong, Edna Hatlestad Hong,
Margaret Hanson Eubanks '38, Gladys Glendening Andrews '38.

14.
HOWARD V. AND EDNA HATLESTAD HONG 1912– AND 1913–

Jack Schwandt

Who are Howard and Edna Hong? New members of St. Olaf College may find themselves asking the question.

They may notice a sign in Rølvaag Library pointing to the Kierkegaard Library; and they may be told that it is a gift to the college from the Hongs and an outstanding research center. Or they may hear that the Hongs recently completed the translation of a many-volume edition of Kierkegaard and that earlier the couple won the National Book Award for Translation. They may even catch a glimpse of the Hongs, or meet them, and surmise that they are storied members of the college.

Their story is indeed important for anyone who becomes curious about St. Olaf and seeks to know more about the college.

The story begins at St. Olaf. Howard Hong, then a graduate student at the University of Minnesota, came back to his alma mater to give a talk about student newspapers and noticed the humor column in the campus newspaper, the *Manitou Messenger*. The columnist was Edna Hatlestad. She had grown up on a farm in Taylor County, Wisconsin. After graduating from high school in nearby Medford, she first attended normal school there for a year and then taught country school for three years to earn money for college. He was born in Wolford, North Dakota, but grew up in Willmar, Minnesota, and graduated from high school there before matriculating at St. Olaf, from which he graduated in 1934.

They were married in 1938, the year he received his Ph.D. from Minnesota and one day after Edna graduated from St. Olaf. Her father, thinking of his daughter's marriage, lamented that Edna would waste her education. But four months after their wedding, the couple hitchhiked to New York and then took a ship to Copenhagen, where he studied Danish.

In the summer of 1933, before his senior year at St. Olaf, he had read Ibsen's *Per Gynt* and *Brand* and discovered the greatness of these plays. His interest in Ibsen then led him to Kierkegaard. Later, as a graduate student at Minnesota, he had found his way to David F. Swenson, the great Kierkegaard scholar, and to his course, which was patterned after Kierkegaard's *Stages on Life's Way.* Edna quickly discovered that she had become a "bigamist," as she puts it, a woman married to two men, Howard Hong and Søren Kierkegaard. So she learned Danish too. Their lifework had begun.

They were in Denmark on the strength of a one thousand-dollar fellowship from the American-Scandinavian Foundation, though President Lars M. Boe had already appointed Howard Hong to the St. Olaf faculty. He thus began his teaching career with a leave of absence. According to him, he was "the only faculty member gone the first year he was here."

He bought a tandem bicycle at a police auction in Copenhagen, which the couple used on a delayed honeymoon trip through Europe in the summer of 1939, amid portents of war. When they returned to the United States that fall (with the bicycle and twenty dollars saved from the fellowship), they learned that Germany had invaded Poland. World War II set the stage for a new phase in their life, one markedly different from what at first seemed in store for them. Their first translation, of Kierkegaard's *For Self-Examination*, was published in 1940. Their first child was born in 1941 and their second in 1942. Thus the dual life they planned—family and Kierkegaard—began. But Howard Hong registered as a conscientious objector, although he was threatened with losing his job if he persisted. He did not back down. Instead, he turned to working with prisoners of war, first in the United States for the American Friends Service Committee and then in Germany for the War Prisoners Aid of the World's YMCA. Kierkegaard's *Works of Love* informed his understanding of this grueling work.

After the war, he began his work with refugees. By the end of 1946, nearly one million people who had been displaced by World War II remained in Germany. About 185,000 of them were Lutherans, chiefly from the Baltic states. A group of eight Latvian pastors urged the Lutheran World Convention (predecessor of the Lutheran World Federation) to help; and American representatives of that body established a service to refugees. Howard Hong was named to head this service. From 1947 to 1949, he was the Director of the Lutheran World Federation Service to Refugees in Germany, and simultaneously Senior Field Officer of the Refugee Division of the World Council of Churches. At the same time, he established three International Lutheran Student work camps in Germany, which were forerunners of the Peace Corps.*

The Hongs became intimately familiar with life in the refugee camps, and with the stories of the refugees about ravaged homes, persecution, and flight. They also went with their children to the concentration camp at Dachau in 1947 and visited the crematorium, where they found this inscription on one of its walls, left there by "some GI Pascal," as Howard Hong called him:

> They were mixed together when the world was made—the murderer and the lover. This is the eternal journey of a man. He gets tricked and bamboozled, and he louses up his life. But if it is a sadness to be a man, it is a proud thing, too, and no demon ever foaled can know that great journey.

Their work in Europe bore fruit back home: they helped resettle 250 displaced persons from Latvia in Northfield alone. The Latvians have remembered the Hongs in quiet yet eloquent ways. For many years, the buffet in their home has been graced by an elaborately carved wooden candelabrum with a brass plaque that marks it as a gift from "the grateful Latvians." And a painting by a Latvian refugee hangs in their living room. *The Last Concert* depicts Latvia's foremost cellist in a prison-camp barracks and playing for the last time, his hands having been ruined by the rough labor forced upon him in the camp. The painting is a gift to the Hongs from the painter, Augustus Annus, who had been a professor at the University of Riga. Most recently, the Republic of Latvia conferred the Order of the Three Stars (for the three districts of Latvia) on Howard Hong, the highest honor Latvia gives to non-Latvians.

The conclusion of their refugee work also marks the end of what they have called the "longest interlude" in their translating career. During this interlude their family grew: it now included six children, two of them adopted from a Latvian family. Two more children were later born to them, bringing the total to eight. Be it noted, then, that they took seven years from their abundant life and gave it to the service of prisoners and refugees.

As if in return for what they gave to others, their own work in all its variety flourished. Edna Hong began a legendary thirty-year stint as a Sunday school teacher at St. John's Lutheran Church in Northfield. Her teaching there is but one sign of the faithful congregational life of the

*Most of the details in this paragraph come from Richard Solberg, *Opening Doors: The Story of Lutherans Resettling Refugees* (St. Louis: Concordia Publishing House, 1992).

Hongs. She later wrote a history of the congregation for its one hundredth anniversary in 1969. She reached a wider church audience by resuming a practice she began before World War II. Between 1939 and 1963, often in collaboration with her husband, she contributed fourteen stories and meditations to *Christmas: An American Review of Christmas Literature and Art*, published by Augsburg Publishing House.

She also wrote a series of imaginative historical sketches of Northfield that were first published serially in the *Northfield News* and then as a booklet, *The Paving Block Stories* (1955), which marked the town's centennial. These projects were a local prelude (and no less important in her judgment for being local) to the twelve books for which she has been widely acclaimed.

Perhaps the best known of these books is *Bright Valley of Love* (1976), which has been published in ten countries. In it, we follow the movements of Gunther's "pilgrim soul." He is a deformed boy with a "flippering walk" and "crazy crooked hands." He was cruelly used by his family, but grows up in Bethel, that worthy Lutheran institution of mercy whose work continues to this day. Grace triumphs in his life, and Bethel survives the Nazi threat to exterminate its residents. Edna and Howard Hong knew Gunther; and she avers that her story is true. True to his life, true to that terrible time in Germany, and true also to her epigraph from Kierkegaard's *Works of Love*: "To love forth love is to build up. But to love forth love means precisely to presuppose that it is present at the base."

As Edna Hong's readership grew, she began to get invitations to speak at various places and for various occasions: at churches and church retreats, before women's groups, at seminary convocations and college chapel services, for high school graduations, and before learned gatherings. She has accepted as many of these invitations as she could, and gives freely of herself when she does speak. She resists the label of "Kierkegaard scholar" at these venues, as she otherwise always has; and her speeches seem designed to prove her point. Here she is, before an audience of sophisticated folk, introducing herself by saying that her "mind still shipwrecks on the shoals of philosophy," though she is married to a philosopher, and claiming that she is "not quite sure what a thesis is"; even more, "as for hypotheses, if one of them approaches me, I turn and flee." Her speeches are exuberant and wildly funny, unconventional and in a distinctive idiom, yet well honed by the disciplines of Christian life, and not least of all by Kierkegaard, who she says "feeds me constantly." These speeches disclose a woman who has found her own voice.

And no doubt about it, Howard Hong's rich, plummy voice is his own. His students know that voice, have not forgotten it, and their lives have been affected by it. Perhaps they caught a sense of what he once said when he was approached about a job that would have taken him from the classroom and from St. Olaf: "my heart is essentially in teaching . . . for I really believe our need is on the deeper levels" of what students "think, feel, and believe . . . [so] my question is: what form can my work as a teacher best take?" Harold Ditmanson, one of his students, saw how he answered that question in the classroom, and wrote memorably about it when Howard Hong retired:

> Philosophy took on a peculiar quality of excitement, due in part to Howard's own temperament and in part to certain pedagogical techniques. The teacher's enthusiasm made the subject seem important. It was as though he had received a revelation or made a great discovery and felt that what truth had done for him it could do for others as well. Memories come flooding back of Howard pacing the floor, covering the blackboard with incredible diagrams, or rocking back and forth from heel to toe, with arm extended and thumb and forefinger pressed together as though shaking the dirt from an imaginary radish, and saying "Radish, *radix*, radical, root—to be truly radical is to get at the root of things."

This is Howard Hong's vocation: "to get at the root of things." It is a calling that attracted students to his courses. His teaching helped make the philosophy department one of the most distinguished in the college, not least of all as measured by the number of its students who later earned doctorates in philosophy and cognate fields.

He searched for "the root of things" in other areas of college life as well. He was the chair of a faculty committee—Clarence Clausen, Harold Ditmanson, Albert Finholt, Nora Solum were its other members—that undertook a thorough study of the St. Olaf curriculum. Their work was supported by the Ford Foundation and the results were published as *Integration in the Christian Liberal Arts College* (1956), which in the words of Harold Ditmanson "will remain a monument to the clarity and comprehensiveness of [Howard Hong's] philosophical vision." This book gained a national reputation it still enjoys, though to Howard Hong's regret its recommendations did not take root at St. Olaf. Why not? Among other things, the book urged the college to reject the allures of both careerism and "university ambition." Instead, "let the Christian liberal arts college have the courage of its convictions—to be a college of liberal education with a Christian philosophy radiating from its center" (82). And so as David Hume said of another such inquiry, his own *A Treatise of Human Nature* (1738–1740), this one also "fell dead-born from the press."

Howard Hong was undaunted. He had another and entirely practical way of expressing the conviction that is at the heart of *Integration in the Christian Liberal Arts College* and of the constitution of St. Olaf. The curriculum study observes that the church college is "a very necessary arm of the Church in the Church's never-ending battle against the secularization of life." But observation tells us that the everyday life of a church college, busy as it is, can easily lapse into amnesia and become habitually secular. Knowing this, Howard Hong attended daily chapel regularly. He maintained this practice for many years and knew that it took time to do so. His practice is all the more noteworthy because he is a man who has never wasted time, whose daily life has always been well disciplined. Here too he went to the root of things.

As he has in the Kierkegaard translations for which he and Edna Hong are best known. Kierkegaard is a prolific and many-sided author. His *Papirer*, or journals, run to twenty volumes in the Danish edition and are both the workshop for and a commentary on his published works. Little of this material was available in the English-speaking world until Indiana University Press published the Hongs' seven-volume edition of the *Journals and Papers* (1967–1978). It is a carefully edited selection from the *Papirer*. Four volumes are arranged topically and have concise introductions to each topic by the Hong's revered friend the late Gregor Malantschuk. These volumes are followed by two autobiographical volumes, arranged chronologically, and by an index volume. A "monumental contribution," one observer rightly notes.

As this project came to its conclusion, and near the time Howard Hong retired from teaching, he convinced Princeton University Press of the need for a uniform, critical edition of Kierkegaard's published works. He was appointed the General Editor of this edition. The results are the twenty-five volumes of *Kierkegaard's Writings* (1978–1998), with the index volume to follow, all but four of which the Hongs translated. Each of these volumes contains a scrupulous historical introduction, the text with cross-references to the pagination of the standard Danish edition, extensive notes, and a supplement with a generous selection of material from Kierkegaard's journals, and an index. When this series began, one notable scholar observed that it "will now become the definite presentation of Kierkegaard in our language," and no doubt he is right. When the series concluded, the *Times Literary Supplement* (London) said of it and them: "All honour to the Hongs: *Kierkegaard's Writings* is one of the outstanding achievements in the history of philosophical translation."

After Kierkegaard died in 1855, his library was sold at auction; and a catalog of that auction was published in 1967. Howard Hong used that catalog and his own index of Kierkegaard's books as he attended book auctions and scoured antiquarian book houses throughout Europe to reconstitute the exact editions of the books in Kierkegaard's private library. The books he bought over many years, together with microfilms from the Royal Library in Copenhagen and other Kierkegaard material, including secondary works, make up the Howard V. and Edna H. Hong Kierkegaard Library, which they gave to their college. It is an extraordinary gift. When it was officially announced at a convocation in 1976, William H. K. Narum, another former student of Howard Hong's and a longtime colleague, spoke on behalf of the college and said that the "Hongs honor us by entrusting [this library] to us."

Such is Howard Hong's voice and such is his presence. Such is Edna Hong's voice and such is her presence. The promise and importance of their lifework has been widely recognized. That first American-Scandinavian Foundation fellowship has been followed by other fellowships, by honorary degrees, and by other awards. To name only one of these: in 1978, Queen Margrethe of Denmark made them Knights of the Order of Dannebrog.

The citations that accompany these awards and degrees often point to the life of Howard and Edna Hong, as well as to their work. They "have touched the lives of many in distinctive ways" and "have lived lives dedicated to fundamental questions," says one of them. Another notes that "wherever they have lived [they] have always opened their doors to people—young and old—students, teachers, and internationally known scholars." This steady practice "has made them as well loved as they are respected." Yet another, speaking particularly of Edna Hong, observes that "she is a doer of good deeds, one who has, in the midst of raising a family of eight children, translating and writing and speaking," always been hospitable "to those in need, whether . . . a distracted St. Olaf student . . . or a distracted matron. . . . Some of the needy have required an evening of care, but some have required months, years, of Edna Hong's time and energy, and she has given it freely."

In Northfield, the center of their hospitality is their remarkable house, first located on the campus near the site of Ellingson Hall and since 1961 next to Heath Creek on the western edge of Northfield. The college's plan to build that dormitory created a dilemma for Howard Hong. If his house remained on campus, the new dormitory would be five feet from his front door. But the house could not be moved. That was the conventional wisdom about a house whose walls were made of limestone slabs cemented together. But against that conventional opinion, the intrepid Howard

Hong found an equally intrepid house mover named Ollie Wren; and they moved the house off the hill on which the campus sits to its present location, where its parts were rearranged according to the design of the Northfield architect and former St. Olaf student Bob Warn.

Howard Hong had built and furnished the house himself, with help from many students, from native limestone and various other materials he salvaged over the years. Examples abound. He built the dining room table from a walnut log he found in a ditch in Arkansas, when he was working with prisoners of war; he bought the living-room window, which originally let light into a bar, at an auction; he made a hickory log that once grew on their property into the shaft of a staircase; and again at an auction, he rescued a fire escape from a Minneapolis building, scheduled for demolition, and made another staircase of it.

Both on campus and at Heath Creek, the house has been an integral part of the life that the Hongs have shared generously with students and others. The young Harold Ditmanson, for example, went there regularly for a philosophy class. He later recalled that "their home was solid, intimate, and simple," which gave him "the impression that for Howard and Edna plain living was the necessary accompaniment of high thinking." Not "high thinking" simply or primarily, he knew; for this house is and has been in the service of charity, Christianly understood. It now has a new name. It is the Kierkegaard House. Its apartments are now regularly used by visiting scholars who are working in the Kierkegaard Library.

Another building figures prominently in the lives of Howard and Edna Hong: Trinity Lutheran Church at Hovland, Minnesota, on the North Shore of Lake Superior, where they have spent their summers for many years. This congregation is housed in a church that was built during the summers of 1947 and 1948. The project began in conversations in 1946 between Howard Hong and members of this congregation, whose original building had fallen into disuse after a highway near Lake Superior had been moved farther inland. He took the story of this congregation back to campus, a group of St. Olaf students made plans to become a work group, and Arne Flaten with help from his former student Ed Sövik (then a graduate student in architecture at Yale) designed the building and later made its stained-glass window. Men from the congregation cleared the land for it and helped pour its concrete footings; the students hauled water from the lake for mixing the concrete; and they helped split both rocks from the lakeshore and local timbers and brought them to the building site. The students stayed in the cabin of a pioneer named Mons Hanson, whom many of them remember well to this day. They also remember the inspiration they took from Howard Hong and the experience of living with the Flaten family and building a church.

So singly and together Howard and Edna Hong have been builders and restorers: of a church, of a house and a way of life consonant with it, of a family, of a college and one of its best departments, of a distinguished research library, of lives ravaged by war and by other traumas. And with all of this, their long and intricate dance with Søren Kierkegaard, and their construction of a highway on which Kierkegaard pilgrims travel. Any reader of the foregoing sketch might reasonably wonder what holds the varied parts of their life together. Howard Hong once answered the question, though of course not directly, when an interviewer asked him if he was "religious." "Well, 'religious' and 'religion' come from the Latin *religio* which in its verb form means 'to be bound.'" Everyone, he noted, is "bound to one thing or another. Some people worship their figures. Others worship God." No pride of intellect here, but rather the Archimedean point Kierkegaard notes by which to take the measure of the world and of one's own life and work: to be bound by the confession of the Triune God.

Early in their life, Edna and Howard Hong wrote a story for "children of all ages" called *Muskego Boy* (1943). Here we are told about an immigrant family that came from Norway to the Wisconsin territory, where they founded the Muskego congregation. The grandmother of the family, profoundly grateful when a congregation is established and a pastor called, misses the old country and is apprehensive about the new. She repeatedly urges her grandson Mikkel not to forget God and the church in a land where a new freedom would make it easy to do so.

The grandmother is aware of the differences between the old world and the new. But are those differences any greater than the ones between the world of Muskego and our own? The question can be asked, for Howard and Edna Hong move between a world descended directly from the grandmother's and the world of today's academy. They are at once parochial and cosmopolitan: citizens of Northfield and of Copenhagen, communicants of a congregation and through it of the church, members of a college and of the republic of letters.

Here then is a practical task for St. Olaf College, not least of all for its leaders. How well and in what practices does this particular college remember the grandmother's profound gratitude and what she knows must not be forgotten? If against the conventional wisdom of the day Howard Hong can move a stone house from Manitou Heights to Heath Creek, we might hope against the conventional wisdom of ours that the answer is "Yes, it remembers."

Harold Ditmanson in Boe Chapel, late 1950s — St. Olaf Archives

15. HAROLD DITMANSON 1920–1988

Walter Stromseth

Though institutions outlast their individual members, they draw their continued life from persons who share and shape their historical development. Harold Ditmanson was such a person. A member of St. Olaf's religion department from 1945 until his retirement in 1986, he saw the college as a personal "crusade, an anchorage, a home, and a reason for being."[1] During his long academic career he served as department chair, member of the Founding Committee of the Paracollege, chair of the Centennial Study Committee, member of three presidential search committees, and in many other leadership roles. He once commented that if all the reports he had written were laid end to end, they would likely reach to St. Louis and back. An eloquent spokesman for the college, one who clearly articulated and exemplified its educational mission over several decades, he enjoyed the respect of the entire St. Olaf community—students, faculty, and administrators alike.

The adopted son of Thorwald and Anna Ditmanson, Harold grew up in Ladysmith, Wisconsin. His early development was markedly influenced by his father's example and advice. On his fourteenth birthday, he received a collection of paternal admonitions, poems and thoughts as a guide to living well. Thorwald inscribed the collection: "to help you be a good citizen and a good Christian," assured "that you have served well, that your friends have found you true, that your foes have found you fair, that your motives have been right."[2] In looking toward college, Harold "never really wanted to go anywhere else" than St. Olaf, owing both to his father's urging and his own attraction to its academic program as well as its religious and musical traditions.[3]

Harold enrolled as a St. Olaf freshman in 1938, beginning a relationship with the college that was to last his entire life. An exceptional student, "Dit" (as he came to be affectionately called by almost all who knew him) excelled in debate as well as extemporaneous speaking and served as president of the student body. His election to that office provided a mark of his characteristic modesty. Running against his close friend and debate partner, Clifford Swanson, he proposed that each should campaign for the other, which resulted in an electoral process unique in college annals.[4] To a question about the distinctive value of his undergraduate experience, he responded: "I found faculty members who were embodiments of what they 'professed,' both academically and religiously. . . . One was liberated from the limitations of provincialism and prejudice and enabled to become a more complete person. The entire program nourished moral perception, informed commitment, and the ability to live with complexity and uncertainty. . . . At St. Olaf it was possible to grow as a literate, moral, and spiritual being through knowledge of the best that has been said and thought."[5]

While an undergraduate, Harold met and courted Jean Hanson, an honor student and fellow debater. They married in 1943 and subsequently reared four children: Barbara, Mary, Anne, and Mark. As in many academic households, Dit would play with the children in the evening, then retire to his study for late-night class preparations once they were in bed. But their father's encyclopedic learning and penchant for lengthy commentary were not lost upon his children. Once Mary brought a question to her mother, who suggested she ask her father. Mary's response was, "I don't have that much time."[6] The marriage became a rich partnership of shared interests and mutual support extending over forty-five years. Their devotion to each other and their nuclear family was joined with remarkable openness to the wider human family. Throughout their life together, the Ditmansons' home provided a place of convivial hospitality where new faculty and students were welcomed into the St. Olaf community.

Upon graduating from St. Olaf in 1942, Harold attended Luther Theological Seminary and received his B.Th. degree. Ordained into the Lutheran ministry, he briefly served a parish in Forest City, Iowa, while simultaneously teaching in the departments of religion and speech at Waldorf Junior College. But in the fall of 1945, Reverend Ditmanson received a call from St. Olaf's President Clemens Granskou inviting him to serve as a one-year replacement for Professor H. B. Hanson of the religion department, who had suffered a heart attack. With the return of World War II veterans and the expansion of both student body and faculty, Ditmanson's temporary appointment became permanent.

Despite the pedagogical demands of his initial year, during which he taught seven courses each semester in a six-day week with eighteen class hours, the new professor reported later that "after teaching, I knew immediately that this was what I really wanted to do."[7] His commitment to college teaching never flagged, even through his first five years on the St. Olaf faculty when he taught classes of one hundred students or more and enrollment in his always popular courses approached five hundred each semester. Combining these heavy academic responsibilities with continued graduate work, Professor Ditmanson received the M.Th. degree from Princeton Theological Seminary in 1948 and the Ph.D. degree from Yale University in 1956.

Beyond the classroom, but in keeping with his lifelong commitment to undergraduate education, Ditmanson singled out the college curriculum as his "main on-campus interest," out of concern "that it should have breadth, coherence and life."[8] As a result, his was a major voice in decades of discussion about St. Olaf's distinctive character and calling as a church-related, liberal arts college. In the 1950s he helped write St. Olaf's widely read curricular proposal, *Integration in the Christian Liberal Arts College*, and coedited the book *Christian Faith and the Liberal Arts*. In the 1970s he was principal author of the college's centennial self-study, *Identity and Mission in a Changing Context*. Dit's curricular interests were evident again in his convocation address opening St. Olaf's one hundredth year. On that occasion he argued that the curriculum should be seen as more than an arrangement of learning experiences in particular disciplines, since it intends also to cultivate specific values such as curiosity and detachment, rational doubt and disciplined reasoning, intellectual versatility and independence, toleration and "the disposition to honor rather than scorn others."[9]

For generations of students, these values were exhibited in Dit's courses. Widely known for their clarity, comprehensiveness, and depth, his lectures were a model of critical commitment that encouraged his students to take responsibility for their own learning and their own faith in an intellectually mature manner. One of his students reported to President Rand: "When I came to St. Olaf I was a skeptic . . . I leave St. Olaf a Christian who knows what he believes. . . . The reason is Dr. Ditmanson. His classes were the difference for me."[10] Though his primary medium was the lecture, he did not regard knowledge as an inert substance to be stored up or handed on. Rather, he wanted his students to "experience for themselves the disciplined activity of discovery and formulation" and so share in the process of developing new insights and ideas.[11] Accordingly, his discussion of a topic conveyed a sense of considering its issues afresh, as part of a continuing quest for enlarged understanding. This explorative spirit found expression in topical digressions which became his pedagogical trademark, one that allowed him both to address and deepen classroom questions. Students valued his "relaxed yet professional manner," his "capacity to make the subject matter arrestingly interesting," his infectious enthusiasm and obvious "joy in the work of teaching."[12] One recalled: "Dit managed to make the study of Church history and Christian ethics come alive for me . . . I began to realize the depth and richness of Christian thought. . . . His wit and informal teaching style encouraged students to be active participants in class rather than passive sponges."[13] Another noted: "As a lecturer, Dit is often deliberately elliptical. He can obscure his own opinions so that students will not be unduly influenced by his authority."[14] Never pompous or ponderous, Dit wore his erudition lightly. Yet, "precisely because he did not try to be an authority figure, many found in him authoritative insight."[15]

Dit's religious pedagogy was influenced by Saint Augustine, one of his favorite authors. He saw Christian faith not as an authoritarian arbiter of all truth, but rather as a participant in the ongoing human quest for understanding. Hence he understood the godly life, in its intellectual aspect, as a "journey from mental obscurity to as much clarity as humans can imagine."[16] This outlook found expression in his open frame of mind, with its immense range of curiosity and learning, as well as in his passion for clear organization and articulation of thought. But it also grounded his finely nuanced sense of the many-sided complexity of issues and his disciplined assessment of relevant evidence and argument. A voracious reader, he could sit with a book for many hours, taking notes on its key points. This reinforced his prodigious memory and enabled him to provide at will a detailed, critical account of its content. His careful attention to diverse views also contributed to his mediating disposition and his aversion to theoretical controversy fueled by claims to full or final truth. Dit's own intellectual orientation is best described in his characterization of the "middle way" envisaged by St. Olaf's Lutheran founders—an "intellectual middle way between classical intellectualism and undisciplined emotionalism" whose essence was "to see the merits of contrasting positions, to wish to reconcile differences," to hold that persons "may cooperate without reaching full agreement, and to affirm that truth is a unity but to deny that anyone sees the truth in its unity."[17]

Although he taught all religion courses and every class level, Professor Ditmanson was best known by St. Olaf graduates as a teacher of ethics. In keeping with the historical mission of the college, he believed that consideration of basic value questions "should be inescapable within the frame of liberal learning," so that students would be encouraged to develop a critical value orientation.[18] As a lifelong teacher of Christian ethics, Dit emphasized the moral virtues of civility, courage, and compassion as "indispensable means of achieving some decency and humanity" in our

Pope Paul VI and Harold Ditmanson in Rome, 1971 Jean Ditmanson

world.[19] Yet he argued that there is "no distinctively and exclusively 'Christian ethic' . . . no special Christian duty, but only a special Christian urgency to do our human duty well."[20] Nevertheless, convinced that Christian concern for the right and the good required disciplined moral deliberation and discernment, he sought in his ethics courses to foster a mature moral judgment that would not only inform his students' concern for the well-being of others, but also "enhance their own lives, and enlarge their country's capacity to choose wisely and to flourish."[21] For him, as for St. Olaf's founding traditions, "higher learning" was not properly a cultivation of intellect that left students' moral dispositions or religious convictions untutored by critical reflection.

Though he was remarkably open to insights from many sources, Professor Ditmanson's wider professional career as a theologian remained rooted in St. Olaf's Lutheran tradition. Yet, true to its spirit, he contributed greatly to the ongoing reformation of both that tradition and his broader Christian heritage. Through his work on committees, commissions and task forces of the American Lutheran Church, the Lutheran World Federation, and the World Council of Churches, he helped shape an ecumenical orientation within his own and other Protestant denominations, an ecumenical spirit that challenged their earlier sectarianism. Again, his theological interest in the Anglo-Catholic tradition led him to stress the religious significance of the entire creation and to question Protestant tendencies toward a Christianity centered wholly upon the human. Ditmanson was also a pioneer in interfaith dialogue. His national and international roles in Christian-Jewish discussions helped his own and other Christian traditions confront their history of anti-Semitism and reform their understanding of Judaism. In 1987, his work and writing on this issue were recognized through presentation of its first Christian-Jewish Relations Award by the Jewish Community Relations Council of Minnesota and the Dakotas. Never comfortable, he said, "with any theology that rules people out,"[22] his own major theological work, *"Grace" in Experience and Theology*, emphasized the inclusive, reconciling character of grace—that Spirit in which the other is accepted and affirmed, distrust and hostility are overcome, new community is initiated. His life and thought were themselves a means of such grace, a reconciling ministry turned always toward open conversation, increased cooperation, and enlarged community.

As a professional teacher-scholar, Professor Ditmanson carried forward St. Olaf's founding traditions and educational aspirations in truly exemplary manner. But also in his person, he exemplified virtues essential to those who authentically link an institution's past and future. With Luther, but also with the ancient Stoics, whom he admired, he possessed the courage to question his inherited perspectives and practices, the courage to acknowledge their limitations and need of reformation, the courage that overcomes fear of dissent from the status quo. Yet he was also a person of hope—not an easy optimism or blind faith in the future, but a basic trust that through personal commitment and patient discussion traditional horizons can be expanded and questionable practices corrected. Even more, he was a person of subtle humor—not mere levity, though he took playful delight in verbal ambiguity and frequently exchanged with an Oxford friend, Principal Donald Sykes, such newspaper headings as "Fifty Lawyers Offer Poor Free Advice." But his humor also ran deep, since he conjoined serious commitment with refusal to take overseriously his own traditions or his own work. He had a keen eye for human foibles, a bemused sense of the incongruity between ideal aims and historical practice, the gap between personal or institutional aspiration and actual achievement, yet a lightness of spirit able to live with such incongruity without losing heart. Though his courage, hope, and humor were basic human virtues, they were nurtured by his Christian faith and a measure of his faithfulness as a Christian humanist who embodied St. Olaf's distinctive educational calling.

Like the college he served, "founded in faith to render light," Professor Ditmanson's professional achievements were devoted to a glory beyond his own. His persistent striving for greater understanding and academic excellence was tempered by an intellectual humility that acknowledged the encompassing mystery of our human condition, a mystery that in his view "does not diminish as knowledge increases."[23] Together with the religious tradition he shared, his life and thought were a witness to that mystery as a reality of grace, the activity of One whose wisdom and goodness exceed our human knowing or achieving. This spiritual milieu of gracious mystery undergirded Dit's personal modesty, his inquiring disposition, his sense of intellectual life as a journey toward expanded but never complete understanding, his dissatisfaction with the status quo, his persistent poise and self-giving spirit. In the commencement address to St. Olaf graduates written shortly before his death, he depicted personal life as a temporal journey with times of special depth and meaning, decisive "hours of authority" that continue to nourish a person's effort at self-understanding and responsible self-expenditure.[24] But institutions, too, are journeys through time, and in the life and work of Harold Ditmanson St. Olaf has been graced with such an "hour," one that will continue to nourish its collective self-understanding and guide its educational practice. For institutions like St. Olaf are also the lengthened lives of individuals, and the college's unique mission finds enduring expression in Dit's distinctive spirit: a paradoxical joining of deliberativeness and devotion, free inquiry and courageous commitment, critical detachment and compassionate caring, reflective seriousness and playful humor, truthful assessment and hopeful vision.

NOTES

1. "St. Olaf 'Platform' for Study and Work," *St Olaf* 34.4 (August 1986) 3.
2. Rev. Morris O. Wee, Funeral Sermon, June 21, 1988.
3. "St. Olaf 'Platform' for Study and Work" 3.
4. Reported by Rev.Clifford Swanson, tape of "Remembering Dit" Symposium chaired by Professor Joseph Shaw, St. Olaf College, October 17, 1992.
5. Harold H. Ditmanson, "Remarks Prepared for Susan Thurston Hamerski," November 24, 1986.
6. Reported by Jean Ditmanson.
7. "St. Olaf 'Platform' for Study and Work" 3.
8. "St. Olaf 'Platform' for Study and Work" 3.

9. Harold H. Ditmanson, Centennial Convocation Address, September 9, 1973, 8.

10. Sidney A. Rand, Tribute to Dr. Harold Ditmanson from St. Olaf College, June 21, 1988.

11. "Remarks prepared for Susan Thurston Hamerski."

12. Letters from former students Gretchen B. Herringer, Carl E. Braaten, and Kathryn L. Johnson to Dr. Richard Peterson, May 1985, in support of Harold Ditmanson's nomination for the Professor of the Year award given by the Council for the Advancement and Support of Education.

13. Letter from James E. Finholt to Dr. Richard Peterson, May, 1985.

14. Letter from Kathryn L. Johnson to Dr. Richard Peterson, May, 1985.

15. Donald Sykes, tape of "Remembering Dit" Symposium.

16. Rand.

17. Ditmanson, Preliminary Paper on the Identity of the College, prepared for the Centennial Study Steering Committee, undated, 3.

18. Report of the Steering Committee of the Centennial Study, Harold H. Ditmanson, Chairman, Part I, Section 3 ("Liberal Arts"), 11.

19. Ditmanson, Chapel Talk, October 20, 1964.

20. Ditmanson, "Christian Faith and Public Morality," *Dialog*, Spring, 1987: 92,97.

21. "Remarks prepared for Susan Thurston Hamerski."

22. "St. Olaf 'Platform' for Study and Work" 3.

23. Ditmanson, Address at the Inauguration of President Sidney A. Rand, September 16, 1963, cited in Joseph M. Shaw, *History of St. Olaf College*, 1874–1974 (Northfield: St. Olaf, 1974) 515.

24. Ditmanson, "Hours of Authority," St. Olaf Commencement Address, 1988, *St. Olaf* 36.3 (June/July 1988) 10–13.

PART III:

Vocation: How has St. Olaf shaped the lives of individuals?

16.
WHY DID YOU QUIT THE MINISTRY?

Sidney A. Rand

I.

One day during my time in the president's office at St. Olaf, a friend surprised me during a conversation. "Why did you leave the ministry?" he asked. I wasn't ready for a question like that and fumbled my way through what he must have thought was a feeble answer. I had begun my career as a parish pastor and then had spent the following years as a college teacher, church executive, and college president. Had I left the ministry when I left the parish? Had I forsaken my calling?

Another day a senior student sat in my office. He wanted to talk about his future plans. What should he do? How could he know he was on the right job? Was he called to some specific task or career? I tried to give him advice based on my own experience. He should follow where his talents and career hunches led him. He should remember that his life could be one of service in many different occupations. I have not followed his career closely, but I think he is a happy and productive person.

The words *calling* and *vocation* are commonly used in our day to refer to one's occupation or job. They have become attached especially to those areas of work that are less involved with academic concerns. Carpentry or mechanics or hair styling or secretarial work may be a vocation. The law, medicine, or college teaching is less often so designated. What does that mean? Are the so-called professions not vocations? Are the doctors, lawyers, and professors not called to their work, while the secretaries and mechanics are?

Another interesting distinction in the use of these words is found in the fact that they are loaded with religious or theological meaning, and at the same time have been thoroughly secularized and used to apply to work in a way that has nothing to do with religion.

So how shall we who are involved in the work of a college of the church see ourselves and our careers? Are we a called people? Are we professionals or nonprofessionals if we attach the word *vocation* to our jobs? Does the idea of calling add to or subtract from the meaning of what we do?

In the religious sense, the concept of the call is used in at least two distinct ways.

1. *There is the common literal use of the word.* I call someone on the telephone. Mother calls the children to come to eat. They called him John, meaning that the parents named the child. In the Bible, the word is used this way, too. "God called the light day . . ." (Genesis 1:5). "Thou shalt call his name Jesus . . ." (Matthew 1:21). "So Pharaoh called Abram . . ." (Genesis 12:18).

2. *The word* call *is used in Scripture to refer to God's action in claiming those who are his.* God says to Isaiah, "I have called you by name, you are mine" (Isaiah 43:1). Jesus said, "I came not to call the righteous, but sinners" (Mark 2:17). "Therefore, holy brethren, who share a heavenly call" (Hebrews 3:1). "To this he called you through our gospel" (2 Thessalonians 2:1).

In these uses the word *call* means the specific call of God to persons to be his. He calls through personal appearances (Isaiah, Abraham, Jesus), or through the message of his gospel (Paul's letters).

Scripture also uses the word *call* in connection with those called to be God's apostles or special servants. This concept of call is the basis for the church's call of persons into the ministry.

II.

Here we are chiefly concerned with the second use of the word as outlined above. As believers we are a called people. We are called by God to be his, to receive the gift of his salvation, and to live our lives in accord with his will.

But Scripture does not seem to teach that we are called by God to a specific way of making our living or spending our working days. Rather, the implication seems to be that God does not favor one occupation over another or see one kind of work as more pleasing to him than another. Our calling is to be God's people, live that way, serve others that way, glorify God that way—in whatever we do day by day.

Why did I leave the ministry? Well, after much thought I would have been able to say to my friend who asked the question that I did not believe my call to serve God locked me into a Word and Sacrament ministry, but permitted me to serve in other ways. So I always viewed the college presidency as simply another area in which, as a person called by God to be his through Jesus Christ, I could live out my calling as a Christian. I must say I felt the same way about becoming a United States ambassador. I do not believe I was called by God to be an ambassador, or a church executive, or a college professor. I do believe, however, that I was and am called by God to be his child, his forgiven follower, his personal representative in all I do and wherever I make my living. I also acknowledge that each part of my life was a preparation for the next, and that God guided me in each step.

I believe I came to this understanding gradually. As a college student I was led to believe that even as God calls some persons to be pastors (the highest calling, some would say), so he calls a person to be a teacher or an engineer or a janitor or a secretary. Even as a college student I marveled at the filing system God must keep at his disposal in order to match everyone with the right job. In the years since that time, I've found that students generally fall into one of two categories. Some see things as I did. They search and wonder as they try to understand a career choice in terms of their Christian faith. Others, though they may take their faith seriously, do not see career choice as determined by it. In fact, many do not let their faith inform their thinking at all as they survey the careers from which to choose.

All of which means that students need guidance and counsel. Most of all, they need to see and understand the way others conceive of their faith life in relation to their careers. It is in this role that college faculty members, administrators and other personnel can be of help to students as they make career decisions.

It is also from this point of view that we can best plan our roles in the program of St. Olaf College or help the college define its vision and purpose. The challenge for each of us is to see our personal lives in this context, but not let it go at that. We also need to see calling or vocation as a basis for what we do together as an educational institution.

At least one more thing needs to be said. Students are also called. They, with us who serve as teachers or administrators or in other staff capacities, live their lives most productively, and most Christianly, when they see themselves as called persons whose current call is to live as responsible students. Calling or vocation does not wait until a person is a college graduate. Students are called now, not simply when they contemplate a career choice or enter on a career. They are part of the community known as St. Olaf College, a community which needs always to clarify its understanding of calling as it relates to the goals and programs of the college.

Two books which I have found helpful in clarifying my understanding of calling are *A Theology of the Laity* by Hendrik Kraemer (Philadelphia: Westminster Press, 1958) and *Our Calling* by Einar Billing (Minneapolis: Augustana Book Concern [now Augsburg Fortress Press], 1952).

17. STANDING AROUND IN THE DARK

Kathryn Ananda-Owens

If my passion is indeed my vocation, I will concede that God called me at the Wisconsin Union Theater when I was eight years old. My mother says I was banging on a piano long before that, but I can trace the onset of my professional interest in music to the Union, and a concert by Rudolf Serkin that included, specifically, Beethoven's "Waldstein" Sonata. Serkin radiated so much joy during his performance that I thought to myself, "I want to do that." Twenty-some years later, I have survived a doctoral program in piano performance. My music making has taken me to China and will shortly take me to Europe. It landed me an assistant professorship at St. Olaf as well as a performance on the same piano Serkin played that night. On paper, I look like a perceptive and dutiful Christian who identified her life's purpose at an early age and single-mindedly pursued it. In fact, I am no such thing.

I am a reluctant Christian. Not a reluctant pianist, but God has certainly had to lead me by the nose to a career in the arts. Look at my college applications and you'll find indications I once thought I would major in physics. Look at my degrees and you'll find a B.A. in economics. Look at my twelfth-grade California Occupational Preference Survey and you'll find evidence that I should have been a bricklayer. (I like to work with my hands.)

Physics and bricklaying were no match for music. Economics, however, fought the good fight. I've been fascinated by public policy for as many years as I've been involved with music. It took a book and a crisis over my honors project in economics during my senior year of college to make me recognize that my interest in the social sciences was about safety more than it was about passion.

I was working on my thesis, a model of political action committee spending, and looking for material for a private reading in economics to fulfill the last requirements of my major when I accidentally ran across the then recently published book *If Women Counted*. Its author, Marilyn Waring, probably didn't intend to derail my thesis. Nevertheless, her book made me ask a lot of questions I'd overlooked while blithely assimilating the fundamentals of capitalism back in Econ 101. Why does a woman's housework carry no value in economic models unless she does it in someone else's house? Why are acres of rain forest valued more cleared, as cattle ranches, than in their natural state as carbon sinks and reservoirs of biological diversity? I thought I had enough material for a private reading on issues of gender in third-world economic development. My adviser thought otherwise.

Maybe he was right. Maybe I had a sociology or women's studies project on my hands, one with no economic relevance whatsoever. Meanwhile, my questions were snowballing out of control, perilously close to those carefully constructed economic theories I'd been nurturing for four years. Try modeling in any field when you can no longer take your givens for granted and you'll know what kind of progress I was making on the thesis. I faced three choices. One, I could write the thesis I wanted to write, questioning more than modeling, which would likely prove worthless in the eyes of my adviser. Two, I could write the thesis my adviser expected, and hate myself for brushing my uncertainties under the carpet. Three, I could drop the thesis altogether and focus on my senior recital. Bach, Beethoven, Scriabin, and Debussy. The chance to get out on stage and do what I loved and maybe radiate some joy in the process. I dropped my thesis. The senior recital was worth it: joy is its own reward.

Had circumstances been slightly different, I might not have felt free to abandon my honors project. The previous December had found me interviewing in Chicago as a Rhodes finalist from Wisconsin. My Rhodes essay stated that I wanted to spend two years reading economics at Oxford. (What I suspect I really wanted was to receive an award that would guarantee me success and an abundance of self-esteem for the rest of my life.) I managed to repress warnings that the Rhodes guaranteed neither piano lessons in Britain nor access to an instrument. What possessed me to consider *willingly* spending two years without the daily solace of the piano I cannot now imagine. Yet there is no question in my mind that, had I been offered a Rhodes scholarship, I would have accepted it. There is also no question in my mind that, had I been offered a Rhodes scholarship, I would no longer be a pianist. I would be an attorney, or a policy wonk, or a banker. I would be castigating myself constantly for having sacrificed what I truly loved in order to gain recognition, approval, and the illusion of financial security. (Ironically, doing what I love has brought me varying doses of all three.)

I was not one of the four Chicago-region Rhodes scholars named that year. The two-day interview process left me and most of the other candidates crushed, dazed, and disappointed. I was confused as well. After a second interview (unscheduled, given at the prerogative of the selection committee, and a frequent though not infallible indicator of success), I'd been staring out the window trying to get the words and music to "Amazing Grace" out of my head. Not two minutes later, the selection committee entered the room and announced the committee's choices. You do the math. My brain started its rendition of "Amazing Grace" at the precise moment someone in the next room removed my name from the list of those still under consideration. I couldn't believe some inner voice had the audacity to suggest to my conscious mind that I was better off without the Rhodes. Four months later, of course, I was to acknowledge that I would be miserable for the rest of my life if I didn't pursue music professionally. In retrospect, I'd have to say my personal Rhodes sound track was highly appropriate.

My acknowledgment nonetheless aroused more internal doubt, reluctance, and resistance than it did faith. So many "shoulds" surrounded the decision between economics and piano. I had mentally categorized a future in economics as a career in public service. I categorized anything to do with the arts as somehow selfish and frivolous. My graduating class was full of idealists going off to medical school to become rural doctors, or to the Peace Corps to volunteer, or to literacy programs in America's inner cities. I went off to grad school feeling guilty for developing my artistry and teaching skills while others were off saving the world. Faith presented itself in the knowledge that there was nothing else I *could* do. I knew that a significant part of myself would be dead to the world (and thus of no use for saving anybody) if I chose not to follow my heart. There is no describing in words the way in which my heart and soul are drawn to music. In musical terms, the pull I experienced was that of a 4–3 suspension (in a major key), a moment in tonal music with only one possible resolution. I figured if this was not a message from God about my calling I didn't know what was and might as well follow my heart until I heard some sort of cosmic "Whoa!"

The reluctance and doubt of the past have been converted to mere uncertainty. I no longer believe that art is frivolous. I believe it is one of the profoundest ways we as humans express and connect with our humanity. The creation and re-creation of art are the greatest acts of thanksgiving for the human experience I know. They are the most powerful tools I have for connecting with the sacred, and the only tools I have, other than life itself, for doxology. I still don't know why God has called me in this time and place to do what I do. I'm grateful for the opportunity to live this uncertainty at St. Olaf, where a biblical context and a community of faith surround my questions about vocation. I'm grateful to be at a place where vocation is discussed.

I've grown to feel, in these discussions, a strong kinship with the Old Testament's Samuel—Samuel as a child. My experience of vocation has been very much like hearing a voice call my name in the middle of the night. I'm not sure I really hear the voice, and I'm not entirely sure it calls my name. Then the call comes again, and again, and I eventually tire of waking up and doing Jungian dream analysis, so I figure I should answer. Someone else says the voice is the voice of God. I can believe that, but even after I say, "Here I am," I'm still standing around in the dark in my bare feet wondering what all the noise is about. Maybe someday I'll figure it out. Meanwhile, I've got a concert or three to play, and quite a few students coming through the door with questions of their own. One of them wants to learn the "Waldstein" Sonata. At least God knows where to find me.

18.
I JESU NAVN

Mark L. Nelson

A couple of years ago I was driving south on France Avenue in suburban Minneapolis near the Southdale shopping center, which is a six-lane stretch of road with many stoplights (too many, by some estimates). I found that I was being tailgated by one of those "aggressive" drivers in a huge, black four-wheel-drive vehicle. Frantic to get somewhere, he kept weaving in and out of traffic and finally passed me going about sixty miles per hour in a thirty-five miles per hour zone. I thought, "Where on earth are you going?"

He made record time—to a stoplight just two blocks from the point where he passed me. There, I slowly pulled up alongside him and calmly rolled to a stop. When the light turned green, his tires squealed, and he took off again, for two more blocks where he hit the next red light. This time I thought, "What in heaven's name are you doing?" This pattern repeated itself for several more intersections, until we reached I-494, where he headed west at warp speed, and I coasted onto the freeway some distance behind.

It occurred to me that maybe I should ask myself these same questions, in a larger sense. "So," I thought, "where on this earth are *you* going? And better yet, what in *heaven*'s name are you doing?"

As an officer of an insurance company in Minneapolis, my professional career has never matched up very well with my religion/philosophy major at St. Olaf, and I've often felt that something was missing. Most of my work is focused on negotiating business contracts with HMOs and organ transplant hospitals across the United States. There are insurance conventions to attend, sales presentations to make, and endless employee problems to solve. I'm on the road thirty weeks a year and spend a lot of time in airports eating cold popcorn while CNN Headline News drones from a nearby TV. It' s not quite what I had envisioned when I attended St. Olaf in the early 1970s and studied Martin Luther, Paul Tillich, Abraham Heschel, and Søren Kierkegaard.

This was on my mind during a recent family vacation to Arizona. I took a personal side trip to visit Dr. Carlyle Holte, my former St. Olaf adviser and now retired Professor of Religion, in Sun City (which, next to Northfield, probably has the highest concentration of retired Lutheran ministers outside of Wittenberg, Germany). As we sat squinting at each other in the afternoon sun, I was complaining about the health care insurance field. With its Byzantine regulations, liability exposures, competitive markets, and client entertainment requirements, it wasn't very fulfilling. It didn't have the kind of meaningful existential connectivity that I imagined when I used to sit in class thinking about those really BIG issues like interpreting Scripture through *Anfechtung*, grasping the *mysterium tremendum*, pursuing I-Thou relationships, and resolving the teleological suspension of the Ethical. Basically, the issues that no one has ever heard of at the Mall of America, and when you try to discuss them people stick their fingers in their ears and hum. Carlyle looked into the blue sky and said, "Well, I suppose it's like the old Norwegian farmer who struggles out of bed at 4:30 on a winter morning, puts on his dirty work clothes, lights a lantern, and trudges through the snow to go clean out the barn with a shovel." He paused to make sure I was listening. "And as he slides the heavy barn door to one side he mutters, 'I Jesu navn.'"

Aha. Norwegian words, I presumed. Unfortunately, I took Spanish. And got a C+.

It took a minute to register, but then I remembered sitting in my grandmother's kitchen in St. Paul as a boy. She had a Norwegian table grace inscribed on a wooden wall plaque with rosemaling:

"I Jesu navn, går vi til bords. . . ."

"In Jesus' name," it began, "give us this bread."

Martin Luther was not recorded as having said anything about the insurance industry. He did, however, have a great deal to say (too much, by some estimates) about a person's vocation and the role of the individual in fulfilling his or her various stations in life. Luther scholars officially call it the "Doctrine of Vocation," with a capital D (see Gustav Wingren, *Luther on Vocation*).

Rather than exalting only priests and nobility, as Europeans were prone to do in the sixteenth century, Luther's theology held that all offices or stations on earth are ordained by God—teacher, printer, mason, sheriff, housekeeper. If you are blacksmith, taught Luther, be the best blacksmith you can be, for you are carrying out the intended order of creation. In the twenty-first century, the same might be said of professional athletes, stockbrokers, parents, computer programmers, entertainers, day care workers, and so on.

One way to think about it might be that in our vocations we're kind of like the Blues Brothers: on a mission from God. *Where* we are ultimately going on earth may be right where we are, and *what* we are doing may be occurring in heaven's name whether we recognize it or not. Luther would not pay much attention to the type of station we hold, but how faithfully and conscientiously we fulfill its duties and responsibilities to make a positive difference. As David Whyte put it in his book on poetry in corporate America, *The Heart Aroused,* each individual can "nudge the world infinitesimally in the direction of good" in every action taken, from the moment we turn off the alarm clock in the morning to the way we design a product or deliver a service.

Most of us with a Lutheran heritage or a St. Olaf education probably recognize that our decisions are, to some degree, guided by an unspoken commitment to respect other people and make a contribution to society. Having a calling or vocation may be the gift that comes with the days we are given, and through it we fulfill, in Luther's terms, a divine purpose. Achieving stature or success may be merit badges on the uniform of the calling.

I used to be an aggressive driver, weaving in and out of traffic and tailgating other drivers. But as I think back on it, I had little idea where I was going. I wanted to *get* somewhere and work on a few big issues.

These days, I think that there may be no bigger issues than showing my five-year-old daughter how to make a bird call by blowing on a blade of grass held between your thumbs, helping my son learn how to throw out a runner trying to steal second base, cleaning week-old apple juice out of the front controls of our VCR, holding my wife after our fourth successive miscarriage. And maybe the list could also include the process of negotiating business contracts in "good faith" and preserving or expanding a few jobs for individuals and their families.

So now on cloudy winter mornings after I park my car and trudge through the snow to the office thinking about a legal dilemma or an abrasive competitor or a three-day business trip that must be faced, I pull open the heavy front door of our building, and sometimes say under my breath, "I Jesu navn."

Thanks, Carlyle.

19.
MISSION AT ST. OLAF

Judy Skogerboe Hyland

St. Olaf College has always been conscious of its special mission as a college of the church. During its long history, there have been faculty and students who have taken seriously the mandate of Jesus, "Go ye into all the world and preach the Gospel to all creatures." This sustained interest in global mission is evidenced by an impressive roster of more than sixty St. Olaf graduates who have served in overseas missions, including well-known names like Ronning, Landahl, Syrdahl, Martinson, and Sövik.

I came to St. Olaf in 1932 with a general interest in world mission that became an intense personal call to serve during my years at the college. There, many influences led me to mission. The weekly fellowships in Ella Hjertaas's studio caused me to think deeply of my place in the work of the kingdom. We had student fellowship gatherings at the home of Pastor Stavig, pastor at St. John's Church in Northfield. His house overflowed with students—all the way up the stairway, packing the floor of his living room. Gert Sövik, St. Olaf German professor and postwar relief worker, was always an inspiration for mission work. We had a spiritual emphasis week every year. In addition, there was the student volunteer movement and the retreats they organized.

During my senior year the student volunteer retreat took place in a private home in Minneapolis, where we talked about missions and prayed all weekend. On Sunday the sermon was given by a missionary from India, who spoke on the topic "When You've Lost Your Ax Head." This was based on a story about Elisha. A worker was cutting wood to make a shelter, and while he was chopping, the head on his ax flew off into the deep river nearby and sank from sight. He thought his work was over; he had lost the tool he needed. What do you do when you lose the tool you need for your work? the missionary asked. Elisha prayed for the man, and the ax head came up out of the water. The missionary used the story as an example: in doing God's work we may begin a job with enthusiasm, but we may lose our ax heads, the ability to carry on the work. At that point we need to pray to God to restore the ax heads; in other words, to renew the impetus and power to continue the work. This story affected me very much. All of us were questioning all the time how best to serve the Lord with our lives. We had a clear sense that we should live for more than ourselves.

These experiences fanned the flames of interest in mission that had been sparked in my home in Erskine, Minnesota. I first got the idea of going to China during my childhood. Missionaries came to visit once a year and stayed at my parents' home, since my father was the pastor of the church. They impressed me with their passion for their work and the joy they derived from it. To be a missionary seemed to be the greatest job in the world. I wanted to be one. I wasn't the only one affected by the visiting missionaries: no fewer than seven missionaries came out of that small town of six hundred people and went overseas to such far-flung places as South America, Africa, China, and Japan.

It may be that missions were romanticized at that time. I remember singing from our Lutheran hymnal about the "benighted heathen bowing down to stick and stone." Today this "benighted heathen" might as easily be found in white Lutheran Minnesota as in any of the countries we thought of in the 1930s as mission "fields." He may be a highly educated person with an advanced degree from an American university; we met many such people in Japan during our years there. Whether he is highly educated or not, if he has no God and no faith, he is without hope and in need of help. According to Dr. Roland Miller of Luther Seminary, there are 2.5 billion people who have not been reached by the gospel, and the number of non-Christians in the world today is increasing.

The need is as great, if not greater, but the face of missions has changed very much. Today in most countries there is a national church with national leaders. The missionary today needs some very special qualities such as patience, love, and humility and certainly, creativity. So far, both church and mission have much to learn in their working relations.

St. Olaf students today are different from those of prewar times. They have a global view. Many have traveled abroad and experienced other cultures. In the 1930s, the longest trip I took was from Erskine to Northfield. The horizons of the women students especially were very limited. Unwittingly, we were caught up in the "hat-gloves-and-bag-to-match" culture. The focus of the future for many of us was not too unlike that of a Midwestern girl who, after a few months in college, quit, saying to her dean, "I came to get went with, but I ain't." Of course, it would have been said much more elegantly by a St. Olaf student! But in spite of our narrow vision, we had a world outlook. At St. Olaf we took seriously Jesus' command that we should go out in the world and preach the gospel to every creature. If thinking of service on the overseas mission field, the men would go to seminary and become preachers, and the women would go to a Bible school and become "Bible Women," or take the medical route and become nurses or doctors. They were professionally religious.

I had no idea when I left for China in 1940 the extent to which I would use everything I had learned in my liberal arts education at St. Olaf. Nor did I have any idea that I would take a ten-year detour to the mission field, as we did because of World War II. When I left for China, I left my fiancé behind, and the plan to marry him when he arrived in China a year later to join me as a missionary under the Lutheran church. Before our plan could become reality, I found myself in a Japanese prisoner-of-war camp in the Philippines, where I had gone to avoid the Japanese army and to study Chinese to prepare myself for my work. In the prison camp, I found what I had learned at St. Olaf very valuable. We had 130 children in the camp who drove everyone crazy by playing war games over our feet. A few of us took them out to the tennis courts for several hours each day and told them stories. I exhausted every bit of literature I had ever absorbed: from Horatio Alger to Shakespeare and the Bible. And when that lost its luster, I told them about my exciting childhood in Erskine. Eventually, we were allowed to conduct school, and for half a day we were allowed to use the books we had brought into camp. But soon they were confiscated and so we began school again, in some classes without any books at all. I taught junior high English one year without any textbook. I reconstructed plots, poems, and novels from memory. We dramatized the bits of literature we could lay our hands on—scenes from Shakespeare's *Midsummer Night's Dream*, *The Birds' Christmas Carol*, and O. Henry's short stories. I also studied Chinese and Greek all the time, anticipating a lifetime of missionary work in China.

During the thirty years my husband and I spent in Japan, beginning in 1950, there was nothing I had learned at St. Olaf that I did not use. University students came to our Student Center in Tokyo for help with papers on the religious imagery of T. S. Eliot's *Waste Land*, or on Shakespeare, or for lessons in Old English. I was often called on to help revise theses which had been rejected because of their poor English. My experience in forensics and debate proved useful all the time.

Typical of our experience was the Japanese university student who visited us every day and felt very superior to us, who were stumbling through a Japanese language primer with sentences such as "This is a book," and so forth. One day when my husband came into the room where we were talking, I thought, We'll show this superior young man that we know something he doesn't know. I spoke in Norwegian to my husband. To my dismay, the student jumped up from his chair and joined in the conversation! He had spent two years in Denmark, and was quite fluent. But one day he came and was less haughty than usual. He was going to have his final exam in English literature that week, and he had not prepared at all. He asked for my advice: what should he study in two days that would prepare him for that test?

I had never been good at guessing my own college professors' minds, but I said, "I think you should have an overview, a good outline of English literature—the periods, writers, characteristics, dates, and so on."

He said, "That sounds like a good idea, but where can I find such an outline? Would you make one for me?"

So with some help from my literature book, I gave him a pretty good outline.

He thanked me for that, but he said, "I should have something specific, too. What would you guess would be a question they might ask?" With more confidence than wisdom I said, "I would concentrate on the poets of the Romantic period, if I were you."

He thanked me profusely and left. I thought maybe I had seen the last of him. But he returned in a few days, bowed very low, and thanked me. There had been two questions on the final exam. One was to give a general survey of English literature. The other was a question about the poets of the Romantic period. This was interesting, but I don't think he ever became a Christian. One does many things in the name of human relations that don't result in faith.

Today there is much greater opportunity in mission for the professional in many areas: technology, science, humanities, and the arts. St. Olaf students, with this kind of training, could spread out into the world in banks, offices, industries, and universities. From these secular positions, they could wield untold impact for Jesus Christ.

Mr. Tabei, a graduate student at prestigious Keio University, was very much like the engineer we met on New Year's Eve at a Buddhist temple, who told us, "We are all homesick for God." That homesickness led Tabei san to a saving faith in Christ. At his first appearance at the Student Center, he reached eagerly for a Bible saying, "I am interested in the Bible because I am on a search for God." Unfortunately, that search became very brief because in a few weeks he graduated and entered a big corporation. With deep disappointment, we saw that young man leave. In a few weeks, however, he returned to the Center. His face was pale and haggard. He looked as if he had not had much sleep. He said, "I've just quit my job." That was almost unheard of in Japan. We asked him, "What are you going to do now, then, Tabei san?"

He picked up a Bible from the desk, saying, "I'm going to read and study this book until I know why I am living." That dear man came to the Center every day and sat there reading and studying the Bible for one year. He wanted to find out for himself what God was saying, so he asked for very little help. He studied the Bible from Genesis through Revelation three times, and when he had finished the third time, he said quietly, "Now I know that Jesus is the Son of God and the Savior of the world, and I know he is coming again, because this is the only thing that makes sense out of history." And he added, "Now I want to confess my sins and receive Jesus Christ." His search for God had ended.

St. Olaf is uniquely situated to produce people with this kind of faith. It offers its students the best of secular education, plus an opportunity to know Christ in a saving faith, and certainly it equips them with the Word of God. In speaking with groups of St. Olaf students today, I am impressed with their wide knowledge and their interest in the world. St. Olaf has an awesome potential for mission that needs to be awakened. I tremble at the possibilities, when St. Olaf graduates fan out into the world with their degrees and expertise, doing their work and passionately making Christ, who has brought meaning to their lives, known around the world. The professionally religious person still has a place, but to make the gospel effective today, it must be reinforced by secular professionals who bring to the world not only their expertise but also their passion to make Christ known.

20.
SOME THOUGHTS I HAVE IN MIND WHEN I AM PROFESSING

James Farrell

I had a vocation once, but I lost it. I grew up Catholic, and a vocation meant only one thing: boys could become priests, and girls could become nuns. When we prayed for vocations, this is what we had in mind. And so did our parents and grandparents. My grandmother Farrell didn't like my parents calling me "Jim," because she feared that a nickname would interfere with my career as a cardinal of the church. Whoever heard of "Jim Cardinal Farrell"?

For a long while, I was, in fact, attracted to the priesthood. But I was also attracted to politics. For a young Catholic, the 1960 election was heavenly, and—even after the Kennedy assassination—politics seemed like a promising profession for a person of my faith. When I applied for admission to Loyola University in 1967, therefore, I said that I wanted to study political science because I wanted to be president of the United States. (I still thought that you had to know something to be president.) Having lost my vocation, I was looking for another, and I guess I still am.

If vocation is a call from God, I must say that God didn't call me person to person. I never heard a voice from heaven, or sizzled in a bolt of lightning. I came to history and American studies and St. Olaf by accident—or by serendipity, which is the term I prefer. Because Loyola needed enough men to match the number of women at its Rome Center, I spent my sophomore year in a junior-year-abroad program. I hitchhiked a lot, and people asked me questions about America that I couldn't answer. Curious, I turned to American history for answers. I also got shut out of all the political science classes when I came back to Chicago, because, even though I had been enrolled in a Loyola program, they made me register dead last as a transfer student. To kill time, and to find an occupation that might occupy me until I was old enough to become president, I enrolled in education courses. And so I blundered into the bully pulpit of the classroom.

I went to graduate school in history with the same purposeless passion. My wife Barb was in graduate school in psychology, and I needed something to do to keep myself busy while she was studying. History was a good choice, because every day there's more of it to study. Eventually—very eventually—I received a degree in American Culture, a combination of history, literature, art, and music. By the time I graduated, I was already at St. Olaf, hired as an interdepartmental clone to replace faculty members on leave—in history, American studies, art history, and education. I had never heard of St. Olaf when I applied here, but it's become an organic part of my life and vocation. Maybe serendipity is just another name for providence.

For me, teaching at St. Olaf has been a chance to answer the questions that life has posed for me. I want to be able to explain to myself why we act like Americans. I want to explore the politics of American government and the politics of everyday life. I want to contemplate the goodness of the so-called good life. I want to see why I act the way I do, and how I might act better. I want to practice and propagate traditions of thoughtfulness, which should be the primary product of colleges. Fortunately for me, St. Olaf is an institution that also engages these issues, and my students are people curious about the same kinds of questions.

Teaching is a peculiar form of work, because it makes a convocation out of our vocations. At St. Olaf, my vocation intersects with those of my friends and colleagues, with administration and staff, and—most importantly—with students. In the classroom, my vocation as a professor offers provocations to students following their own vocational paths. The main elements of college classes are reading, writing, and speaking, each of which brings us into conversation with people, past and present, who help us see why we act the way we do. Each of the disciplines of the college is designed to help us answer the main question of a college education: "What does it mean to be human in a particular time and place in the universe?" History suggests that we act the way we do because dead people told us to. Dead people established the ideas and institutions—even the language—that we use. Reading history, then, is a way of having conversations with dead people, a way of asking them what they had in mind, and what we have in our minds. Sometimes, especially in American history, we learn directly why we think the way we do; in other cases, history gives us "perspective by incongruity" on our own lives by showing us fully human beings who act on different assumptions altogether.

I am a professor of history, but I don't think that professing a discipline, by itself, constitutes a vocation. When my friends introduce me to other people, they often say that I teach history. This is true, but I prefer to think that I teach *students*, who are a peculiar form of human being. When I'm teaching, I try to be mindful of the personhood of these young people. For me, that sense of personalism helps me keep my work in perspective. History in the abstract may be a profession, but history in the persons of my students is a more profound and interesting matter. When the stories of the past become intertwined with the stories that students bring to my classes, then history really happens.

At a place like St. Olaf, professors like me notice that their students learn more than we teach—and that much of that learning is unrelated to our classrooms. First-year students, especially, report that they learn a tremendous amount about living on their own just by sharing a room with a person who, until September, was a total stranger. They learn about different human purposes and work habits, and varying definitions of diet and cleanliness. They experience the joys and sorrows of time management, money management, and stress management. They feel the pangs of doubt and the consolations of religion. They reap the hard-earned benefits of a residential college.

For the most part, it's my vocation to let students learn these lessons on their own. But when, in their class journals or in office hours, students ask questions about these issues—and other issues of human belief and behavior—it's my job to tell them my partial truths. In many ways, I think that we profess not just by teaching but by example. In a wonderful essay called "Some Thoughts I Have in Mind When I Teach," Wendell Berry contends that "the best relationships of teacher and student are those that turn into friendships. In friendship the education machine is entirely circumvented and removed from consideration, and the two minds can meet freely and fully. The student comes to know the teacher, which in my opinion is a thousand times better than knowing what the teacher knows. The teacher ceases to function merely as a preceptor and becomes an example—an example of something, good or bad, that his [or her] life has proved to be possible."

For me, this means that part of my vocation is to offer who I am as well as what I know to my students. When students ask—and generally *only* when they ask—I can offer my story as one way of making sense and making meaning in the world. White, male, heterosexual, married, middle-aged, middle-class, suburban, Catholic, confused, critical, contradictory—I am a possibility for my students, just as historical figures are also models for our own thinking and action. When we are studying the politics of housework in American studies, it's useful for students to know how Barb and I have worked this out. When I'm teaching environmental history, it's OK for them to ask why I drive a distance to work. Along with their parents and pastors, their friends and relations, I am exemplary—and not always positively. Indeed, it's important (and both humbling and consoling) to know that, in some ways, it's a good thing for me to be a bad example for students. I am an example, good *and* bad, of some possibilities in American life.

Part of my professing happens in classrooms, but some of it happens in dorm rooms and living rooms and cars. That's because, like most faculty, I'm a writer. In America, the culture of college usually includes an injunction to professors to "publish or perish." Professors pass on knowledge in the classroom, but they're also supposed to shape knowledge in books and articles presented to their academic peers. The problem with this academic publishing is that, too often, it's "merely academic," meaning that no one really cares about our abstruse theories and stories. In my own life, I've tried to present my scholarship in other ways to larger audiences: in Chautauqua presentations as a nineteenth-century Minnesota pioneer; in lecture series at places like Holden Village and Bjorklunden; at Elderhostels; and, more recently, in "Dr. America" commentaries on WCAL.

Most of the time, writing is a way of discovering what I think. At this point, for example, which is a few pages into a first draft of this essay, I'm still not sure where I'm going. Writing is, for me, a form of play, a way of "serendipping" between words and my experience to see if I can make some sense of them. Writing is where I don't come out to play; I go in to play. In an essay, especially in an exploratory essay, play is what we pay to see. The word *essay* means "to try out," and an essay is where we try out different voices and ideas. Sometimes, we try on other people's ideas, dressing in what we might call intellectual drag.

Sometimes, however, writing is just a drag. Writing a book is a pain in the butt, and in the lower back, and the wrists and forearms. It's carpal tunnel syndrome, and it's tunneling to the brain. It's the extra strength headache, the one that sneers at Tylenol™ and Excedrin™. I sit in front of my computer monitor, and I'm sure that it is monitoring me. "Vegetative state," it bleeps back to the mother ship. The cursor blinks like a demented lighthouse, while another idea crashes into the writer's block. My fingers touch the keyboard, but they are not in touch with my brain. I am not writing; I am writhing.

Then, when I least expect it, the writing amuses itself with my mind, taking possession of me. I find that the writing wires my brain for double tasking. I can be thinking about one thing, and, all of a sudden, a sentence slides sinuously into my synapses. Often, when I'm otherwise occupied in my morning shower, my neurons just keep on composing. I even find that I write when I am asleep. Dreams just before dawn often turn out to contain first drafts of phantom phrases. I seldom need an alarm when I am writing.

At its best, writing is pure play. Play, says my dictionary (playing with my expectations), comes from a root meaning "to take up one's promise or responsibility." But it means "to move lightly, rapidly, or erratically; frisk; flutter." It means "to have fun, amuse oneself." Or "to make love playfully" (foreplay and afterplay, I guess). Or "to perform on a musical instrument." And "to perform on a stage." This means, I guess, that I take up my responsibilities as a writer not by taking myself too seriously, but by amusing myself.

Writing is also, for me, a musical performance. I love the rhythm of a good sentence, the harmonies of a well-constructed paragraph or page. (The word *page*, for example, is pasted onto that last sentence as much for the pulse of the alliteration as for any addition of meaning; and this sentence, you'll notice, doesn't flow nearly as nicely as the last one.) I like to play with metaphors and puns and allusions, because they are the bargain basement of writing; you get two meanings for the price of one.

Culturally speaking, writing is a way of recording words, a way of making ideas available for reading and reflection. Writing is a point of connection between one person and another person, the two of them engaged in a dance that neither of them entirely controls. At its best, it is a conversation in which the worlds and words of the author come into contact with the worlds and words of people with the *author*-ity of their own experience, whether or not they ever write it down. Like teaching, writing is a place where vocation becomes convocation. At its best, our books and articles can be both profession of faith and a calling to both writer and reader.

When I first became a college professor, I didn't think of it as a vocation; I thought of it as a job. In America, most of us are happy to have a job, which is a position for which we get paid. A job is a piece of work. In fact, in the nineteenth century, the term *job work* meant "piecework." The word *job* comes from a Middle English word meaning "lump," and is related to our word *gob*. In the eighteenth century, Samuel Johnson defined a job as "petty, piddling work," and for many Americans, the definition still fits.

A lot of Americans do this petty, piddling work because companies pay us for it. We are part of the "Great Compromise," in which twentieth-century Americans have told employers that "we will perform stupid, dehumanizing work as long as you give us enough compensation to purchase the private compensations of a 'good life.'" We focus on the extrinsic rewards of work, because the intrinsic rewards are often so paltry. College professing is different. If you're smart enough to be a college professor (which, frankly, isn't all that smart) you know that there isn't much money in it. But there are intrinsic satisfactions that compensate professors like me, and some of the most significant are spiritual and religious.

After a few years of professing, I began to think of it as a career, which, in America, is the upward trajectory of jobs over time. For most Americans, a career is primarily private; it is a person's advancement within social boundaries, and it often leads to social and geographical mobility and the uprooting of communities. A "career culture" requires ambitious, calculating individualists who want to get ahead—leaving the rest of us, by definition, behind. At a certain point in my careering, I would have left St. Olaf behind for a so-called better offer.

In my time at St. Olaf, I've increasingly come to think of my career as a vocation. When I have time to think deeply about my work—which is not as often as I'd like—I think of it as a calling from God to help create the kingdom of God on earth. Vocation gives us a way of thinking about the cosmic and communitarian aspects of work, and it invites us to think about the gift of creation, the creation of our own gifts, and the ways in which our gifts might be applied to the purposes of the creation. A vocation is a call from God, to use God's gifts for her glory, and for the good of the community, including the poor. A calling can never be purely private, nor can it be purely vocational in the narrow sense of the word. A vocation is God's call to work in the world, not just at work, but in all of the settings of our lives. If we believe in vocation, we are all at work now, because we are all engaged in thinking about our work in the world. Perhaps, therefore, instead of saying that we are "at work," we should say that we are "on vocation."

For me, this idea of vocation is intimidating, because it means that a person must be dedicated to God's project and not just the projects of American capitalism. The more I think about it, the more I think that God's main projects are justice and reconciliation. If a job doesn't have justice in the job description, I sometimes think, then it's probably not a vocation. If it isn't religious in the root sense of the word, it's probably not a vocation. Religion comes from the Latin *religare*, which means "to bind together." At its root, therefore, religion is a science of connectedness, binding people to God, people to each other, and people to God's creation. At its root, religion is radical, because it works against the disconnectedness of modern (or postmodern) culture. Sometimes college professing lets us make these connections, helps us to see our responsibilities to God's creation. But there are many days when I wonder if my work is really radical enough to be a vocation.

While I've been at St. Olaf, I've also come to think of my work as a profession—and, to some extent, a profession of faith. In America, a profession is a generally understood as a service occupation, usually prestigious and often enriching, in which professionals employ their expertise and their judgment to assist people who are considered clients. The ethics of professionalism require professionals to act in the client's interest, even when other options might be easier. Lawyers, doctors, and college professors are among America's professionals.

Beyond this cultural definition of professionalism, I also think of teaching as a profession of faith. At Loyola, I took a course on the Pauline Epistles from a priest who never used the word *God* without appending the parenthetical expression "if there is a God." At first, I thought it odd that a priest should be unsure about the existence of God. But then it occurred to me that, even without rational certainties, he was leading his life *as if* there were a God, a remarkable act of faith in itself. Since then, I've been dubious about dichotomizing faith and works. The way we act *is* our act of faith. Each of us is an example of how faith acts in the world. Increasingly, it seems to me that work is not just how we experience faith but also how we express it. "For the Shaker craftsmen," Thomas Merton once observed, "love of God and love of truth in one's own work came to the same thing, and that work itself was a prayer, a communion with the inmost spiritual reality of things and so with God."

James Thurber once said that it's more important to know some of the questions than all of the answers. In *The Reinvention of Work*, Matthew Fox provides some of the questions we should pose about the spirituality of work. Here are my favorites:

> Is my work real work or just a job?
>
> Do I experience joy in my work? Do others experience joy as a result of my work?
>
> Is my work smaller than my soul? How big is my soul? How big is my work? What can I do to bring the two together?
>
> How does my work connect to the Great Work of the universe? Is my work actively creating good for others? Who profits [in both senses of the word] from my work?

How is my work a blessing to generations to come?

How does my work affect the environment?

What do I learn at work?

What is sacred about the work I do? Which of the classical seven sacraments most characterizes the work that I do?

If I were to leave my work today, what difference would it make to my spiritual growth? To the spiritual development of my colleagues at work? To the spiritual development of my family and friends?

What am I doing to reinvent the profession in which I work?

These are tough questions, the midterm self-examination in the course of life. At this point in my life, I expect I would still flunk. But having lost one vocation and gained another, having abandoned a life of Holy Orders for a life of disorder and thoughtfulness, I still have time to learn.

21. CROSSROADS

Angela Goehring

> The place God calls you to is the place where your deep gladness and the world's deep hunger meet.
>
> Frederick Buechner

Before St. Olaf, the only constant I knew in my life was change. It wasn't until I claimed St. Olaf as my own community of believers and fellow friends and scholars that I realized how God had always been a constant throughout my life. As a navy brat throughout my childhood, I had no choice but to follow my family around the world, moving every couple of years, never allowing roots to settle deep. Finally at St. Olaf, a place "rooted in the Christian Gospel," I understood roots to mean more than where one resides, but the foundation for life, from which a life of service branches.

Somehow, somewhere along the line, I knew I wanted a liberal arts education. My family had lived up and down the East Coast, but mostly in a liberal arts college town in Brunswick, Maine, where my roots started to settle on the banks of the Androscoggin River, and I dreamed of carrying books through hallowed halls and having class with grass between my toes. Soon enough, we were plucked out of our comfortable life in the woods, to the bustling city of Tehran, Iran, and then back again, to the East Coast and then the Arizona desert. In each of these places, we sought out Lutheran communities, which seemed to be the only welcome, common thread throughout. Still, I just dreamed of stopping long enough to breathe and then perhaps leave again by my choice . . . to change the world, to make a difference, to find a place where my deep gladness meets the world's deep hunger.

And then, somehow, I chanced upon St. Olaf. Through reading college materials, I was struck by St. Olaf's academic excellence and "commitment to a liberal arts education, rooted in the Christian Gospel, and incorporating a global perspective." The St. Olaf Choir concert in Phoenix of my senior year in high school confirmed that these were indeed good, honest folk. But I never visited campus, much less

Minnesota or the Midwest. I just showed up on the first day of Week One. It had never really occurred to me to visit, since everywhere else I had lived (never having a say in the matter), I had been determined to suck the marrow out of life. And once here, I knew I had come home.

For now, just a few years after leaving with diploma in hand, I'm back on the Hill. As a counselor in the admissions office, I find myself at the crossroads where students seek to choose for themselves where they will claim as their community. What an exciting meeting place to be! Many of them seek change and growth, yet wish to keep their constants, their roots as they are. Somehow, because transition has been a household word as long as I can remember, I thrive on meeting students in transition, at their own crossroads. As I remember years ago, I hungered for a place to stay still. Now whether students come from mobile pasts like mine or from a lifetime on the fourth generation family farm in southwestern Minnesota, they still hunger for a place to call their own . . . and perhaps a place where God calls them to.

Through each of my transitions, I've been reminded of God's constancy through the words from the last verse of the beloved Epiphany hymn:

> How good, Lord, to be here!
> Yet we may not remain;
> But since you bid us leave the mount,
> Come with us to the plain.
>
> Lutheran Book of Worship #89

Sometimes St. Olaf led me to the mount . . . a place to pursue truth, to dance a psalm, to wander through creaking elms in Norway Valley or meditate under creaking beams in Boe during windstorms, to breathe in the lilacs on Thorson Hill. Sometimes St. Olaf led me to the plains . . . to work to pay for my education, to grapple with radical changes in my choice of major (thanks to shepherds Carrington, Hoekstra, and Schwandt and the Great Conversation flock), to work with Habitat for Humanity to build homes for the hurricane victims in South Carolina, and to walk through the slums of Nairobi.

Whether St. Olaf serves as mount or plain, we must turn to our mission and remember that "it offers a distinctive environment that integrates teaching, scholarship, creative activity, and opportunities for encounter with the Christian Gospel and God's call to faith . . . [and that] it encourages [students] to be seekers of truth, leading lives of unselfish service to others; and it challenges them to be responsible and knowledgeable citizens of the world."

Never before have I lived daily with the reminder of St. Olaf's mission statement (which I've now nearly memorized!) as I have working in admissions. (In fact, I don't believe I ever knew our college's mission statement while a student.) But what continually amazes and delights me is to hear how obvious our mission is lived out, as evidenced by comments made by prospective students and applicants when asked "What brings you to St. Olaf?" and "Why did you choose St. Olaf?" These responses I find most satisfying to me in my daily work. Again and again they describe our community as having a "sense of purpose," of fostering the "whole" person, a place preparing you for life (not just a livelihood). They describe an honest place where people "look you right in the eye," P.O. boxes don't have locks, and coats and bags are strewn across the Fireside Lounge. We know that St. Olaf's mission will continue to be lived out by students who choose to come here because of what we are, rooted in the Christian Gospel, and because of what we strive to be.

Frederick Buechner describes God's call as a "place where your deep gladness and the world's deep hunger meet." And so I ask myself—must my deep gladness be confined to just one? Certainly not. My deepest gladness is found in the saving grace of Jesus Christ. And yet, my call—where God calls me—has been a constant change. I have been called and have served as a teacher, a missionary, a counselor, and still ask the questions, Where should I be? What should I do? James Thurber says, "It is better to have some of the questions than all of the answers." Oh, that the Lord would guide my ways to live out the answers. I may come upon countless crossroads, and serve others as they meet theirs. Wherever I am—whether mount or plain—whatever I do, may I say with firm voice, How good, Lord, to be here!

22. BREATHING MY CALLING

Patrick Cabello Hansel

It is a little after 1:00 A.M., and my neighbor's house is on fire. Thank God they're all OK, but smoke is beginning to seep into our house, and I can't get back to sleep. I was up at 5:15 this morning, to accompany a family to Parkview Hospital, to be with them as the life-support equipment was taken away from their wife, their mother, the rock of their family. I'm not even sure of all that went on during the hours of this long day, but I know it has made me rejoice in my calling as a pastor, and also wonder why it is I am following that call.

Becoming a pastor was the farthest thing from my mind when I entered St. Olaf in the fall of 1971. I had been raised a Roman Catholic, had dreamed of being a priest as a boy, but had been a militant atheist since I was fifteen. Why did I choose St. Olaf? To tell you the truth, my friends from high school were going to Catholic colleges, and I wanted to go to a school with women. And St. Olaf seemed to be more interested in me as a football player. Such were my priorities at age eighteen.

I was also interested in justice, in peace, in struggling for a better world, and I hadn't yet met many Christians who really cared about those things. I started to meet a few at St. Olaf: students and faculty. I started to read the Bible, not in a religion class, but at late-night bull sessions in Ytterboe. Howard Hong and other philosophy professors helped me critically think about a lot of issues. I wasn't ready to be a believer, but I thought the man Jesus was pretty cool. Then I went to Chicago, for the Urban Studies Term.

It was in Chicago that I both had my worldview expanded and the very limited nature of my human powers exposed to me. While I was working as a community organizer—and loving the city to pieces—everything I put my trust in crumbled: love, job, relationships, money, health. It was in Uptown Chicago—reading 1 Corinthians 13 by myself—that I came to experience God's love *for me* personally and fully.

Fortunately—I didn't see it at the time, but now I can—I had to come back to St. Olaf to finish my senior year. It was during a Paracollege semester on the topic "The Church and Social Change" that I was able to integrate my passion for justice and the city with my intellectual pursuits. (Thank you, John Stumme, for making me read the Neibuhrs and *centuries* of Christian writers on ethics.) I interned at an inner-city church in Minneapolis, and I learned to pray again.

I have been a pastor for nearly thirteen years, all of it in the inner city, and while this day was fuller than most days, it can illustrate why I thank God for this calling, and also why I often wonder what God is up to.

This day I talked with a teenager who is being bounced from mother to father and back again. Threatened in one house, neglected in the other. I tried to resolve a conflict between two teachers in our after-school program. I wrote a grant application to expand our environmental work with our preteen employment program. I visited the sick, and tried to speak words of hope to the family who has lost the dearest person to them. I worked with a staff team to plan new workshops on domestic violence and women's health. I took some time to pray: mostly: God, help me! That was the morning.

In the afternoon, I planned a local action with a leader—a man who came to know Christ in jail—in which we will attempt to gain better policing and sanitation from our city government (we won, by the way). I worked on two sermons: one for the funeral, one on the Spirit of God bringing liberation to the city. I talked with a key leader whose husband is back using crack. I was hugged by about thirty children in our center. I got yelled at by just one person.

At 4:00 P.M., I practiced with thirteen children from our children's choir. They sang a number of *coritos* in Spanish, and "Children of the Heavenly Father." We've been working on dealing with distraction by "Spirit Breathing" (a technique I formulated ten minutes before practice, but have been thinking on, or breathing about, for years), and of course today, we were interrupted many more times than usual. Two of the girls brought a tape they had been practicing with for weeks and asked if they could sing it in church on Sunday. It's by the Spice Girls. Hmmm. I believe in contemporary worship, but puhlease!

There were more visits, prayers, phone calls, letters, I'm sure. Now it is late, now I am trying to practice relaxation breathing. I thank God for this day, and I wonder: Is this calling to the gospel the same one I heard as a boy? The same one on the Urban Studies Term? The same one in chapel services as a returning believer? Between the breath of life leaving Felipa in the hospital this morning, and my neighbors gasping for breath tonight, how has the breath of the Spirit been moving around here?

Luther says the gospel is not the gospel unless it is "for me." I know that from the room in Uptown Chicago, and I know that without God's breath, I am lost. I wouldn't have made it through this day without knowing Christ is with me. I read the text for Sunday's sermon: Jesus in Nazareth, proclaiming the Spirit; and I also know that the gospel is not the gospel unless it is "for all of us." Especially the blind, the poor, the prisoners, the oppressed.

God has given me the privilege of working in the city for nearly twenty years, as a layperson and now a pastor. I have known incredible persons of faith, of real joy in the midst of struggle. I thank God for the people and forces that have shaped my passion and developed my gifts for service. I think of the hymn phrase: "Spirit of the living God, fall afresh on me." That is what has been happening this day, and for these many years.

23. TEACHING—THE LORD'S TRUE CALLING

Kathy Wilker Megyeri

When I was a high school student almost forty years ago, I had little tolerance for my old female teachers with their thick-soled shoes, protruding stomachs, sagging breasts, gray hair, and bifocals. I wondered why they didn't retire and give young teachers whom I could relate to a chance to teach and make learning fun.

Now, more than three-and-a-half decades later and facing retirement, I've become the teacher I used to criticize and laugh at so very long ago. I wear cushiony Easy Spirit orthopedic shoes every working day. My stomach, breasts, and rear not only protrude, but sag. My gray hair demands brown dye every month. Like a '65 Mustang in for repairs, I was hospitalized twice last year, and I cope with bifocals.

What's forced me to face my own professional mortality is that when I observe this year's batch of new teachers, I realize how dated I've become. I still prefer whole-class instruction to groups. My classroom writing models come from literary classics instead of rap lyrics. I still grade papers with a red pen. I'm serious and content-oriented, not "fun." But I like to think that I'm a good mentor, that I grade fairly, and that most students appreciate my stern demeanor and realize it's my way of wanting them to take school as seriously as I believe it should be taken. Also, I believe that even though I've grown tired and old in their eyes, I still have contributions to make in the classroom and to their lives. I love introducing adolescents to good literature, observing their writing mature throughout the year, seeing a student's poem printed in a school publication or local newspaper, watching an enraptured class stare open-mouthed at a student-made video, and reading a composition written by a trusting pupil who admits feeling abandoned and heartbroken the day no one wanted to sit with him at lunch.

I truly admire those who now begin their careers in education. Teachers are faced with ever-increasing incidents of violence and criticism for our students' high failure and dropout rates and low test scores, but these same teachers face huge enrollments of special-needs students, teens who are shuttled between two sets of parents, youngsters who have been ignored, abandoned, and abused, and still others who speak little or no English. These educators spend their own money on teaching supplies in spite of earning an average of $36,000 a year. They are faced with the mandate of incorporating service-learning experiences in their curricula, planning for school evacuations following bomb threats, coping with block scheduling and ninety-minute classes, demands for more competency testing, installing metal detectors, and pleas for year-round schooling while completing paperwork at home most nights and weekends. They watch more funds being spent on computers than on textbooks, and they know that few beginning teachers plan to remain in the classroom for thirty years as they have. To describe the plight of today's teachers, this sign hangs in our faculty lounge:

> If a doctor, lawyer, or dentist had twenty-five people in his office at one time, all of whom had different needs, and some of whom didn't want to be there and were causing trouble, and the doctor, lawyer, or dentist, without assistance, had to treat them all with professional excellence for nine months, then he might have some conception of the classroom's teacher's job.

In spite of the frustrations and joys of teaching, St. Olaf has long had a reputation for employing fine educators and training even better ones. Most of our college's alumni in one way or another have been inspired by a professor they had at St. Olaf. The one instructor most responsible for my becoming a high school English teacher many years ago was Associate Professor of English Emeritus Graham Frear, '47. After serving in the Marine Corps during World War II, he began a fifteen-year career teaching secondary biology and English at Northfield High School. In 1962, he joined St. Olaf's English faculty, and in 1986, he retired. During his years of teaching in those rooms above St. Olaf's library, he taught me American literature, structural linguistics, semantics, and introduced me to S. I. Hayakawa, one of America's greatest semanticists, a writer, a U.S. senator, and a college president. Frear also showed me that high school students need to be repeatedly exposed to good literature, so I copied his technique of filling my classroom with quality magazines, books, and paperbacks—material students could borrow, read in class, or even steal. Most of all, Professor Frear taught me about professional excellence because he believed that what we did mattered. He convinced me that teaching is the profession that most benefits society and impacts most positively on youth. Even today, 57 percent of Americans cite teachers as the greatest contributors to society as opposed to 25 percent who cite the medical profession and only 1 percent who cite lawyers (Ad Council, 1995). Although teachers may receive little respect in the classroom, teens tell phone pollsters that teachers play a critical role in society. They rank just below parents as teens' favored role models; 86 percent of students say teachers are "very important" to a good society and rank them above scientists, business owners and managers, politicians, writers, artists, poets, journalists, professional athletes, moviemakers, and rock musicians (Gallup Organization's *National Youth Survey; Attitudes Regarding Society, Education, and Adulthood*, 1996).

Frear calculated that during his St. Olaf teaching career, he administered 6,308 exams, evaluated 9,533 papers, taught eighteen different courses to over 2,006 students, and worked with 409 English education supervisors, including my cooperating teacher at North High School in Minneapolis. He did not include the hours of paperwork, committee meetings, and conferences. He once wrote me,

> Teaching was always my way of attempting to impart attitude and dedication more than skills. I'm certain I became a teacher largely through attempting to do what I would have wanted done with me as a student. The teachers I remember were the ones who conveyed a sense of purpose and enthusiasm more than were centered on subject matter.

Thanks to his example, my enthusiasm for the subject still wins me rave reviews on students' end-of-the-year evaluations, but it's getting harder to maintain that enthusiasm now that I'm aging while my students remain fifteen years old year after year. When I started my teaching career, one of the best units in Maryland's curriculum was the "Bible as Literature." It taught students to understand what John Steinbeck meant when he claimed his novel *The Pearl* was a "parable"; what a character in Lorraine Hansberry's *Raisin in the Sun* referred to when she said, "Thirty pieces of silver and not a coin less"; what forty days and forty nights" referred to in the title of Iyanla Vansant's book *One Day My Soul Just Opened Up: Forty Days and Forty Nights toward Spiritual Strength and Personal Growth*; and what Helen Keller meant when she wrote, "Words made the world blossom for her, like Aaron's rod with flowers." But the "Bible as Literature" unit became controversial because many parents felt it smacked of "religious indoctrination," so the unit was abruptly dropped from the curriculum, and the thousands of Bibles our county had purchased were donated to the Gideons to be placed in local hotel rooms. Over the years, students forgot that Christ was the world's greatest teacher, that teaching was a "calling" for many of us as a way to serve God in daily life, and therefore that teaching deserved respect. Now, students aren't learning biblical allusions anywhere—not from home, school, or church—so to them, "Aaron's rod" means his "hot car," "forty days and forty nights" lacks any meaning whatsoever, and, as they say, "only God knows what a parable is." Very few of my students regard teaching as a "calling" worth considering because news anchorwomen, rock stars, and football players are worth so much more. As one of my students wrote, "I considered being a teacher, but now I know I do not want to be a high school teacher. I would find teaching the same subject all year round, year after year and day after day, boring and very hard." Other professions offer more money and more glamour to most of today's graduates.

Still, I've lived with bell schedules, parent conferences, starting new school years in September, and finishing old ones in June so long that I know no other life. Tenured teaching brings academic freedom to me, for I can read for school and write for publication, two great loves in my own life. Of course, teaching fifteen-year-olds to enjoy reading and writing as I do is a yearly challenge, and, admittedly, some school years are more successful than others. But I know that the day I leave teaching, I leave the vitality of youth and won't daily witness the joys of discovery I see in these teens as they experience "new beginnings": passing their driver's tests, falling in love, ordering class rings, making the honor roll, scoring a winning touchdown, attending homecoming and prom, signing each other's yearbooks, or walking proudly across the stage to receive their diplomas and wave a last good-bye. Maybe I'm reliving my youth each year through these students and that's what keeps me from changing the constant in my life—teaching.

Unlike Professor Frear, I don't have the courage to count the numbers of classes taught, parent conferences attended, papers graded, and chaperon duties supervised. I still keep an old copy of *Up the Down Staircase* by Bel Kaufman on my desk, which was the subject of my St. Olaf admissions essay that I wrote as a high school senior so many years ago. Now, the book seems as trite and dated as my essay, but I keep it because it was the first book on real-life teaching that I remember reading. However, my own experiences have been just as colorful. One is the humbling incident of reading one student's end-of-the-year evaluation that said, "You would be a great teacher if only you would update your wardrobe." The other recollection is a student's reply when asked what advice he would give for improving my class the following year. He wrote, "Do just what you did to us this year—give 'em hell!"

A few of my classmates from my years at St. Olaf (class of '65) are still in the classroom as I am; roommate Barbara Berg Swenson in Chaska, Minnesota, and Mary Emmons Timm in Plainview, Minnesota. The acclaimed director of St. Olaf's theater, Patrick Quade, who sat beside me in every drama class taught by Dr. Ralph Haugen, has recently advanced in his career to lead St. Olaf's International Studies Program. And whenever I teach Tennessee Williams's *Summer and Smoke* to my students, I remember classmate Charles Kahlenberg, who made his acting debut on the little stage in the basement of Ytterboe Hall in that same play. He went on to become a Hollywood actor of note, and whenever I hear his voice in some movie, voice-over, or TV production, years are swept away, and again, he's Dr. John Buchanan in the play telling Alma Winemiller, "I'm more afraid of your soul than you're afraid of my body." My students chuckle at that line, perhaps because the teen reader can't deliver it as sonorously as actor Kahlenberg, or maybe they see a nostalgic gaze in my eyes for years gone.

These fellow "alumni/teachers" are dedicated and excellent role models crafted by St. Olaf. They are like candles which light others while consuming themselves. They are ignited by the curiosity of children, they like literature and young people, and they know they make a difference in lives. Teaching is their mission, their "calling," and, like Christa McAuliffe, they can claim, "I touch the future; I teach."

Perhaps Professor Frear characterized the Ole-trained teacher the best when he recommended the profession to me so long ago:

> Teaching is a good way to make a living. Not only does one enjoy the process itself (how lovely the sound of one's own voice) but it's like being a "doorkeeper in the house of the Lord," which is authoritatively stated to be better than sitting in the "seats of the scornful."

24. WHO AM I?

Kristine Carlson

"Get your education," my grandmother would say to me. A Norwegian immigrant to this country, she served as a missionary in Madagascar. Widowed there with six children, she returned to work as a nurse at Northfield Hospital, putting her children through St. Olaf.

My parents, too, would say to me, "Get your education." On a meager pastor's salary, they sacrificed to put four daughters through college. When they would say to me, "Get your education," they told me, with their use of the pronoun "your," that education was mine to get and, even more, that for me to be "me" was to be educated. From the time they bought me a St. Olaf sweatshirt when I was seven, I knew that, for them, St. Olaf embodied the education which was mine to get.

So it's no wonder I chose to attend St. Olaf: I was born inside a story that sent me. And it sent me to St. Olaf to ask not, "What career will I have?" but, "Who am I?" My story told me that in my response to that question would lie my vocation.

I came to St. Olaf in the fall of 1970, from my home in Brooklyn, New York. In high school I had been deeply affected by the peace movement and the women's movement. I encountered a different mood on the St. Olaf campus: these issues seemed still nascent, especially the role of women. I had come from an all-girls' high school where girls were the only ones talking in and out of class and where all but one of my teachers had been women. In my St. Olaf classes, women students seemed to me not to talk much. My whole first year I had only one female professor, my piano teacher, Margaret Birkeland. Often confused by this culture, I considered transferring.

In the end, I stayed—because I had begun to love St. Olaf in deep ways that continue to this day. What happened for me was that I met people who cared about me and encouraged my gifts and passions. Teachers like David Wee and Ron Lee guided my skills as a thinker, reader, and writer. Miss Birkeland nurtured my musical ability. Their studio and classrooms, and those of many other teachers, were places where I matured intellectually and aesthetically. Students like my roommate, Mary Austin, offered me wonderful friendships. Cliff Swanson, the campus pastor, didn't give up when I showed little interest in the life of Boe Chapel. Eventually I was participating in daily and Sunday worship and serving on the church council.

In addition to learning about myself, I also learned more about the story of St. Olaf. I was inspired by stories about Edna and Howard Hong, for instance, who had gone to Europe after World War II to help resettle refugees. Such events from St. Olaf's past, as well as my daily life, showed me that I was part of a community following a vocation. Many of its members were involved in education as part of a calling, a calling that sought to address our entire lives, inside and outside the classroom.

As a result, when I graduated my response to the question "Who am I?" was most of all, "I am a daughter of God."

It was the "daughter" in my response that I left St. Olaf to explore. In a graduate program in English, I planned to study women and literature and prepare to teach. My plans abruptly changed three years later, when I experienced a powerful and profound call to ordained ministry. The entirety of my response—"I am a daughter of God"—had indeed revealed to me a vocation.

After two years of seminary studies, I found myself once more packing for a move to St. Olaf. I had been assigned to the St. Olaf Student Congregation for my year of pastoral internship. I was anxious before I began. I didn't know how I could ever be a pastor, a preacher, a spiritual counselor to people who had been my teachers and administrators. During my first weeks back, I discovered, humbly, that I did not make myself their pastor: they claimed me and made me their pastor. This has been for me an important insight about vocation: the community calls us into our calling. For me, it was St. Olaf that called me into being a pastor.

The other profound event for me vocationally was when my husband and I had our first child. We stayed up all night after he was born, the three of us now, lying in bed together. When I think of that night I have a physical sensation of a shift, as if the room moved, but it was really my point of view shifting. I have loved, and struggled with, the entirety of my vocation: career, marriage, children, self. My choices have put me on the pastoral "Mommy track," I suppose, but I have made these choices recognizing that the whole of my life is my vocation.

Living out a vocation can be costly. My grandmother was widowed as she followed her vocation: I knew this from my story. But I learned also from my story that the faith which takes us into the hard demands of a vocational life is also the faith that sustains and gives joy and hope.

A daily witness to me of such faith is a quotation from Howard and Edna Hong that hangs on a yellow Post-It™ on my mirror. They were asked what they had learned from their refugee work in Europe that they would want to tell their grandchildren. They replied: "When everything seems dark—the past is cut off, present conditions are miserable, and the future is utterly impenetrable—one must simply say, 'With God all things are possible,' and venture forth." With such faithful words, people of St. Olaf continue to direct and uphold me in my vocation.

We Lutherans assert that "the finite is capable of bearing the infinite." The theologian George Forell claims that this is important for our understanding of vocation: that who we are, what we do in the ordinary, daily events of our lives, conveys Christ. This is the perspective on vocation that I began to see at St. Olaf.

It was toward the end of her long life that my grandmother was encouraging me to "Get your education." In midlife now, I know better the depth of education that I think she hoped for me: it was this sense of vocation, that in all we are, we are bearers of Christ.

25. LIVING WITH FAITH—I DON'T HAVE TO SING THE BLUES

Deborah Liv Johnson

It was May of 1977. I was sitting in my freshman dorm room on the ninth floor of Mohn Hall, staring out the narrow window, wondering if I had made the right decision to stay at St. Olaf. In two weeks we would all return home for the summer, and I had been so sure that I needed to transfer, to return to California, to pursue the music industry in Los Angeles. That was before I met Professor David Wee and learned about the Paracollege.

I never regretted staying at St. Olaf, and through the Paracollege, my desire to pursue both creative writing and music became a reality. I truly thrived. It was the perfect opportunity for an independent, self-starting student who wanted to test several facets of her creativity. It was also the beginning of a faith that God could work small miracles, and I have been living with that faith ever since.

Upon graduating from St. Olaf in 1980, I dove into the music business as a performer, all the while juggling a stewpot of jobs—everything from teaching school to bartending to painting houses to clerking at a shipyard. In the late 1980s, I received a call from a man in Nashville who was interested in signing me to a major record deal. He was very direct. "Now, honey, we want you to come down here to Nashville to record. We'll choose the songs and the musicians and how you'll look. You just sing pretty and we'll take care of the rest. You have one hell of a voice and we can make you a star. So call us in a couple of days, honey. Here's my secretary's name and number."

I never called. My mother and a few friends accused me of being stubborn because I might as well just sing what they wanted—I could always choose my own material later on . . . after I became a big star. But I was a songwriter and an interpreter and I knew that if I didn't like the material, it would come across in my voice. I had just been hired as a copywriter and editor for a small publication, and I decided to start my own record label on the side. Then I could record whatever I wanted. Something in my gut told me to follow my heart and my faith. I didn't know where I was headed but I figured it would be a good ride.

It's been ten years since the birth of Mojave Sun Records. I'm not a big star, although I do get recognized in the grocery store now and then, usually while I'm squeezing the bread. I've recorded four CDs and I make my living as a musician, record producer, and label owner. I've been able to record songs about old friends, a song about my mother and being born in Tanzania, a song written for Ann Bancroft in celebration of her historic 1993–1994 Antarctic expedition, and fun songs about old trucks and falling in love and having the blues.

Last summer I took my biggest risk of all—a CD of old hymns. I'd be lying if I told you that everyone was jumping up and down with excitement about this project. In fact, I got strange looks from some of my longtime fans. "Hymns, huh? Well, gee, that does sound interesting. [pause] Well, what's your project after that? Something that really cooks, maybe? Heh, heh."

It's easy to translate the meaning of "interesting" when it relates to an artistic project. I was already feeling nervous about the recording. For one thing, my voice was totally exposed. Most of the selections were produced bare-bones. I was also worried that everyone might think I was a "born-again," since religion had become so politicized. And most importantly, I wondered if I had enough relatives to buy the CD to pay off my loans.

There was no need for all those worries. During the first three months following its release, my new CD was outselling everything else I'd done. I'll admit that I didn't know why I was supposed to record those hymns, but I knew I had to do it. Just like I knew I was supposed to stay at St. Olaf and develop as a writer and songwriter and performer. I didn't know where that little hymn project would take me, but I had faith that God would reveal it to me. A major record label wouldn't have let me record a bunch of old hymns in a million years. But that's why I have my own label—there are better reasons for doing things than simply to make a buck. I know that God has a lot of other surprises in store for me, so I keep asking and praying and looking for signs.

All this from a gal who is pretty quiet about her faith and her beliefs. I even get embarrassed when someone says, "Praise the Lord." Maybe that's my Lutheran upbringing—kind of quiet, kind of restrained. But those hymns were too beautiful to keep under wraps. Now they're exposed and I'm exposed and who knows what I'll record next. I'm just keeping the faith—something St. Olaf taught me to do a long time ago.

26. SERVANT-LEADERSHIP: THE VOCATION OF A LUTHERAN DEAN

James L. Pence

The Call

I was in graduate school the first time a pastor invited me to preach on a Sunday morning. Honored by the invitation, I said "yes" without worrying much about the challenges of preparation. After all, explicating a biblical text and saying something about its meaning for people's lives couldn't be much different from teaching *King Lear* to undergraduates!

For reasons that I no longer recall, I selected the Old Testament reading for the day as my text: Isaiah 6:1-8. What I do remember is the great difficulty of coming to a satisfactory personal understanding of Isaiah's behavior. Never having been touched on the lips by a live coal held in the hand of a six-winged seraph, and never having heard the voice of the Lord, I did not understand Isaiah's ready response, "Here am I. Send me!" I was, after all, a graduate student completing a dissertation in anticipation of entering an inhospitable job market. My professors badgered me to look only for tenure-track jobs in reputable places and to seek assurances that I would not have to teach too many writing courses. For my career's sake, they argued, I needed to find a job that would allow me to concentrate on my own writing, not the writing of undergraduates. It seemed to me that the Lord was asking Isaiah to teach freshman English full-time in an open admissions college with little professorial entitlement and no hope for the security of tenure. Why was he so eager to go?

My research into the call of Isaiah for that Sunday sermon led me to the idea of "the call" in Hebrew scriptures and to Luther's concept of Christian vocation. In many ways, I have spent the past twenty-five years deepening my understanding of Isaiah's behavior and shaping my own. My pastor's request for pulpit supply turns out to have been a life-changing event for me. I sometimes wonder if the congregation knew that my sermon on the call of Isaiah was really about my discovery of vocation.

It was a deeply personal sense of vocation that informed my decision in the spring of 1996 to leave Wartburg College, where I had served as dean for six years, to accept the position of Vice President and Dean of the College at St. Olaf. In coming to St. Olaf, I believe I accepted a call to serve the church as the dean of one of its greatest colleges. I have learned that my vocation as a Christian is to love God and serve neighbors, particularly those who teach; to be immersed in the dynamic ambiguity of the created world, especially the world of higher education; and to practice servant-leadership, by extending the mission of St. Olaf as a national liberal arts college of the church.

Over the years, it is true that I have devoted a good portion of my professional career to investigating the history, traditions, and values of church-related colleges. It is also the case that I meet regularly with deans of church-related colleges in various professional associations, and that I interact frequently with Lutheran clergy and laypeople who have long personal histories of ties to Lutheran colleges. I do read widely in the literature of leadership development and servant-leadership, a personal discipline I have worked hard to maintain since my 1985–1986 year as an American Council on Education Fellow. In some ways, coming to St. Olaf was a logical career move.

But a career is not the same as a calling. Is it possible to *choose* a calling? I think it is possible to say "yes" or "no" or "not now." It is also possible to live out one's calling in specific places and times and in certain ways. Based on personal experience and careful study, I have concluded that church-related colleges offer a distinctive opportunity for deans to practice servant-leadership. In academic communities where both learning and faith are highly valued, the model of servant-leadership fits well. And in a Lutheran college, where the dialogue between learning and faith is central to community identity, the paradox of servant-leadership is just one more paradox with which we live!

Goals and opportunities for professional advancement notwithstanding, however, I felt a little bit like Isaiah when President Edwards phoned to offer me the dean's job at St. Olaf—not knowing if I were up to the task, on the one hand, but trusting, on the other hand, that I was called by God to exemplify faithfulness through servant-leadership. I said "yes" to the vocation of a Lutheran dean.

The Practice

The practice of servant-leadership manifests itself in three important contexts for me: personal, professional, and organizational.

The first context is *personal*: as Dean of St. Olaf, I believe that I must both *administer* (as in manage and direct) and *minister* (as in serve or give help); I must act in simultaneously *administrative* and *ministerial* capacities; and I must privilege the pastoral dimensions of the office of dean.

A pastor friend of mine once called my attention to this passage in a book written for the continuing education of clergy:

> Leadership: The creation and articulation of, the focusing attention on, and the developing commitment to a vision of what God is calling the congregation to be and to do—and the concrete form its mission in the community should take—marks the excellent parishes. Such leadership is primarily and indispensably exercised by the pastor(s). It is rooted in the pastor's self-awareness of being called by God to exercise the office of ministry and refined by training in the various disciplines and tasks of pastoral ministry. It is exercised through an ordained minister's constant interaction with people in pursuit of bringing the Gospel to bear on their daily lives.[1]

I see many parallels between pastoral and decanal leadership. As dean, I interact constantly with the faculty in pursuit of bringing the mission of the college to bear on the daily life of the campus community. Exercising my training in academic disciplines and academic management, I aim to provide leadership for the academic program, the concrete manifestation of the college's mission. I carry responsibility for inspiring academic vision among the faculty and focusing their attention on issues of academic integrity. At St. Olaf, academic integrity means faithfulness to mission; mission involves "what God is calling the college to be and do."

In the storied history of St. Olaf College, notable presidents and legendary faculty members have shaped the institution according to a compelling vision of residential, coeducational Christian education in the liberal arts. One must read only a single speech by Lars Boe or hear a distinctive hymn composed by F. Melius Christiansen or read an essay by Bill Narum or have a lively conversation with Howard Hong to understand this point. Anton Armstrong is often quoted as saying that the mission of the St. Olaf Choir has always been to celebrate music making as a gift from God. I came to St. Olaf eager to pitch my tent among the saints of the past and the present—all those who share the vision to advance our distinctive mission: a distinctive education in the liberal arts that incorporates a global perspective and offers opportunities for rich encounters with the Christian gospel. That is what God is calling this college to be and do.

I came also with views on academic leadership strongly influenced by Luther's words in *The Freedom of a Christian*:

> A Christian is a perfectly free lord of all, subject to none.
> A Christian is a perfectly dutiful servant of all, subject to all.

I am convinced that the vocation of a Lutheran dean is *both* to champion academic freedom *and* to expect academic responsibility. In the exercise of my vocation, I *both* administer policy *and* minister to people. I immerse myself in the culture of the college, and offer critiques of cultural practices. My personal goal as dean is to express my Christian faith in loving service to neighbor, especially those neighbors who serve on the faculty. I often do that by asking myself, "What would Jesus do?"

On occasion, this personal goal brings me into conflict with the professional demands of the position and the organization. St. Olaf College, after all, exists in the earthly kingdom. Deans have to make decisions about people and budgets. At St. Olaf, as at many colleges and universities, deans are often the bearers of bad news. Over the years in administrative positions, I have learned that loving service to neighbor, for deans, requires the ability to ask hard questions and to give messages to people that they really do not want to hear. Professional competence is essential in the dean's office.

The second context, then, is *professional*: as Dean of St. Olaf, I must exercise *moral*, *legal*, and *political authority*. Competence in the legal and political realms is easy to describe although not always simple to achieve. Competence in the moral domain is more difficult to explain and to demonstrate, but for the servant-leader dean, more important.

Soon after I became dean at Wartburg College, a regent advised me that my primary duty as dean could be summarized in a single sentence: "Do what's right and do it right." In a college of the church, she suggested, the moral authority of leaders is and should be connected to principles of right and wrong, issues of conduct and character. In a college of the Lutheran church, she said, moral authority derives from understanding the point of view that education is a gift from God. With that understanding in mind, she argued, a Lutheran dean needs to be *both* a disciple for education *and* a disciple for Christ—living continuously in the dynamic space between reason and faith.

Sidney Rand, the former president of St. Olaf, taught me the same lesson in a different way. Rand once wrote that "the administration of the Christian liberal arts college needs to be above all in the hands of *educators*."[2] I believe President Rand's comment gets at the importance of establishing moral authority in the dean's office. Deans who are educators need to be teacher-scholars. Some deans manage to maintain scholarly interests in their disciplines and to teach while serving as dean. I have not been able to sustain professional activity in teaching writing or teaching Shakespeare and keep up with the demands of academic administration. Students deserve well-prepared professors, not merely well-intentioned ones!

I also believe that the current state of affairs in higher education requires my full-time attention to academic administration. St. Olaf needs me to know as much as I can about St. Olaf and its future; so my subject matter now is St. Olaf as a postsecondary institution and higher education leadership, and my students now are faculty members and administrative colleagues at St. Olaf and elsewhere. Establishing myself as a teacher-scholar means immersion in the discipline of educational administration as it is practiced in the liberal-arts sector of higher education. To that end, I subscribe to higher education journals; read books about leadership, management, and organizational culture; write essays on topics related to faculty personnel policies and the theory and practice of academic administration; make presentations at national conferences on issues of academic leadership; and serve in leadership positions in organizations such as the American Conference of Academic Deans.

In the literature about leadership I first encountered the works of Robert Greenleaf, who makes the point about moral authority of servant-leaders in this way:

> Prophet, seeker, and leader are inextricably linked. The *prophet* brings vision and penetrating insight. The *seeker* brings openness, aggressive searching, and good critical judgment—all within the context of the deeply felt attitude, "I have not yet found it." The *leader* adds the art of persuasion backed by persistence, determination, and the courage to venture and risk. The requirements of leadership impose some intellectual demands that are not usually measured by academic intelligence ratings. They are not mutually exclusive, but they are different things. The leader needs three intellectual abilities that may not be assessed in an academic way: one needs to have a sense for the knowable, to be prepared for the unexpected, and to be able to foresee the unforeseeable.[3]

As I reflect on these experiences, I realize that a regent, a president emeritus, and a former AT&T executive have helped to shape my views about the moral contexts of deaning. I believe that my Christian faith strengthens me for the work of being a dean, but the work itself is manifestly secular. My faith motivates me to immerse myself in the messy life of college administration. This life is messy because all human action is flawed. Faith reminds me of my own human frailty and the need for grace and forgiveness. But my professional responsibility to the college inspires me to deal with the problems at hand by asking myself, "What leadership is expected of me in this situation?"

In the messy world of colleges, deans cannot escape issues of legal and political authority. Professional competence in dealing with legal matters and expertise in handling campus politics are expected in the dean's office. I do think that Lutheran theology provides helpful insights into the challenges of law and politics in higher education these days. Luther's concept of Law and Gospel, for example, addresses the need for civility and justice among the diverse peoples of the earthly kingdom. His idea that humans are both saints and sinners has helped me handle personnel conflicts with heightened recognition of the complexities of human relationships and with sure knowledge that the "other side" is part of the whole story. The notion of vocation informs hiring decisions, especially in determining the extent to which candidates for positions explain how they think they can contribute to the mission of the college. And Luther's understanding of the finitude of human activity serves as a reminder of the incompleteness of academic solutions and the comfort inherent in President Edwards's favorite Luther quotation: "Be a sinner and sin boldly!"

At a national meeting sponsored by the American Conference of Academic Deans in Washington, D.C., in March of 1999, I made a presentation entitled "Changing the Way We Change: Helping Faculty to Think Strategically about Institutional Welfare." Part of my talk included ten tips for deans who seek to provide leadership for change. Here are two of the tips I mentioned:

—Be gracious and merciful, slow to anger, and abounding in steadfast love.
—Combine a belief in yourself with a decent doubt; have a passion for the job and an awareness of other worlds; combine a love of people with a capacity for aloneness—practice the paradox of leadership.

The first tip is an excerpt from the Lenten verse sung by the congregation prior to the announcement of the gospel in the worship services of the *Lutheran Book of Worship*. The second tip is a paraphrase of the argument of Charles Handy's *The Age of Paradox*,[4] a management book with what I would call a "Lutheran" bent.

My vocation as a Lutheran dean calls me to exercise moral, legal, and political authority in professional contexts as a servant-leader, informed and (I think) enriched by the theological influences of my faith tradition. I still expect to be judged, however, on my professional competence as a disciple of education. St. Olaf, after all, is an organization of the earthly kingdom.

The third context for servant-leadership is the *organizational* one: as dean at St. Olaf, I must *make decisions for the common good*. I approach my work as the dean with an assumption that the whole is greater than the sum of its parts and that the long-term welfare of the academic program is my special concern.

In *Common Fire*, ethicist Sharon Parks and three colleagues write about ways to "kindle a common fire and forge a new synthesis of practical wisdom" in an increasingly complex world. The book describes a study of people who lead committed lives dedicated to the common good:

> Such people have learned to trust appropriately and act with courage, to live within and beyond tribe in affinity with those who are other, to practice critical habits of mind and responsible imagination, to manage their own mixed emotions and motives, and to live with a recognition of the interdependence of all life—manifest in a paradoxical sense of time and space. They help us imagine ways of building a more promising future.[5]

This is the kind of committed life I think the dean of St. Olaf has to lead—for the sake of the academic programs for which the dean is responsible. As a liberal arts college in an increasingly competitive marketplace, St. Olaf needs its dean to help imagine ways of building a more promising future. To do that, the dean must keep focused on the needs of the organization.

One of the greatest challenges of being dean at St. Olaf, especially in these times of concern about financial constraints, is negotiating the territory between *college as organization* and *college as community*. The college is, of course, both. The dean, however, is not only an organizational leader but also a community member. Keeping focused on the strategic needs of the organization frequently brings the office of the dean into conflict with the interests of people in the community. This is the paradox of servant-leadership—*both* in its fullest expression *and* at its sternest test.

Church-related colleges are usually small and often in rural locations, qualities contributing to the powerful sense of community and interest in questions pertaining to the common good. Although St. Olaf, with nearly three thousand students, compares favorably with a number of comprehensive universities in the Midwest, organizationally it "thinks" and "acts" like a community: the small, residential, liberal arts college it was founded to be.

In a book written to orient new faculty to Lutheran colleges, Ernest Simmons, Professor of Religion at Concordia College, Moorhead, uses Luther's view of the distinction between law and gospel to explain a theological influence on the understanding of community in colleges of the church:

> In Luther's view the law . . . has a civil or ordering function in the world. Such orderliness is an expression of God's creation and prerequisite to the

> health of the earthly kingdom and its inhabitants. Civil law is the social expression of natural law found in the creation. All people are subject to these laws, whether Christian or not. A particular implication of this formulation was Luther's insistence that in the earthly kingdom the Christian is called to make common cause with all people, including those of other faiths, in providing for a just and healthy world. This view allows, indeed requires, that believers transcend religious and political differences for the sake of the common good.[6]

Transcending differences for the sake of the common good is a very difficult task for most people. It is extremely difficult for academics, in part because we rarely agree on a definition of the common good! On the one hand, the St. Olaf faculty has a long tradition of transcending differences for the sake of a commitment to the study of cultural differences in the curriculum. On the other hand, the faculty also has a long tradition of independent action in the forum of the monthly faculty meeting, where the "common good" may devolve to the "specific good" or the "particular circumstance."

I have found that disciplinary or departmental loyalty of faculty exists in creative tension with institutional loyalty in most postsecondary institutions. Deans are the ones called upon to negotiate conflicts between individual or departmental interests and college-wide needs. In most colleges, it is also true that the perspectives of faculty members often conflict with those of administrators. Deans are the ones who bridge the gap between the two stakeholder groups. On most campuses, trust—or rather, lack of trust—is a major impediment to organizational effectiveness and to community health. Deans are the ones in the middle of dialogues about trust.

St. Olaf College is not different from most colleges these days. Like my counterparts around the country, I am a dean engaged daily with the challenge of focusing the attention of the faculty community on the needs of St. Olaf as an academic organization. Where I may differ from my counterparts is how I approach deaning: from the perspective of servant-leadership as a manifestation of my sense of Christian vocation.

My vocation as a Lutheran dean calls me to make decisions for the common good by using a variety of servant-leader practices, such as those identified by Larry Spears, CEO of the Greenleaf Center for Servant-Leadership: listening, empathy, healing, awareness, persuasion, conceptualization, foresight, stewardship, commitment to the growth of people, and building community. It also requires effective use of modern management practices, such as those employed by Peter Drucker, Peter Senge, Charles Handy, Peter Vaill, and Stephen Covey. To be faithful to my calling, I believe that I must learn to live personally and, by extension, publicly with the paradox that the college is *both* organization *and* community. I know that I cannot solve this paradox, or make it disappear. It is a part of me, my position, and the age in which we live.

The Response

Over the past nine years, I have formed some strong opinions about the value of Lutheran higher education and the principles of deaning in Lutheran colleges and universities. When I read a copy of the talk given by Richard Hughes of Pepperdine University at the annual Conference on the topic "The Vocation of a Lutheran College" in 1997, I thought immediately about the application of his words to "The Vocation of a Lutheran Dean." The concluding remarks from Hughes's talk are worth quoting at length:

> Finally, I want to make a few observations regarding the dilemmas you inevitably face as you seek to interpret the Lutheran vision to potential constituents.
>
> In the first place, because the Lutheran tradition thrives on paradox, ambiguity, thoughtfulness, and reflection, it is difficult to explain a Lutheran institution that genuinely lives out the Lutheran worldview. As the director of development for one Lutheran institution told me a couple of years ago, "It's tough to market ambiguity." This is all the more true in a "sound bite" culture such as ours. How can one possibly explain a Lutheran institution to a potential student or potential donor in a sound bite?
>
> While in one sense this may seem like a disadvantage for Lutheran institutions, in another sense this may well be your greatest asset. Because your theological resources are unique in the world of church-related higher education, and because those resources can do so much to sustain the life of the mind, Lutheran colleges and universities have the potential to grow into absolutely first class institutions of higher learning. This means that while you may not be able to explain to potential donors or potential students all the intricacies of the Lutheran worldview, you can explain that Lutheran colleges and universities offer a first class education where the life of the mind is nurtured, where all questions are taken seriously, where critical thinking is encouraged, and where a diversity of cultures is valued, and that these virtues all grow out of your commitment to the Christian faith.
>
> In my view, you occupy a unique and enviable position and I wish you well as you seek to implement these tasks.[7]

I am not sure I agree fully with Hughes's assertions about a Lutheran worldview, but I do agree with his assessment of the value and the potential of Lutheran colleges and universities. It has everything to do with vocation.

After all these years, I think I do understand Isaiah's response to the Lord's question: "Is there anyone I can send? Will someone go for us?" The angel's touch carries with it words of special significance: "This has touched your lips. Your sins are forgiven, and you are no longer guilty." After this experience, Isaiah hears the Lord's question and immediately says "yes" to the call. Only afterwards does he find out the details of the job description:

> Then the Lord told me to go and speak this message to the people: "You will listen and listen, but never understand. You will look and look, but never see." The Lord also said, "Make these people stubborn! Make them stop up their ears, cover their eyes, and fail to understand. Don't let them turn to me and be healed."

Without pushing the identification between the call of Isaiah and the vocation of deaning too far, I do see similarities. On the surface, Isaiah's task seems to be to bring about a hardening of the people of Israel and thereby to ensure their destruction. What we know, however, is that God's purpose was not to destroy Israel but to save it by calling the people to be faithful. Empowered by a strong vision and touched by God's love and the message of grace and forgiveness, Isaiah springs into action in the ambiguous, paradoxical, and confusing world of human affairs.

If there is such a concept as "The Vocation of a Lutheran Dean," it surely thrives on paradox, ambiguity, thoughtfulness, and reflection. I believe it is possible to serve in a dean's office and maintain a commitment to the life of the mind. I think I can ask hard questions and engage respondents in dialogue about issues that matter. I aim to value diversity of cultures and people and love all neighbors, even (or maybe, especially) those with whom I disagree. And, by the grace of God, I publicly trace these virtues to my commitment to the Christian faith. It just may be that my vocation as a Lutheran dean begins and ends with the simple message of servant-leadership: "Here am I. Send me."

NOTES

1. Daniel V. Biles, *Pursuing Excellence in Ministry* (Washington, D.C.: Alban Institute, 1988) 9.

2. "The Administration of the Christian Liberal Arts College," in *Christian Faith and the Liberal Arts* (Minneapolis: Augsburg, 1960) 83.

3. Robert Greenleaf, "The Servant as Religious Leader," *The Power of Servant Leadership*, ed. Larry Spears (San Francisco: Berrett-Koehler, 1998) 120, 124.

4. Boston: Harvard Business School, 1994.

5. S. Parks, L. Daloz, C. Keen, J. Keen, *Common Fire: Lives of Commitment in a Complex World* (Boston: Beacon, 1996) 19.

6. Ernest Simmons, *Lutheran Higher Education: An Introduction for Faculty* (Minneapolis, Augsburg Fortress, 1998) 27.

7. Richard Hughes, presentation for "The Vocation of a Lutheran College," A Conference for Faculty and Administrators at ELCA Colleges and Universities, Carthage College, Kenosha, Wisconsin, August 7, 1997.

PART IV:

The Future: How can church colleges best serve students in the present world, particularly a college with St. Olaf's history and background?

27. CALLED TO SERVE

Mark U. Edwards, Jr.

In America from the seventeenth through the early twentieth centuries, churches founded many of our great institutions of higher education in the conviction that, since God was the source of all Truth, the pursuit of truth through study, argument, and investigation was part of honoring God and God's creation. Of course these Christians had practical goals as well. They wanted higher education for their children to prepare them for the work of the world. They also hoped that higher education would assist in making their children good citizens and prepare them for life in general. When thinking of their church community, they trusted that church-related institutions of higher education would also prepare future pastors, ministers, and other church leaders. Further, they saw these institutions as places where serious questions about matters of faith could be asked and answered; an unexamined faith was suspect to many of these pioneers. Finally, since many of these founding churches were also distinguished by ethnic identity, they also saw themselves as having a stake in higher education as a means of preserving and celebrating their ethnic heritage.

Much of this has changed since World War II.

The Secularization of the Academy

In recent decades colleges and universities founded by churches have become secular in approach and identity, and the founding denominations have not protested much. Christians increasingly have sent their sons and daughters to secular and public institutions, apparently no longer as concerned as their forebears were that institutions of higher education should help young adults develop a mature faith or prepare people for leading roles within the church. In some quarters, Christians may even have abandoned the hope that institutions of higher education should educate people for citizenship or life in general; it is enough if institutions of higher education prepare their graduates for a job, preferably a highly paid job.

The loss of religious perspectives in higher education has other sources as well. As a practical matter, when the founding denomination is no longer able or willing to provide sufficient numbers of students and other resources to a college or university, the institution is usually forced to broaden (and often secularize) its mission and its outreach. This has happened to church-related colleges throughout the nation, and especially on the coasts.

Other causes have also been at work. If one spends time, as I have, at a research university such as Harvard and then at a college of the church such as St. Olaf, it becomes readily apparent that what might be termed "professional formation" at the research universities socializes faculty in ways often inimical to the values and identity of the college of the church. When newly minted Ph.D.s arrive at St. Olaf, we must spend considerable effort resocializing them to the values of a liberal arts college, and especially to the values of a liberal arts college of the church. There is, for example, a crucial difference between educating a student to think historically—encouraging a habit of mind—and educating her to be a budding professional historian through immersion in professional secondary literature, methodology, and research technique. The difference is a concern of liberal arts colleges. Further: at a college of the church, explicit discussions of faith and belief do, in fact, have a place in the classroom so long as intellectual rigor is maintained. The propriety of such discussions is challenged at most research universities. We at liberal arts colleges of the church are not always successful in our attempt to resocialize colleagues, and the secular and disciplinary spirit of the research academy can subtly and not so subtly erode the distinctive character of a college of the church. This is also part of the trend toward secularization.

For some observers, this is a salutary trend. They can point to the violence and division engendered throughout Western history by religion. They can point to ethnic tribalism (such as in Bosnia), religious intolerance (which was strong in America just a generation or so ago), and Christian practices and beliefs that hindered the search for truth (for example, regarding evolution). For much of the early history of American higher education, there was little place for Catholics or Jews in the leading academic institutions. For these and other reasons, then, some observers argue that in our increasingly diverse world, higher education must remain above the fray, relying on procedural values of reason, scientific experiment, and "secular" discourse to allow otherwise exclusive and potentially opposed groups to talk to each other. The academy becomes in their view an important part of the "public square" where secular rationality allows productive, socially beneficial intercourse across ethnic, religious, and ideological boundaries.

These views dominate much of academe. In their extreme form they rule out of bounds all claims of fact or moral validity that arise from religious conviction. In a more moderate form, they allow the introduction of ideas and moral claims in academic discourse if these ideas and claims can be justified in secular (rational) terms, whatever their ultimate source or grounding in religious tradition.

The Stake of Religious Communities in Higher Education

Religious communities, whether Christian or Jewish or Muslim, need to question whether these trends are healthy either for their own self-identity and values or for the well-being of higher education and society generally.

This exclusion of religion from higher education relegates faith to the private sphere and treats it, as the lawyer Steven Carter has put it, like a hobby, that is, as an interesting private inclination that has no, or should have no, relevance when entering the public square (or the public academy).

Such exclusion may either force the religious individual to deny much of the grounding of her moral and intellectual being or to contort her beliefs into an alien form that just happens to fit the rules of reason and evidence accepted by the secular academy. These rules, while extraordinarily productive in scientific research, represent only one way of human knowing. The religious individual has a powerful interest in insisting that her claims of knowledge, while based in part on different notions of reason and evidence, have a rightful place in intellectual and academic discourse along with other convictions that also fail the narrow test of scientific rationality but nevertheless represent respectable and widely held views within the academy. Religiously based convictions should not be the sole metaphysical claims excluded from academic formulation and debate.

There are also practical considerations. Like it or not, Christians must learn to survive within a larger pluralistic environment. To survive, much less to flourish, within modern America, they must learn how to maintain their distinctive beliefs while living peacefully with difference. They need to be concerned about preserving their identity in the face of secularizing trends, consumerism, and the effects of the mass media. Becoming socially homogeneous by accepting the "secular" rules of "public square" or secular academy is no solution, or at least no solution if churches wish to perpetuate themselves. More to the point, there is little future for these communities in cutting off the intellectual side of religion and in reducing faith to matters of private emotion. If they abandon the academy to secularism, they will be abandoning a precious part of their own heritage.

For these and other reasons, churches and other religious communities need to become reengaged with higher education. If they do not, they run a substantial risk of further decline and marginalization within the academy and modern American society.

Higher Education's Interest in Religious Communities

Enlightened self-interest cuts both ways. Churches need to reengage institutions of higher education. But secular colleges and universities may also find it beneficial to rethink their position vis-à-vis religion.

Throughout the Western world and especially in America, higher education owes at least a historic debt to Christian denominations. Most of today's colleges and universities were founded by churches. The idea of the university has its origin in the intellectual aspirations of the medieval church. And as the historian Mark Schwehn has shown, many of the mental attitudes and virtues upon which the modern research university depend—faith, humility, self-denial, charity, friendship, recast in secular guise—have their origin in religious belief.

To the extent that this historic dependence is true, it may be asked whether these virtues may be sustained beyond a few generations without the presence of the religious community that nourished them in the first place. This question is a subset of the larger issue of whether much of civil society depends upon virtues that are religious in origin and require religion to be sustained over the long term. Are we in the academy, to put it bluntly, living off borrowed capital?

However we answer this question, we must acknowledge that religious diversity and conviction is a fact that will not go away by being ignored, silenced, or belittled. So what is the academy to do?

First, let us recognize that Christianity can never return to the dominant and dominating (even persecuting) position that it once enjoyed in the academy in the nineteenth and early twentieth century. This is a good thing. But now that room has been found in the modern academy for many diverse perspectives, there is no reason that Christian perspectives should not once again have a role in academic discourse much like any other perspective such as varieties of Marxism or feminism or capitalism. The same would be true for other religious perspectives such as Judaism or Islam.

Second, it is crucial to allow for diversity *among* institutions as well as *within* them. There is a danger that in seeking the needed diversity *within* every institution of higher education we inadvertently promote an unhealthy homogeneity *among* institutions. There must be room within the more than 3,600 institutions of higher education in America for colleges like St. Olaf and universities like Notre Dame that maintain a strong connection to their founding religious community and reflect that connection in both curricular and cocurricular offerings. These institutions need to be seen neither as anachronisms nor as second-class academic citizens. Rather, they enrich the larger academic community by the particular perspectives they bring to the academic enterprise.

Religious perspectives, once allowed back in the academy, will enrich discourse and assure that a vital part of life, including intellectual life, is not suppressed for what are now anachronistic reasons. This is not merely a matter of "fairness." There are real gains to be made by once again allowing religion—all religions—a place in the academy.

Religious perspectives can enrich moral deliberation, put the search for knowledge in a larger perspective, and help young men and women combine the pursuit of a career with a larger quest for human wholeness and service to others.

The Lutheran Contribution: The Case of St. Olaf College

If you accept the need for explicit religious perspectives in higher education, what might be contribution of a Lutheran college such as St. Olaf?

Darrell Jodock has suggested five closely intertwined features that should characterize a college in the Lutheran tradition:

1. It serves the community and educates community leaders.
2. It strives for academic excellence.
3. It honors freedom of inquiry.
4. It embraces the ideal of the liberal arts.
5. It organizes itself as a community of discourse.

As Jodock recognizes, none of these characteristics is uniquely Lutheran, but they all are well grounded in traditional Lutheran theology and especially the theology of Martin Luther himself, the denomination's reluctant founder. Rather than retrace ground that Jodock has already superbly covered, I want to suggest some additional theological elements that distinguish a Lutheran approach to higher education.

Colleges and the Two Kingdoms

In the Reformed tradition as in evangelical Christianity—the two traditions, I might add, that have dominated American religion and shaped our understanding of church-related colleges—there has been a tendency to wish to conform the world to the church (or, more narrowly, the college to the church). In Lutheranism, at least of a nonpietistic variety, there has been greater willingness to recognize a difference between the individual and the world and to distinguish between the norms for individual Christians and the norms for institutions. Much of this distinction has been expressed in the language of the "two kingdoms" or "two governances" of God.

From a Lutheran theological perspective, as Jodock points out, higher education resides properly within the secular realm where justice is sought and reason, one of God's greatest gifts to humanity, offers primary guidance.* Situated within this realm, we in higher education are called to pursue truth with all the intellectual rigor at our command. In this respect a Lutheran college shares goals similar to those of secular colleges or universities. We all seek to approach the "truth" of what we are studying.

An example should serve to illustrate the role of "reason" within Lutheran higher education and suggest how the Lutheran approach differs significantly from some Reformed or Evangelical stances.

Within both secular and church-related institutions of higher education, a biology class should examine, say, recombinant DNA within the naturalistic paradigm of modern science. Reason, evidence, and the standards of proof are the guiding principles. This applies to both a Lutheran

*We need, however, to be careful when translating Luther's understanding of the secular realm and reason from the early sixteenth to the late twentieth century. The intervening history has changed the meaning of crucial terms. For example, Luther operates with the assumption that the secular realm is God's creation and that God acts within this realm both directly (by sustaining creation, by establishing and upholding the natural working of creation through what are sometimes termed natural laws, and by intervening, on occasion, in the normal working of things through miracles) and indirectly (through the power of government and the exercise of reason, which is God's gift to human beings). By way of contrast, many moderns, under the impress of Enlightenment rationalism and its modern variants, would view the "secular realm" as autonomous and subject to analysis and control through the application of reason. Some go so far as to place in the category of subjective and private and even unknowable all things that cannot be determined through the scientific application of reason. There is no place for God or for revelation or for a distinctly Christian perspective in this approach.

and a secular college, both of which should advocate rigorous scientific inquiry. This is the way "scientific truth" (among other "truths") is discerned within the "secular realm." To be sure, Christian conviction may prevent scholars, including Lutheran Christians, from accepting, for example, the metaphysical assertion of naturalism that denies "that there exists or could exist any entities or events which lie, in principle beyond the scope of scientific explanation." But it remains possible for a Lutheran Christian scholar to work within a framework that explains the working of the world solely according to natural causes. Since many Reformed and Evangelical scholars would disagree, some further exposition is necessary.

In his recent book, *The Outrageous Idea of Christian Scholarship*, the Notre Dame historian George Marsden argues that a Christian perspective *should* make a difference in scholarly results. Coming out of the Dutch Reformed faith, Marsden identifies with the tradition which traces a line through Augustine, Thomas, Calvin, and the Reformed tradition. Some have labeled this tradition "sapiential" in its understanding of God and God's relationship with creation and human knowledge. Lutherans come from a more "voluntaristic" theological and intellectual tradition and, as a result, are more modest in their expectations of the difference a Christian perspective might make in scholarly results. Let me illustrate the difference with two examples drawn from Marsden and dealing with questions of epistemology, or the study of how we know what we know.

Consider the Christian (and Jewish and Muslim) belief that God is the creator of heaven and earth. Marsden contends that the "doctrine of creation . . . has important implications in the field of epistemology. . . . For one thing, if God has created our minds as well as the rest of reality, then it makes sense to believe that God may communicate with us in nature as well as in Scripture, even if as 'through a glass darkly.' In such a theistic framework, we have reason to suppose that God would have created us with some mechanisms for distinguishing truth from error, however darkened our hearts and puny our intellects" (88).

The historian in me recognizes in this argument an echo of a late-medieval debate concerning the relationship between God and the world. In this medieval debate, the existence of what Marsden calls "some mechanisms for distinguishing truth from error" rested on the scriptural testimony that human beings were created in the image and likeness of God. This "image and likeness" was thought to be most fully expressed in the human mind, which, modeled on the image and likeness of God, was, as it were, able to "think God's thoughts after God." At issue, then, was the relationship between God's "thoughts" and the created world. Put simply—although the matter is not simple at all—is the world comprehensible because the world was created by God, who is rational and who created the human mind in the image and likeness of God's own rationality? If so, then human minds, created in the image and likeness of God, should be able to understand the world in which we find ourselves; much of the skepticism of modern society needs then to be rethought by Christians. Further, the relativism in much of academia should also be challenged by a certainty, however dimly perceived, guaranteed by a rational, creator God.

But in the medieval debate there was an alternative. Is the world as it is because God simply *chose* to make it as it is? God, in this view, could have made it otherwise. In this latter case, we cannot assume that because our minds are like the mind of the world's creator we can understand the world, or, more extreme, that we can deduce how the world should work. Rather, we must use our minds to discover the way in which God *chose* to make the world. We are given no epistemological guarantee. Lutherans and others in the "voluntaristic" tradition are left with (admittedly fallible) reason, experience, and experiment—the sharpest tools of the modern academy.

Here is another example of how those in the Reformed and Lutheran traditions may take different positions regarding epistemology: "Christians," Marsden argues, "who affirm that Jesus was not only human but also fully divine must presuppose that the transcendent God, the wholly Other, the Creator of heaven and earth, can appear and be known in our ordinary history. Most of modern thought, by contrast," Marsden continues, "assumes something like 'Lessing's ditch': that one cannot get from the contingent truths of history to the timeless metaphysical truths of religion. Acceptance of the incarnation, however, seems to presuppose that we *can* know about the transcendent through ordinary contingent means, such as the testimony of others and evidence drawn from our own experience."

Here the difference between the Reformed position and the Lutheran may be one more of degree than of kind. From Martin Luther's perspective, the incarnation may tell us more about our limitations, and God's graciousness, than about our ability to, in Marsden's words, "know about the transcendent through ordinary contingent means." Luther was convinced from his reading of Scripture that God became a human being in Christ Jesus because we incarnate human beings cannot by our nature understand transcendent matters except (and even then imperfectly) through material (that is, incarnate or fleshly) means. The incarnation, for Luther, is not a testimony to our ability to know. Rather, it is testimony to God's willingness to accommodate God's self to our inability to know. Because we finite, contextualized, historical human beings cannot by our nature understand the transcendent or absolute or unchanging, God chose to come to us in way that we could understand, namely, in an embodied, historically contextualized, linguistically and culturally conditioned manner, namely, as a first-century Palestinian Jew named Jesus. Both Reformed and Lutherans may conclude, then, that the infinite can be glimpsed through the finite, but the Lutheran is likely to draw far less warrant from this than the Reformed.* "Lutheran epistemological humility" is the phrase recommended to me by Ed Langerak of the St. Olaf Philosophy Department. This "humility" allows Lutheran colleges to work comfortably within the modern academy's notion of academic freedom.

So what, then, is the difference between Lutheran higher education and secular higher education? The Lutheran difference, I submit, lies not in the content but in the people, and the doctrine of vocation is at the center of this difference.

Vocation and Colleges

Jodock has pointed out the importance of "vocation" in Lutheran higher education. Let me elaborate a bit on his point. People in Martin Luther's day spoke of a "call" or a "vocation" to the office of priest, monk, or nun. God, it was thought, "called" people *from* a life in the world *to* the more demanding, and spiritually superior, life of the clergy. Other occupations were not "callings" or "vocations" in this special sense.

As it happened, Martin Luther's new understanding of justification transformed this understanding of vocation or calling. Following Paul,

*By the way, the Lutheran difference with the Reformed and Evangelicals goes deeper still. Consider again the example of the biology class and recombinant DNA. When we move from the question of how techniques of recombinant DNA can prolong life or heal disease to the question whether we should prolong life with these techniques, we move into the realm of ethics. From a Lutheran theological perspective, most ethical questions are themselves located in the "secular realm" since they involve the reasonable application of principles to specific circumstances. Ethical decisions, in other words, are prudential decisions that can be answered just as well by non-Christians as by Christians. To be sure, in a limited number of cases the principles may be distinctly Christian, but most ethical principles are shared by many religious traditions and not a small number of secular traditions as well. So a biology class at a good secular institution should also allow the raising of ethical questions; a Lutheran institution certainly will. We should not differ significantly on this score either.

Luther declared that we are justified by faith apart from works of the law. We are made right with God, that is, reconciled and justified, not by a process of spiritual growth accomplished by the doing of good works in a state of grace—the leading theological view of Luther's day—but solely through Christ's death on the cross. We are justified when we accept in faith and trust God's promise that Christ has died for us. We can do nothing on our own behalf. Even faith in God's promise of salvation through Christ is a gift of the Holy Spirit. It is not a "psychological work" lying within our power.

You can see that this new understanding of justification could transform the idea of unequal vocations. As long as Christians understood justification as a process of spiritual growth, it made sense to say that the life, say, of a nun was spiritually superior to the life of a wife and housekeeper, or the life of a priest was spiritually superior to the life of a butcher or baker or candlestick maker. The nun or priest was living a life that better promoted spiritual growth. But if, as Luther put it in Latin, salvation comes *extra nos*, that is, from outside of ourselves, then our salvation depends not on what we do but on what God has done for us. Everyone, be she a nun or a housewife, be he a priest or a butcher, depends equally on Christ's reconciling sacrifice. We all have the same, singular spiritual call, to love God and serve the neighbor in whatever we do.

This one, singular Christian vocation has implications for vocation*s* with an "s." And Luther was quick to spell out this implication for his hearers and readers. He argued that all occupations were equal in God's sight. The housewife, or butcher, or baker is pursuing a vocation, a calling, that is equally pleasing to God so long as it is lived in faith in God's promise through Christ and in loving service to the neighbor. In this way Luther took the notion of a "calling" or "vocation" to the superior life of the clergy and extended it to all Christians at work in the world. All Christians have the single Vocation or Call that in turn is lived out in many vocations or callings.

The Lutheran Difference

It is this understanding of calling that can offer definition to a specifically Lutheran view of college education. In a profound way Lutheran colleges, when true to their heritage, are helping young people to find and develop their vocations in this specifically Lutheran sense. This is largely a secular task but with an important religious dimension. How is this accomplished?

While I cannot specify a number or percentage, I am convinced that Lutheran schools need to have a significant proportion of the faculty and staff who are self-consciously living out their Christian calling in service to students and to each other. They model and teach what we want to encourage in the students themselves, an understanding that a vocation is far more than an occupation, that careers should be seen as callings in which we exercise our God-given talents not merely to earn money or status or personal satisfaction but also, and primarily, to serve the neighbor.

There also needs to be a larger context in which education occurs, a context that encourages by example and opportunity a view of life larger than a career and of service wider than self-interest. Regular worship in a centrally located chapel is a beginning, but only a beginning. A liberal arts college, when true to its Lutheran heritage, should give its students an experience of *community* different from the individualistic autonomy that characterizes much of American life today.

Jodock discusses at length the importance of community for Lutheran higher education. A student is educated so she might serve the community. A student's vocation or call is to service of the neighbor in community. A Christian is freed by grace from worry about one's own salvation in order to serve others. The liberal arts aim for "not just a freedom *from* restraints that stifle individual liberty but also a freedom *for* creative, ethically sensitive, responsible participation in a community." And so on.

Community at Lutheran colleges (and elsewhere, of course) is constituted by shared experiences and common practices, tempered by respect for difference. Further, such communities engage in everyday activities that subtly teach and embody the fact of interdependence and the importance of being mindful of the needs of others.

The subtle ways in which everyday activities at a Lutheran college may convey important social, moral, and even potentially religious messages can be illustrated with a simple contrast drawn from St. Olaf's experience. In his essay on changes at the college, Robert Nichols observes that over the last twenty-five years "the animating Christian activity common among students took place through the varied musical programs, especially the choirs, more than in the intellectual dialog of the classroom or in daily chapel." Nichols may rue this development, but I am more sanguine. Over a third of our students participate in musical groups during their four years with us. These ensembles give our young people the experience literally of harmonious cooperation. Individual performers subordinate their talents to a common good. Beautiful music is the goal, cooperation without competition is the means. There are no losers: only winners, both the performers and the audience. The whole is larger than the sum of its parts. And our students experience the power of harmonious cooperation at such a deep level that it colors their approach to life in general. The fact that much of the music performed is sacred music adds significantly to the benefit.

Unfortunately, our students' experience of making music together—and the social and even moral lessons it tacitly teaches—is becoming increasingly attenuated for the rest of our society. Where we once heard music only if we produced it ourselves, or at least watched and heard real human beings make music, now through the "miracle" of electronics, our stereo systems or, more isolating yet, our Walkmen, we can experience wonderful music divorced from any immediate human cooperation. In such circumstances many of us no longer learn from music the truth of its production, namely, that music asks people to subordinate narrow self-interest to achieve a common goal, that music depends on human cooperation and in that cooperation something is produced that is greater than the simple sum of its parts, that music with its harmony is at least one appropriate metaphor for the functioning of a healthy society.

To return to my example of the biology class. The Lutheran difference from the secular academy lies largely not in the content of the class or the scope of the argument but in the teacher and the students and in the broader context in which education takes place. The teacher needs at least to understand the Lutheran commitment to calling and be willing to help the student think through his or her professional or career goals in light of this larger consideration. Preferably, the teacher should be living out his or her own Christian calling as a biologist and teacher who seeks both to be the best biologist and teacher possible and, as a Christian, to love God and serve the neighbor in all that he or she does. At a Lutheran college the students, too, should be thinking through their own vocation, their own calling, even as they educate themselves for careers and for life in general. And the experience of community at these colleges should convey some sense of the world's true interdependence of both people and the rest of creation.

Our Norwegian Heritage

In conclusion, I need to say a few words about St. Olaf's Norwegian heritage and the continuing role it plays in furthering and deepening the mission of the college.

True communities have a memory, a set of shared stories, that helps shape identity and character. So, too, do liberal arts colleges with strong traditions such as those found at St. Olaf. For us those stories come out of our Norwegian Lutheran past. Our Norwegian heritage is celebrated solemnly at Founders Day, in the names of the buildings around us, in the special curricular offerings such as the Norwegian language and Scandinavian history, and in the story of those who founded a college to help Norwegian immigrants become Americans. But it also is recalled with humor and playfulness with such things as the Ole "fight polka," "Um, Ya Ya," and with jokes about lutefisk and lefse, and with stories about Ytterboe the Dog. Our Norwegian heritage gives us a sense of grounding in times past and reminds us of those who planned, labored, and sacrificed so that we might teach and learn.

Overseas Study

Some aspects of this Norwegian Lutheran heritage continue to shape the college ethos. For example, as several of the biographies illustrate, St. Olaf has always enjoyed a strong engagement with contact, education, and service outside our national borders. President Boe, for example, was actively involved in the predecessor body to the Lutheran World Federation, and Howard and Edna Hong provided exemplary service to war refugees in the United States and in Europe. Nichols rightly sees this world involvement together with a modernist missionary tradition, exemplified by such St. Olaf leaders as President Granskou, as one important source of St. Olaf's extraordinary international studies program. As we move into the twenty-first century we need to nourish this important tradition while doing some corrective work on what Nichols has termed "modernist missionary attitudes" that slight cultural and language preparation.

A College for Immigrants

St. Olaf was founded by Norwegian immigrants who sought to prepare their young men and women for lives of worth and service within their new home, America, while preserving and passing on the cultural treasures and values of their former homeland. In the decades ahead, much of the growth in the college-age population in Minnesota and the Upper Midwest will occur among other, more recent immigrant groups who would like opportunities for their children similar to those sought by our Norwegian forebears. With its history and values, St. Olaf is well positioned to continue its immigrant tradition and reach out to the children of the new immigrants and offer them an opportunity through education to enter into lives of worth and service.

Governance

Another aspect of our Norwegian Lutheran heritage may lie in the arena of governance. Until quite recently, presidents felt free to identify a St. Olaf graduate as "one of the chosen"—Boe's phrase in correspondence with Agnes Larson—whose destiny would be to create the college of the future. For example, of the nine faculty "shapers" of St. Olaf College profiled in this volume, President Kildahl tapped F. Melius Christiansen and Ole Edvart Rølvaag. President Boe, the embodiment of the "take-charge" president of the old school and St. Olaf's most influential president, did the same for Emil Ellingson, Agnes Larson, Arnold Flaten, and Howard Hong. President Granskou appointed Harold Ditmanson. These appointments were, for the most part, done on the president's authority without benefit of search committee or faculty approval! Truly, through World War II and beyond, presidents shaped the St. Olaf faculty in a way that more recent presidents can only wistfully admire.

This presidential authority, while common at many schools in the decades before World War II, may have persisted longer at St. Olaf. Combined with a vigorous Norwegian-American concern for equality and a suspicion of hierarchy and bureaucracy, it has shaped St. Olaf's culture into the present day. Nichols captures this cultural legacy with remarkable insight:

> As a college of the American Lutheran Church, St. Olaf shared the new church's sometime belief in itself as a big, if somewhat quarrelsome, family, suspicious of bureaucracy and structure, but nonetheless confident in authority exercised in a personal way by its leaders. This helps to explain something that I poorly understood in my first years at the college: why so many faculty regarded the administration with a deep suspicion that it was running the college simply for the benefit of a secretly growing number of bureaucrats, when in fact the college had one of the lowest ratios of administrators to faculty and students among the consortium of colleges to which it belonged. At the same time, the president exercised considerable authority and did so in a manner that commanded genuine respect. The president was paterfamilias of the church college family. As family, or community, St. Olaf offered intimacy and sense of belonging; but family, while personal, could also be arbitrary, unpredictable, and often paternal: not the ideal combination perhaps for guiding Lutheran higher education through the civil, women's, and personal liberation movements that have dominated the second half of the twentieth century in America.

The tradition of the president as paterfamilias, while richly documented in this volume's biographies and a contributing factor to much of the school's historic accomplishments, has been changing for some time and needs to change further to fit the needs of the twenty-first century. In the years ahead, faculty and administration must craft a new relationship situated between benevolent paternalism and governance exclusively by vote of the whole faculty. While appropriate governance will continue to require both presidential fiat on rare occasion and vote of the whole faculty on frequent occasion, the college should work toward a governance system where crucial information is regularly shared, where those with responsibility and authority to make both administrative and faculty decisions consult widely and take advice seriously, and where the right to be consulted is not confused with the right to decide and the concomitant accountability for the decisions made.

The Gap between Aspiration and Achievement

In his essay on Harold Ditmanson, Walter Stromseth observes that Ditmanson "had a keen eye for human foibles, a bemused sense of the incongruity between ideal aims and historical practice, the gap between personal or institutional aspiration and actual achievement, yet a lightness of spirit able to live with such incongruity without losing heart." This states eloquently what everyone needs when dealing with the incongruity between the ideal and the reality of colleges of the church, and especially St. Olaf College. While we can speak of our Lutheran Christian ideals—service to community, the quest for academic excellence, honoring free inquiry, embracing the liberal arts, the search for community, to offer Jodock's list—and simultaneously celebrate our Norwegian distinctiveness, we must recognize ultimately that we are sinful individuals who, ineluctably, compose a flawed human institution. Rather than being glum at this inevitability, we should recall Jodock's salutary observation that our unmerited adoption by God calls for us to cultivate a sense of humor. We must not take ourselves, our ideals, or even our college too seriously. With God's gracious and unmerited assistance, we'll muddle through somehow. It is better to aim at unattainable ideals and fall short; when reaching for the stars, we may at least get a piece of the moon.

Society's Continuing Need for Colleges of the Church

In my inaugural address in October 1994, I spoke on society's continuing need for colleges of the church. My remarks then are still applicable, I believe, for setting our direction as we move into the twenty-first century.

> While our colleges of the church are no cure-alls for the ills of American society, they do retain some not insignificant ability to restrain the

> centrifugal forces that threaten to fling us apart into isolated individuals who deny the real interdependence of today's world. The liberal arts college has long championed the interrelatedness of all knowledge. Our size and total commitment to undergraduate education challenges both faculty and students to seek ways to integrate the disparate scholarly disciplines into a coherent education. Moreover, the liberal arts colleges have long been avenues for economic and social betterment.
>
> But liberal arts colleges, especially liberal arts colleges of the church, do far more than promote interdisciplinary studies and facilitate economic advancement. At their best they give students an experience of community—a community that builds character. . . . Undergraduate education here at St. Olaf fosters a sense of what true community is all about so long as that education provides extensive interaction among students and between faculty and students. So we must remain a place where the faculty and staff seek to cultivate each student's unique God-given potential. We must remain appropriately small so that large numbers of the community know each other. We must remain residential in character so that the whole person is known and engaged. We must continue to encourage activities and interactions that shape moral character and promote civic virtue. We must be intentional in fostering diversity and in seeking out and recruiting students from all corners of our society. In short, we at St. Olaf must continue our journey towards true pluralistic community, bound together by a shared overarching history and identity—Norwegian-American, Lutheran, Christian—while honoring and celebrating the stories of our various constituent communities as well as the autonomy and individuality of each member of the student body, faculty and staff.

St. Olaf's heritage is distinguished, its legacy enormous, and its potential great. St. Olaf College remains called to serve.

28.
A FLAGGING FLAGSHIP?

Robert Benne

Encounters with St. Olaf

My first encounter with St. Olaf College was through its choir, which toured northeastern Nebraska when I was in my mid-teens. The choir sang at the municipal auditorium of Fremont, Nebraska, a town then of fifteen thousand that brought many traveling attractions to our part of the state. I can remember being enthralled by the quality of the choral presentation, the elegance and dignity of the white-haired director (who may have been the great F. Melius, though more likely his successor), and the moving rendition of its final piece, "Beautiful Savior." As a beneficiary of that fine Midwestern tradition of choral training in the high schools (even the smallest), I had already acquired enough musical experience to appreciate something special.

Furthermore, St. Olaf had a kind of mystique for me because it was named after a Norwegian king. Though our part of Nebraska was heavily Lutheran, we didn't name our colleges or churches after European saints or kings. We were far too American and egalitarian for that kind of thing. Moreover, not many Norwegians settled in Nebraska; the Germans and Swedes were far more numerous.

That mystique was magnified when I went off to Midland Lutheran College and was taught by one Herman Gimmestad, a graduate of St. Olaf. I was an English major and Gimmestad was my main teacher and adviser. While he did teach standard American, British, and world literature courses, his passion was teaching two "minority" interests: the literature of Iceland, especially its sagas, and the literature of the Great Plains. Looking back now, I can see that such emphases were central to his calling as a professor. Not normally given to emotional displays, "Gimme" would really get into the Icelandic sagas and the stories of immigrants to the Great Plains. As he read sections from them aloud, his deep voice would rise and his completely bald head would become flushed with excitement.

His enthusiasm for these two interests fired my imagination. I became a lifelong fan of O. E. Rølvaag as well as of Willa Cather, one of Nebraska's heroes. I also vowed I would meet an Icelander when I went to graduate school and then visit Iceland, the home of those wonderful stories. At the University of Chicago I did meet an Icelander, Bjorn Bjornsson, who has not only become a lifelong friend, but who has also invited me to lecture a number of times at the University of Iceland.

So St. Olaf's heritage touched me at an early age and from quite a distance. Later, when I became a seminary professor in Chicago, I taught with a number of colleagues who were St. Olaf graduates, and I taught many students who came from St. Olaf to our seminary. I was impressed by their quality and learned more about St. Olaf. As I got more interested in the challenges of church-related higher education, I came to view St. Olaf, along with Valparaiso, as the two flagships of Lutheran higher education. Rightly or wrongly, I see them that way today, though I think both, along with all other church-related colleges, are being sorely challenged to maintain their character as Christian institutions.

Though I am of quite a different American Lutheran tradition, St. Olaf has reached me in a number of ways. I am honored to have been asked to respond to the volume of writings before us. As one viewing from afar, perhaps I can add something to St. Olaf's understanding of its calling at this crucial juncture of its history.

The Spirit of St. Olaf

What is this "presence" that I have encountered at numerous points in my life and which has been sketched in the various essays in this volume, some of which are the narratives of real "giants in the earth" and more of which are the many "ordinary saints" who have contributed to the larger story of St. Olaf? I would like to characterize the "soul" of St. Olaf in a bundle of qualities that make up what I think is definitive.

A College of the Church

It seems obvious that St. Olaf has always been unapologetically a college of the Lutheran church, though what precisely that means has always been a subject of debate. From its earliest days the college made choices about its particular role as a college of the church. But it has always been committed to the Christian ethos as the context for higher education.

Substantively that has meant that the college as an institution and as a large collection of individuals has lived out of the Lutheran teaching of the calling of all Christians. The idea that all persons have been called by God to use their talents for the good of the neighbor has been central as a defining motif. It comes up again and again in the stories of the "greats" in the past as well as in the stories of the contemporary products of the college, who may be remembered tomorrow as the "greats" of today. Likewise, the college itself has debated consistently through the years the nature of its calling as an institution of the church, witness the title of this volume.

Certainly the intellectual content of the Christian worldview has played a central role in the story of the college in its commitment to a strong battery of courses in Christian theology and ethics. That intellectual content has also been involved in the efforts of Christian faculty outside the religion department to relate faith and learning in their own fields and in the general curriculum of the college. At Midland College I was the beneficiary of the efforts of one St. Olaf graduate who tried mightily to see the Christian meaning in the literature he taught.

The commitment to the Christian practice of worship—of Word and Sacrament, of praise and prayer—has also characterized St. Olaf. A strong, "public" chapel that has been central to the life of the college is a distinctive mark in comparison to those many colleges whose chapel has become either nonexistent or a sideshow.

A College of the Liberal Arts

There is little doubt that St. Olaf has been a college committed to a broad and "liberating" education for its students. Throughout its history, it has required a substantial number of general education courses which have ensured that student minds have been broadened and deepened. Moreover, an emphasis on critical reflection seems central to its educational enterprise, though that critical reflection was always constrained by Christian commitments that prevented that reflection from becoming arid and relativistic.

Even though St. Olaf's reputation in some circles depends on its training of mathematicians and scientists and in others its nurturing of professionals, it has been clear that those fields have always been part of a larger educational enterprise that aims at shaping the whole person.

The college has shown its commitment to the liberal arts in its Paracollege, now seemingly abolished, and its Great Conversation sequences. Both are efforts to give its students an encounter with "the best that has been thought and written."

A College of Music and the Arts

Though St. Olaf is justly known for its majors in all the arts, its choral music has captured national attention. From the time of F. Melius

Christiansen to the present day, the St. Olaf Choir occupies the highest ground among college and university choirs. The choir provided my first encounter with St. Olaf and it was a memorable one. I have heard virtually hundreds of choirs in my life, but the choirs of Cambridge, England, and of St. Olaf stand in my estimation above them all.

Perhaps the many other Lutheran colleges would have developed choirs on their own, but I suspect the model held up nationally by St. Olaf spurred many of them on to build quality choirs of their own. It no doubt also provided a standard at which to aim, and thereby lifted the quality of music at our Lutheran colleges.

In this ongoing commitment to musical excellence, St. Olaf manifests a strong aesthetic dimension in Lutheran higher education, something that is wholesome and distinctive. The Lutheran tradition's identification with profound music is borne magnificently by St. Olaf.

A College of Norwegian Heritage

The curious window in Boe Chapel with the "Fram, Fram—Krossmenn, Kongsmenn, Kristmenn" phrases continues to amaze me. After most Lutheran colleges long ago shed any explicit commitment to an ethnic heritage, St. Olaf still puzzles about how it continues to carry a Norwegian heritage. But then few colleges have an O. E. Rølvaag as a lingering presence amid them and few could draw so heavily on one ethnic group as a constituency. Moreover, unlike the German-background colleges, the Scandinavian ones did not have to prove their Americanism during the First and Second World Wars.

For many years the college could count upon the small-town and rural Norwegian Lutheran churches to supply them with bright and eager students. Lately, that composition, like the composition of America, is more likely to be urban and suburban. Both the Norwegian and the Lutheran character has waned with the country's demographic shifts.

But nevertheless, as Aune has argued, the Norwegian "thing" goes on. It seems that the commitment to that heritage is more than nostalgia, though I am sure there is much of that. Rather, it seems to be consonant with Rølvaag's own conviction that all heritages have something valuable to contribute to America. The Norwegian is no exception. Its egalitarianism, its love of language and literature, its devotion to nature, its appreciation of music and the resonance of its long Christian past are distinctive attributes that add texture to the life of the college.

Another characteristic of the Norwegian religious heritage that deserves to stand alone is its commitment to world missions. The Norwegian-American churches sent out missionaries by the droves, and they returned to this country and to the college to tell the stories of other cultures and climes. This particular thrust seems to live on in the college's commitment to international exposure, to the "globalization" of education, as the current argot has it.

Also, I would argue, the Norwegian heritage has produced a certain personality type that I would wager is still present at the college. Among all the northern European cultures, Norwegians seem more contentious, feisty, argumentative, and individualistic than most. At least the majority of the Norwegian-Americans I have known—many of them St. Olaf grads—are passionate in their convictions and not at all bashful in expressing, advancing, and defending them. They add spice and verve to any debate even as they irritate and bring to naught all expectations for consensus.

These four characteristics—present in strength and quality—make up the St. Olaf mystique. But is the mystique dissolving? For over a century St. Olaf was able to draw upon faculty and students who had been formed in a living religious and ethnic tradition. It could presuppose that formation; it did not have to provide it from college onward. Its embodiment of the four qualities I have outlined above enabled students from those living traditions to blossom and develop from soil that had already nurtured them. In other words, St. Olaf relied on an ethos in its faculty and students that was a presupposition for its Christian, liberal arts, musical, and Norwegian endeavors. What happens when the ethos can no longer be assumed? We will return to that question at the end of the essay.

The Underlying Model

It is my contention that all colleges operate with some underlying philosophy of education, even if it is implicit. Colleges of the church operate with some underlying theological model, again even if implicit. St. Olaf has carried on a continuing dialogue about its guiding theology of education, so its rationale is often more explicit than implicit. The current set of essays do in fact carry on a discussion of explicit theological rationales, especially those by Jodock, Aune, and Nichols. But these do not constitute the formal stance of the college. That formal stance—as well as the debates that went into it—are more likely present in the "think pieces" of the 1950s (*Integration in the Christian Liberal Arts College*) and the 1970s (*Identity and Mission in a Changing Context*), as well as in the latest curricular reflections of the 1990s, of which we have no record in this set of essays.

Since there is no detailed account of either the debates or the documents, I will have to do a bit of surmising. (In the near future I hope to examine these and other relevant documents much more closely in order to get a surer grasp on their theologies of higher education.)

My thesis is that a shift in theological models took place in the 1950s and 1960s, a shift that corresponded to a demographic shift among St. Olaf's students and to the arrival of a more diverse and secular faculty.

Up until that point in the college's history, it seems that the Christian worldview in which the vast majority of students and faculty were formed was *the* reigning paradigm.* This overwhelming consensus, which naturally flowed from the living tradition of the Norwegian Lutheran churches, was not even explicit. It was just there as a dominant ethos. Most of what the college did flowed naturally from that ethos. This is not to say that there were no contradictions between that ethos and what was taught and done, but the dissonance was not visible or strong enough to become a problem.

The Norwegian Lutheran ethos was the glue that held things together. One could call it, to use the types employed by H. R. Niebuhr, a "Christ above Culture Model." The Christian meaning system provided the unchallenged canopy under which everything found its place. The tradition was intact in both the students and the faculty that peopled St. Olaf. Another way to put it, to use the words of Nicholas Wolterstorff, is that reason was employed within the limits of religion. The Christian worldview provided the unchallenged parameters of the college's endeavors. Or, to use the notion of another philosopher, Alasdair MacIntyre, reason (liberal arts learning) proceeded from and within the substance of a living tradition (Norwegian Lutheranism).

When the college expanded in the 1950s and 1960s the tradition began to weaken. New kinds of students arrived. New faculty arrived who were

*By Christian "worldview" I mean a comprehensive view of reality that includes a background theory of the origin and destiny of the world and its creatures, a view of nature and history, an estimate of the human predicament, an affirmation about how humans are saved or liberated, and a rather detailed set of moral imperatives that follow from this comprehensive view. The Christian worldview arises from the biblical narrative which has then been the object of reflection by theologians and philosophers for many centuries. The Christian worldview has been embodied in a venerable and impressive intellectual, artistic, moral tradition. The narrative—and its accompanying worldview—are rehearsed and enacted in worship and cult, in art and music. They form the character and outlook of those who participate in the tradition that both bears and communicates them.

not part of the tradition. The college wanted to "make it" so it emphasized professional expertise wherever it might be found. Fewer Norwegian-background faculty with their M.A.s and lifelong commitment to the college could find their callings there.

Reading between the lines, I would argue that Narum and Hong sensed this loss of integrating ethos. In *Integration in the Christian Liberal Arts College* they pressed for an explicit model of Lutheran higher theological education in which Christian theology would play the organizing role in the integration of the curriculum. But several remarks in the essays in this volume indicate that such a model never took hold. It was already too late to gain consensus on such an explicit Christian model after the implicit model had given way under the feet of the administration and faculty of the college. In order to institute such a model, the college would have had to require a theological consensus among the administration and faculty that would have been regarded as oppressive and closed.

So a new model was put forward in *Identity and Mission in a Changing Context*, shaped decisively, I suspect, by Harold Ditmanson. The first move seemed to be from theology to religious community as the key source of identity. This move was supported by the reflections of Constance Gengenbach. In it, identity was closely connected to religious practice, so the worshiping community took on a central role. Intellectually, the Christ-culture model shifted from Christ-above-culture to Christ-and-culture-in-paradox. Ditmanson embodied this more dialogical, dialectical, and unresolved approach. All human disciplines—including theology—were on a journey toward a Truth which would unify all knowledge. But none had a corner on that truth. Rather, a Christian college provided the context for an ongoing conversation between the Christian worldview and all secular learning. Critical reason was crucial in this approach because neither could trump the other's claims to truth. It had to be argued out. Likewise, the meaning of the college's calling was something to be discussed continuously. Both Ditmanson and Gengenbach identified such ongoing discussion as an important clue to the college's health as a college of the church.

This newer model, though, assumes a faculty and a student body who are willing to give the Christian vision a privileged role in the ongoing conversation. It also assumes that most faculty are interested enough in such a conversation to carry it on, not just to tolerate it.

By and large, it seems to me, St. Olaf has held to this model fairly well. The conversation about the relation of faith and learning continues. This volume itself indicates that the relation of faith and learning is the object of continued, public discussion. The new capstone course in ethics entails an honored role for Christian ethics. Faculty who teach the course must be willing to learn a good dash of Christian ethics. Faith seems to be an indispensable conversation partner.

The Challenge Ahead

Yet, not all bodes well for the future. There are enormous pressures toward secularization that affect all church-related colleges. The so-called Enlightenment paradigm continues to marginalize the Christian vision in the vast majority of church-related colleges, even in many Lutheran colleges. The emerging postmodernism, while it may open doors in secular universities, doesn't offer much to church-related colleges, where the Christian tradition is often held in suspicion for its "hegemonic," "totalizing," and "intolerant" tendencies. Colleges are increasingly broken into departments that prize disciplinary excellence above all. Most liberal arts colleges will be struggling for their existence and may well decide they can't afford to push their religious identities on the hesitant consumer.

Indeed, at least two of the essayists end with a decidedly mixed message about the future of St. Olaf as a church college. Jodock worries about the "homogenization" and "culture of disbelief" which infect our modern world, including St. Olaf. He argues that "the tradition needs to be articulated more clearly and affirmed more intentionally" so that its "core identity can be reclaimed."

Nichols, who is the only writer currently teaching at St. Olaf to offer a systematic interpretation and critique of the college's recent history, ends his essay on a pensive note. He sees the college "moving away from some of its traditional moorings and practices." He sees a discouraging stalemate in many of the college's serious endeavors to find its way into the future.

Could it be that the "Christ-and-culture-in-paradox" theological model is giving way to one in which Christ is just one voice among many, with few privileges whatever? In this situation, which is typical of many church-related colleges, we have a cacophony of voices with little consensus on substantive issues. The best that can be given the Christian perspective is a voice in an ongoing process; the worst is that it becomes an ornament tacked onto the real stuff. But even under the best construal of this model, the dominant ethos is evacuated of public religious meanings and practices. The Christian vision is tolerated in its place; it might even be the object of "religious studies."

In contrast, a genuine "paradox" model is a difficult one to sustain because it counts on the willingness of a critical mass of the college's faculty and students to engage in a continuing quest for truth and beauty in which the conversation with the Christian vision is absolutely crucial. The conversation cannot simply be tolerated by the many for the few who like that sort of thing. It has to be one of burning significance, of "ultimate concern," for a large portion of the college population.

Such a conversation does not insist that all participants be Lutherans, or even Christians. But it does require faculty and students who respect the Christian tradition enough to usher it to the center of the conversation. It also requires a significant number of key persons who are Lutheran—maybe even a number who are of Norwegian extraction—and who are unabashedly willing to be public bearers of the tradition.

Are there enough such persons available to sustain the spirit of St. Olaf? Certainly there are. But the college must be willing to select the kind of faculty and students who fit the bill. It must place persons with this sort of vision into the leadership roles where the selection process takes place, not only for faculty and students, but for administrators and staff. Only then can the delicate flower of Lutheran higher education bloom for another 125 years at St. Olaf. Only then can the magnificent tradition described in this volume move robustly into the future.

29. A CATHOLIC COMMENTARY

David J. O'Brien

Not very long ago comments by a Catholic college professor on essays about Lutheran St. Olaf College, directed at that college' s campus "family," would have been an exercise, probably painful, in subcultural communication. Indeed, the effort at conversation would have involved multiple subcultures. St. Olaf was Midwestern and Norwegian as well as Lutheran. My college, Holy Cross, was Eastern and Irish as well as Catholic, and so was, so am, I. Lutheran colleges related to multiple Lutheran synods, Catholic colleges to multiple religious orders, in both cases engaging quite diverse understandings of knowledge and its responsibilities. Behind both sides was their church, and there the differences were enormous and memories were still charged with passion. We would probably have sought a basis for understanding in philosophy, but Catholicism' s exclusive reliance on scholasticism, "Catholic philosophy," would likely have limited the dialogue. So, after ritual bows to the wonders of American pluralism, we would likely have found ourselves awkwardly confronting differences so profound we would have yearned for the comfortable certitudes of our own campus families.

Yet, if such a dialogue had taken place in the 1920s or the 1950s, we might have found common ground in our shared Americanness. Rooted in immigrant communities, sustained by very different theological and pastoral traditions, we dealt with the common experience of the world wars and with very similar aspirations, our own and those of our students. Most of us probably shared Ole Edvart Rølvaag's worries about the loss of identity in the rush from the edges to the centers of American life, but we knew better than to stand in its way. In fact, more often than not, we shared those aspirations. My own Holy Cross clung tightly to an exclusive mission of undergraduate liberal arts education, but almost all her sister colleges changed their curriculum to meet the needs of ambitious immigrant constituencies, and thus to "serve the church." Like St. Olaf they happily added education, business, and nursing, some added medicine and law, all with hardly a second thought. Change, dramatic enough to signal the end of those multiple subcultures, came as much from inside, our own drive to share in American life, as from external pressure suggested by so many passive voice accounts of "Americanization" or, more loaded, "secularization."

The point is important, I think. Responsible men and women like ourselves, parents and students, faculty and staff, college presidents and pastoral leaders, made Americanist choices. Those choices are clear in the stories told in this book. Let me try to build the ground for a conversation by sharing the Catholic story.

After World War II, Catholic colleges and universities grew dramatically under the impact of America's voucher plan for higher education, the G. I. Bill of Rights.[1] Growth took place in the context of upward and inward mobility, working-class Catholics at the bottom moving up, immigrant Catholics on the outside moving in. Between 1967 and 1972 that process reached its climax as most Catholic colleges and universities transferred responsibility and ownership from religious orders of men and women to independent boards of trustees. This revolution of separate incorporation meant that the religious orders of men and women whose members had built the colleges now entrusted them to lay partners. They gave the charter and the property to these new, lay-dominated boards of trustees, sharing with them responsibility for the institution's academic mission. This broke the legal connection between the church and its colleges and universities. From now on, Catholic identity, for the institutions as for their graduates, would be voluntary and intentional, not subcultural.[2]

The 1967 Land o' Lakes manifesto of a group of Catholic academic leaders clarified the deliberate choice. "Institutional autonomy and academic freedom are essential conditions of the life and growth and indeed of survival for Catholic universities," the statement claimed. At the same time they promised that each college and university would remain "a community of scholars in which Catholicism is perceptibly present and effectively operative."[3] On that basis two long struggles began, one to defend institutional autonomy, the other to ensure Catholic mission and identity.

As for institutional autonomy, the Vatican never fully accepted separate incorporation. From the start there was a seemingly irreconcilable conflict. Academics claimed that in order to be authentic universities, they must enjoy institutional autonomy and academic freedom. Roman authorities argued that an institution could not be Catholic unless it was in some way accountable to the church's hierarchy. The dialogue on this question was complicated by a similar controversy surrounding Catholic theology. The difference has been regularly argued, most recently in relation to the implementation of the Apostolic Constitution Ex Corde Ecclesiae. At times the debate can become very heated, but so far the American bishops and academic leaders have found resolution in dialogue, mutual trust, and shared responsibility, dodging the juridical questions which so worry the Vatican. Rome still has trouble accepting this arrangement.

Equally important, a growing number of Catholic intellectuals have raised questions about the Americanizing process of change surrounding separate incorporation. They worry that Catholic colleges and universities have undergone a process of secularization comparable to that of Protestant colleges and universities at the turn of the century. Their argument is supported by reference to George Marsden' s detailed history of the Protestant experience, *The Soul of the American University*.[4] Historian Philip Gleason lends powerful support to this case in his history of Catholic higher education, *Contending with Modernity*.[5] As the title suggests, Gleason believes Catholic higher education long found its meaning in resisting the process of modernization, and Americanization, such as Marsden describes. Now, in his view, Catholic higher education has lost its way because it surrendered to modernity in the choices made to pursue academic excellence through separate incorporation, academic freedom, and academic self-governance. In short, the critics argue that academic leaders broke their promise that Catholicism would remain "perceptibly present and effectively operative."

Thus the second debate about Catholic mission and identity. There can be no question that many academic leaders took their institutions' Catholicism for granted. As Darrell Jodock says of St. Olaf, they relied on the church and the ethnic community to socialize students and faculty and only found out later that "the tradition must be articulated more clearly and affirmed more intentionally."

Of course Catholic academic leaders knew from the start that they would have to take steps to ensure Catholic identity. They did so in four ways:

1. By regular, public, official affirmations of their Catholic commitments: they said they were Catholic, and they said so often.
2. By the continuing presence of the sponsoring religious community, whose members still provided presidents, administrators, faculty, and staff; no one expected the dramatic decline in numbers which has so reduced their influence.

3. By strong support for campus ministry, whose leaders sustained an active worshiping community, organized service to and with the church, provided constant pastoral care, and exerted great influence on campus culture.
4. Most important, by supporting strong departments of theology and religious studies. In Marsden's account of the Protestant experience, academic study of religion moved off the campus and into the seminary. Catholics made the opposite move—separate incorporation accompanied by a move of theology from the seminary, where it had been taught exclusively by and to priests, onto the campus, where it was taught for the first time to laypeople and undergraduate students. For that generation of Catholic academic leaders, theology, in dialogue with the other disciplines, would be the primary means by which Catholicism would be "perceptibly present and effectively operative."

Vatican pressure and increasing skepticism among intellectuals have sparked in recent years a revived interest in the academic questions surrounding Catholic identity. There is renewed interest in collaboration with the local church, many initiatives to share the traditions of sponsoring religious communities with lay, and non-Catholic, faculty and staff, and curricular initiatives designed to challenge the separatist impulses of departments and professional schools. Perhaps most interesting is the development of interest in Catholic studies, interdisciplinary centers and programs designed to focus responsibility for Catholic intellectual life and share with theology the academic responsibilities of the Catholic mission of individual institutions.

Thus most Catholic colleges and universities face questions similar to those posed at St. Olaf.

1. Implementing the continuing institutional commitment to the faith tradition and to serving the church
2. Maintaining institutional integrity in the context of an altogether proper pursuit of academic excellence
3. Supporting the academic study of Christianity in general and Lutheranism/Catholicism in particular in ways appropriate to the mission of the institution
4. Dealing with questions of hiring, faculty development, and curriculum which arise from these commitments, recognizing that the faculty have primary responsibility for shaping policy on these matters.

In Lutheran and Catholic colleges alike the focus of attention of academics is less the institutional relationships which still besiege administrators and trustees and more on the intersection of faith and the research and teaching which constitute their work, possibly their vocation. Fortunately, there is a revival of interest in these matters among academics, and increasing resources to support Christian intellectual life.

What can a Catholic, preoccupied with this complex set of common problems, say to Lutherans? Let me offer three suggestions for a conversation.

First, both sets of institutions must find ways to serve the church. A generation of ecumenical dialogue has made clear that serious Lutherans and Catholics share a strong doctrine of the church. Neither can settle for the religious individualism so characteristic of American religious culture, and of so many of our own Americanized students. On the one hand, our newly found cultural embeddedness draws us to pastoral strategies which emphasize personal commitment, interior faith, and respect for the religious journey of others. On the other hand, our ecclesial commitments require us to work at drawing our people to worship, to sacraments, to commitment to an authentic community of faith, the body of Christ. Neither pastors nor professors can do this alone. Catholic bishops and presidents worked their way through the last round of debate with the help of the concept of "communio," the church as communion whose members share responsibility for its life and work. Some among us believe that our commitment to church draws us in a confessional direction: we should reestablish our distinctive identity by redrawing the clear boundaries between ourselves and others. And some of our institutions, responding to the specific responsibilities arising from their particular histories, may have to settle for the "mere sponsorship" which so disturbs denominational critics. But most of us share St. Olaf's quest for a third way, rooted in our histories, and in our best aspirations. I suspect we could help one another specify that way in curriculum and faculty development.

Second, Catholics and Lutherans badly need some new ideas about how to bring faith to bear on the public square. A recent report of the Task Force of the American bishops, chaired by the retired Archbishop of St. Paul, noted the failure of Catholic education at every level to incorporate the rich resources of Catholic social teaching. For reasons I cannot fully develop here, I think the concept of vocation, so richly expressed in the essays in this book, may hold one of the keys to a renewal of civic responsibility among Christians. The words of students and faculty from St. Olaf echo those of many of my own students.

A pastoral strategy emphasizing lay vocation was widely discussed among Catholics before and during the Second Vatican Council but somehow was blurred in the postconciliar church. I have attributed this to a combination of restorationist resurgence within the church and evangelical impulses arising from our postimmigrant, middle-class culture. For the former, vocation becomes once more formal service to the church's internal life. For the latter, service to the larger community is overwhelmed by countercultural piety grounded in cultural alienation. Our common desire to find a third way between sectarianism and cultural surrender requires us to resist the segmentation inherent in these impulses, and to explore affirmative ways of renewing ideas of stewardship, the common good and vocation. Here is another area where we might work well together.

Finally, I personally resonate to many of the themes surfaced by Professor Jim Farrell. I hope another common-ground project might be to explore the theological and political meanings of our Americanization. Who, now, are my people? Were the Americanizing choices of those who went before us forms of religious self-destruction? Were they choices for material gain, social acceptance, and self-satisfaction? Or were they about freedom, economic sufficiency, social respect, and shared public responsibility? Did those choices constitute a kind of messy experience of liberation, about which we might theologize? Does the liberation God intends require people to remain peasants, or migrating unskilled workers, or workers in the arts and crafts? Does liberation forbid material advancement, higher education, political participation (except when we are in charge), and the many forms of pluralism it seems are required by human freedom?

Your St. Olaf essays make clear that these are family journeys of which we speak. Judgments about those journeys are involved in most of our discourse about our churches and our colleges. Let's bring those judgments out on the table and ask what we are to make of this historical experience of our American people. In fact, that might be the very best place for us to begin, rather than in our own churches. If a conversation gets started, I hope you will invite this Irish, Catholic, New England American to join you.

NOTES

1. I try to tell this story in *From the Heart of the American Church: Catholic Higher Education and American Culture* (Maryknoll, N.Y.: Orbis Books, 1994).

2. Alice Gallin, O.S.U., *Independence and a New Partnership in Catholic Higher Education* (South Bend, Ind.: University of Notre Dame, 1996).

3. Gallin, ed., *American Catholic Higher Education: Essential Documents 1967–1990* (South Bend, Ind.: University of Notre Dame, 1992) 7.

4. George Marsden, *The Soul of the American University from Protestant Establishment to Established Nonbelief* (New York: Oxford, 1994).

5. Philip Gleason, *Contending with Modernity* (Baltimore: Johns Hopkins, 1996).

30. KEEPING THE FAITH: INTEGRITY WITH YOUR HERITAGE

Keith Graber Miller
and Shirley Hershey Showalter

> I had been my whole life a bell and never knew it until at that moment I was lifted and struck.
>
> Annie Dillard, *Pilgrim at Tinker Creek*

"In their ventures into higher education in America," writes retired Lutheran pastor and educator Richard W. Solberg, "Lutherans have never lacked a theological base for full participation in the intellectual or scientific marketplace."[1] Solberg's remarks, from Richard T. Hughes and William B. Adrian's *Models for Christian Higher Education: Strategies for Success in the Twenty-First Century*, are aptly illustrated in the collection of essays in this volume. By design, St. Olaf's and *Called to Serve*'s vision is grounded in the college's religious and ethnic heritage, historically carried forth by faithful administrators and professors from multiple disciplines, and today lived by teachers and alumni on campus and across the globe.[2] Already longtime St. Olaf admirers-from-a-distance, we were moved by the voices represented here, and struck by both commonalities and differences arising from a common goal but different traditions.

As Mennonite college educators whose tradition is only now beginning to articulate an educational philosophy, we confess to feeling a smidgen of theological envy when we read Solberg's words, and when we encounter volumes such as this. Mennonites were latecomers to the higher education ball, Cinderellas who founded our colleges in the later-nineteenth and early-twentieth centuries, long after most others had begun the dance. While many sixteenth-century Anabaptists were highly educated, they and others in the fledgling movement were martyred by the thousands in the early years of sorting out how radically the church needed to be reformed. The loss of such leaders, and the fact that the primary antagonism toward Anabaptists came not from common folk but from other theologians and philosophers, contributed toward a relatively anti-intellectual stream in our tradition's middle centuries, a stream which still flows through some Mennonite communities today. However, it is possible to build a strong academic tradition out of these materials. To the extent that we can demonstrate wisdom rather than "mere learning," we can draw from and call forth support from the church. We also can challenge the church when the difficult issues of our time require deeper thought and more intense dialogue than perhaps the church alone would give them.

Goshen College, the Mennonite liberal arts college where we are professor and president, was founded as Elkhart Institute in 1894, nearly two decades after Pastor Bernt Julius Muus organized St. Olaf's School. While you and other Protestant and Catholic colleges were doing the higher education minuet, we were out hoeing. When you moved into breakdancing and moshing, we were still folk-dancing. And when we waltzed, undoubtedly clumsily, into the higher education ball, we did so without fully securing our theological or philosophical dancing shoes.

As Theron Schlabach indicates in the *Models for Christian Higher Education* text, "Goshen's place in higher education rests more on what it and its people have *done* than on *words* or *theory*. . . . Mennonites tend to search for truth far less in words or abstract systems than in practice."[3] Speaking to a group of Lutheran educators, Richard T. Hughes said, "It is true that Mennonites do not begin the task of higher education with an elaborate set of theoretical understandings. . . . They begin their task by seeking to implement a vision for radical discipleship that takes its cue from the teachings of Jesus." In light of our tradition's action-reflection orientation, with practice rather than theory serving as the starting point, many of our comments here will be oriented toward practical application of St. Olaf's vision, calling you to be faithful to your vocation.

As we read these essays, we were struck by the overlap between our callings as liberal arts institutions, and by the multiple parallels in our histories and contemporary experiences. Both of our institutions were founded in the last thirty years of the nineteenth century, and although both were designed to serve their respective churches, neither college's mission was primarily to train pastors and church teachers. In its early decades, each institution experienced disenfranchisement from the church, in part at least because of suspicions of progressivism, as perceived by constituents or other denominational institutions. Your links with the United Norwegian Lutheran Church were severed in 1893 in the midst of mergers and tensions with one of your sister colleges. The Mennonite church shut down our college for one full year in 1923, fearing that students and faculty were becoming too liberal. Our first president, Noah E. Byers, had said he wanted early twentieth-century Mennonites to avoid the "intellectual starvation" that comes from rethinking the same thoughts, and he challenged them to open themselves so they could experience "even more the richness and beauty of a large life." Byers knew from his own experience in a university college of arts and sciences that "higher education, if approached from the liberal arts tradition, was understood to be a quest: revelatory, transforming, beneficial."[4] Such a vision, of course, is not always a safe one. After the one-year shutdown, the college reopened the following fall with a slimmed-down student body, a new set of administrators (the incoming president had no college degree when he took the helm in 1924), and a significantly altered faculty. Throughout our history, we've lived with a zesty, dynamic, often energizing tension with our founding denomination, a reality which has kept us deeply rooted in our tradition even while we draw supplemental light from other faiths and the secular academy.

If the articles by Walter Sundberg, Darrell Jodock, and Michael Aune are representative, Goshen College and St. Olaf also share much of the same language in describing our history and mission. Clearly some of the historic distinctions between our traditions—for example, our differing perspectives of two-kingdom theology, and our complementary but contrasting emphases on grace or discipleship—are evidenced in this volume as well as in texts of our past. Although the term *justice* belongs to your tradition more than to ours, we resonate with Darrell Jodock's conviction that one of the purposes of Christian higher education is to enable students "to discern what makes for justice and what preserves and enhances human dignity." And our voices sing in harmony about our primary calling to love and serve the neighbor, and the essence of Christianity having to do with relationships. We speak in unison about our desire to counter the prevailing ethos of American individualism, educating our students to be "increasingly out of step with the attitudes and self-understanding commonly found in our society."[5] We both call our students to transformation, as Jodock writes:

> . . . indeed, a transformation disquieting enough to be daunting for many students. Such an education endeavors to wean them (and their teachers!) from their comfortable, uncritical allegiance to societal assumptions and to entice them into both an intense curiosity regarding the worlds beyond their own experience and an intense desire to make their corner of the globe a better place in which to live.[6]

Amen, Brother Jodock! Preach it! Jodock's words are consistent with St. Olaf's 1954–1956 self-study, which suggests as a model for integration of academic excellence and a Christian outlook a stance of "critical participation"—neither rejection of secular learning nor accommodation to the world.[7]

At St. Olaf and at Goshen College we each speak of incarnation, and community, and the truth emerging "amid the engaged deliberations of people." We call our students to lives of service. We provide opportunities for international education—you through your Global Semester, Term in the Middle East, or Term in Asia, and we through our Study-Service Term in various third world countries in Latin America, Africa, Eastern Europe, and Asia. Such international education is an essential component for thriving in an increasingly interdependent world, for learning what makes for peace, and for appreciating our near and farther away neighbors. The language of "academic excellence" peppers our public and in-house documents, expressing both a yearning and a reality that is increasingly recognized by others. We appear together in honorable lists such as *Peterson's Competitive Colleges*, *Barron's Best Buys*, and *U.S. News and World Report*. We each produce high numbers of doctoral recipients per capita, as reported in the survey Franklin and Marshall College does of 518 liberal arts colleges in the United States. Together we are recognized in books such as Richard Hughes and William Adrian's *Models for Christian Higher Education* and Ann Kelleher's *Learning from Success: Case Studies in International Program Development*. Both colleges have sought to remain faithful to their religious traditions while engaging students in the best liberal arts education possible to prepare them for service in the church and world. And both of us, during the last several years, have been stepping back to examine how this can most effectively be done as we enter the twenty-first century.

So how can church colleges best serve students in the present world, and how in particular can St. Olaf, with its rich embeddedness in the Lutheran tradition, be faithful to its vocation? It is essential to ask such questions as we face a new century and the realities of postmodernity, a world dramatically different from the one our students came from and reentered more than a century ago. Students today, with far fewer roots than their ancestors, are keenly aware of the fragmentation of the multiple, overlapping, sometimes barely cohesive communities from which they've come. They experience, more sharply than most of us did at their age, competing claims for truth, and the potential stress of being less sure of any credible foundations. They have known more brokenness than many of their predecessors have—perhaps the pain of their parents' divorces, or their own; violence and warfare around the globe brought to them instantly via mass media and the Internet; shattered faith in churchly and political leaders who have betrayed the trust of their people.

Our students also are more diverse than they once were—they are far more than Norwegian (in your case) and Swiss-German (in ours). Many are coming back to school in midlife, after raising children or making a career change. Scores from outside of the United States come to learn alongside students raised in North America. Many are from other denominational or faith traditions, with little or no knowledge of their own religious traditions or those which birthed our institutions. Goshen's student body is 63 percent Mennonite, higher than most church-related institutions, including St. Olaf's. Yet we still consider our student body to be much more diverse than it was twenty years ago. All of these realities offer remarkable challenges and opportunities, re-etching or more deeply etching the nature of our institutional vocations.

Several years ago, at a conference on Mennonite higher education at Goshen's sister college in Bluffton, Ohio, Doug Reichenbach, the father of a Mennonite high school student, articulated his image of what he expected a church college to be for his son someday.

"One thing I expect," Reichenbach said, "is inspiration. I expect that if my son goes to a Mennonite school he will be able to breathe in, take a deep breath of, the Holy Spirit; to breathe in a sense of acceptance, to breathe in a sense of the church and the faith. To take a deep breath and feel that he is loved and cared for."

"The second thing I would expect," said the father, "is an opportunity for him to express his imagination." He noted that different language has been used to express such creativity, including the oft-cited (within Anabaptist-Mennonite traditions) "Do not be conformed, but be transformed by the renewing of our minds." "But it is more than thinking," said the father. "I would like my son to find a place at a Mennonite school where his images could be released. Whatever those images are—verbal, artistic, or some other kind of creativity. Someplace where his imagination can let go."

"The third thing I expect," said Reichenbach, "is that he will experience some interrelationship like he has not experienced before. I expect the church school to provide opportunities for community for him. To share himself, to be in a personal relationship with faculty. To be in a relationship with friends, persons from other cultures, and all kinds of interrelationships."

"Fourth," he said, "I expect him to experience identification on two fronts. I know our son needs to leave our household to find himself. I know he has to separate himself from his parental home. I know he needs to find his identity. But more than that I know my son, who has just recently made a commitment to Jesus, needs to understand about whose he is, the Lord to whom he belongs. I expect him to experience that kind of identity but also identification with Christ and Christ's church, particularly the Anabaptist-Mennonite expression of the church."[8]

In a book of this sort, such words likely will make many readers squirm, even if we were to substitute "Lutheran" for each Mennonite reference. Implicit in Reichenbach's image of a Mennonite college is much of our tradition's rich heritage of full-bodied, earnest discipleship; voluntarism; a biblicism which acknowledges the lordship of Christ; pacifism; an ecclesiology of a mutually accountable and covenanted body of believers; a willingness to be countercultural; a wisdom born out of experience and commitment; and a call to peace and multiculturalism. Education modeled after such a charge is, or would be, education toward life-giving transformation—transformation of self, community, and society. Such an educational vision rejects the Enlightenment notion of dismembered individuals, unencumbered selves abstracted from particular formative narratives, commitments, relationships, and communities.

We are not ashamed to seek out, and to serve well, the brightest and best young people emerging from our Mennonite congregations. At the same time, we pray that for all of our students—Mennonites, Lutherans, Presbyterians, Catholics, Baptists, Methodists, "reluctant Christians," Hindus, Buddhists, Muslims, atheists, and others—Goshen's community of faith and learning will develop, as our mission statement and desired outcomes declare: faith that is active and reflective; intercultural openness; the ability to communicate effectively and think actively and strategically; an understanding of the transcendent reality of aesthetic and spiritual experience; personal integrity that fosters the ability to resolve conflict and promote justice; leadership abilities that empower self and others; an understanding of responsible stewardship; a sense of vocational direction; and a healthy understanding of self and others that is reflected in social relationships of interdependence and mutual accountability.

We believe colleges today can best serve their diverse student bodies not by discounting or abandoning their religious traditions, but by remaining embedded in them and drawing on their rich heritages of faithfully seeking after the truth, wherever that truth may take them. We believe that, among the other broader and more inclusive strands of St. Olaf's contemporary vocation, the calling remains to educate well, and shamelessly, Lutheran young people. When done with integrity, with an authentic openness to the insights and critiques of the multiple other religious and nonreligious traditions on campus, all students—and the truth—will be well served. St. Olaf ought not seek to be a generic Christian college, nor simply a liberal arts college with "value-added" benefits, but an unmistakably Lutheran college, proud of its heritage's commitments to education and to bridging the gap between church and world. Lars Wilhelm Boe said in a 1939 chapel talk at St. Olaf, "We are frankly a Lutheran college. We have, thank God, many who do not belong to the Lutheran Church. If you want to come to St. Olaf, take St. Olaf as it is."[9] We doubt whether many administrators or faculty would make that statement so boldly today, but we hope that the institution and its members do say unabashedly, "We are a Lutheran college," and that they understand what those words mean. To be authentic, whatever alterations are made to St. Olaf's future vocation should be born out of the college's heritage.

Allow us to give an extended example of how such a commitment has enriched the educational experience at Goshen College. We note it here because each of us has nationally recognized international education programs, and for both of our institutions the programs emerged from our larger vocations.

Our sixteenth-century Anabaptist-Mennonite forebears, fallible as are their descendants, sought to be faithful to God's call to represent—to re-present, as Rod Sawatsky says in his essay in the *Models for Christian Higher Education* book—the Word in the midst of the world. "From the Anabaptist perspective," writes Sawatsky, "Jesus as the Word made flesh reveals God's will for His disciples, His church . . . so, too, the Mennonite college is to be incarnational."[10] For Mennonites, and for students at Mennonite colleges, such incarnation often is expressed in sweaty, tactile, embodied discipleship, often translated into service and peacemaking. Such service can be broadly defined, though, allowing most vocations (though not quite as many as the Lutheran tradition allows) to be understood as or transformed into loci for Christian service.

Writing in another context, Richard Hughes notes that the Mennonite understandings of discipleship and community are what sustains the life of the mind in Mennonite contexts. "After all," writes Hughes, "if one builds community around a commitment of service to others, one inevitably respects the other and the other's point of view. . . . Clearly, the Mennonite commitment to service-oriented community enhances the life of the mind insofar as it enhances serious conversation with a variety of cultures and with perspectives different from their own."[11]

At Goshen, as at St. Olaf and most other liberal arts colleges today, service opportunities—and options for other experiential and cross-cultural education—abound. On our campus several hundred students voluntarily participate in local community service each year—with Habitat for Humanity; with La Casa, which provides assistance to new immigrant families and others; with The Window, an interchurch agency which provides food for those needing it; with Big Brothers/Big Sisters; and with other community and church organizations. Each year four students live with two developmentally disabled young adults in a college-owned house, in an effort to integrate young people with disabilities into a more mainstream living arrangement. Every summer about a dozen students participate in our Ministry Inquiry Program, which places them in congregations across the country as ministerial interns, and scores of others participate in required practicums, internships, and other experiential learning. Such opportunities are essential for the formation of servant-leaders, graduates who understand that life is about more than their own financial independence or corporate success.

Where service, experiential learning, and cross-cultural education are most clearly institutionalized on our campus, however, is in our Study-Service Term (SST), now more than three decades old. All Goshen students are required to complete a Study-Service Term or comparable international education requirement. While small in numbers (just over three hundred thousand in the United States and slightly more than a million worldwide) and, until relatively recently, limited primarily to European ethnic ancestry, Mennonites and their educational institutions and mission organizations have developed a remarkably international perspective. Such internationalism can be traced, in part, to persecution which frequently forced Mennonites to move from their homelands into strange territories—to the American colonies, Russia, Paraguay, Canada, and elsewhere. It also is rooted in the denomination's pacifism. Because members of the church usually seek conscientious-objector status in times of warfare, they've sometimes been referred to as "anti-American." Mennonite ethicist John Richard Burkholder says this response could better be described as "more-than-Americanism." "Pacifists," writes Burkholder, "consciously adopt a more global worldview than most Americans. They wear tribal identifications lightly and see themselves as global citizens."[12] Transnationalism is, of course, not the exclusive claim of pacifists. At St. Olaf, faculty and students see themselves "as world citizens as well as part of a specific cultural heritage."[13]

SST emerged rather naturally when administrators realized in the early 1960s that more than half of the college's faculty members had taught or worked abroad for a year or more, and about the same number spoke fluently more than one language. Because of their status as conscientious objectors during World War II, many future GC faculty members or their spouses were required to do Civilian Public Service as an alternative to military service. Although generally CPS assignments were restricted to stateside locations, following the war many Mennonites volunteered to resettle refugees and rebuild Europe and parts of Asia. Prompted by a visit by a 1965 accrediting team from the North Central Association of Schools and Colleges, who noted Goshen's "unusual resource," faculty and administrators spawned the SST program in 1968.

As one early summary of SST stated, to be effective, the study-abroad term must allow students to have vivid, firsthand experiences so they can "punch through what has become for many the confusion, impersonality, and vacuity of life in sterile, suburban America."[14] Such an intention—and the desire to place students where the majority are in the minority racially, economically, socially, linguistically, and religiously—necessitates that SST programs be located in third world countries, or places which have been on the receiving end of colonialism. Throughout each academic year Goshen students are in such settings as the Dominican Republic, Costa Rica, Côte d'Ivoire, China, Indonesia, and the former East Germany. Our SST students live with and—to the extent possible—become a part of families. During their seven weeks in their capital city they read, engage, reflect, and journal on their experiences as well as participate in lectures by artists, intellectuals, educators, and theologians from their host country. For the second half of the semester-long program, they move out into the countryside alone or with one other student (again living with families) and participate in low-key service projects, working alongside their hosts, accompanying them as they harvest their crops or care for their ill, elderly, or orphans; teaching and learning; or staffing medical clinics. SSTers recognize that they cannot truly "help" their hosts in a brief, six-week period, and that their main calling is to help those in the villages believe in themselves and draw on their own faith and other resources, working together as communities to bring about change. They also are there to learn, and to take their new understanding of the world though relationships in foreign lands back to the United States, where they can help create better understanding and even, occasionally, better policy.

Wilbur Birky, director of the SST program since 1994, proposes that the Incarnation can enrich one's understanding of the SST vision:

> Let us propose the Incarnation as an act of divine imagination rooted in a profound realization that even God could not know and understand the human condition without entering into it, to experience it in the body. This was a true cross-cultural experience. So a description of at least the early

> parts of Jesus' incarnation applies aptly to the SST experience: it is to give up one's customary place of comfort, to become as a child, to learn a new language and eat in new ways, to be received into a new family, to work in the mundane "carpentry shop," to attend the local house of worship, to question and be questioned, to experience frustration and success, and to learn to serve in the very "thick" of life. This is service-learning in the context of crossing over into the life of "the other." If necessary for God, how much more so for us is this knowledge by experience for compassionate action.[15]

If we can continue to communicate its rootage in our faith commitments, international education programs such as Goshen's Study-Service Term—or St. Olaf's Global Semester or Term in the Middle East or Asia—can appropriately school our students in the virtues and perspectives of Mennonite (and broader Christian) worldviews while expediting their entry into a postmodern world with appreciation for multiculturalism, knowledge of diverse narratives, and commitment to dialogical humility.[16] In an increasingly culturally diverse and globally interdependent world, all of us need to strengthen our international education programs.

We would encourage St. Olaf to continue to allow these opportunities to be ones of cultural immersion, experiences which foster commitments to cross-cultural understanding and peacemaking. Church-related colleges should be leaders in this form of international education, in contrast to those educational institutions which offer overseas experiences solely to make students more marketable. If we are truly concerned with helping students "discern what makes for justice and what preserves and enhances human dignity," our international education programs ought to be distinctive from those of other schools, structurally and philosophically distinct from "academic tourism" to other first world countries. As Ole Edvart Rølvaag wrote a half century ago (as quoted in Michael Aune's chapter in this volume) about his teaching of Norwegian language and literature at St. Olaf:

> I might as well haul manure. If nothing else, it would at least stink. I can scarcely see any difference between St. Olaf College and any other Protestant American college. What then do I have to do here? If we have no special mission, why do we exist at all?[17]

Rølvaag's words contain much wisdom, and although we suspect St. Olaf's primary calling ought not be to pass on Norwegian heritage, the novelist's challenge is one church-related colleges still need to hear.

In addition, church-related colleges with strong international programs also need to work at multiculturalism on their home campuses in order to reinforce the learnings overseas. Attention must be paid to developing diverse student bodies, including international students; students from various Christian denominations as well as those from other religions and nonreligious backgrounds; students from multiple racial and ethnic heritages; and students from other underrepresented groups. Both St. Olaf and Goshen College work hard at such diversity already, though we could no doubt improve. Integrity with on-campus multiculturalism helps students better link the multicultural dimensions of their overseas experience with their college and its sponsoring denomination. Forums for cross-fertilization of ideas should be sponsored, and cross-cultural social relationships should be encouraged through the modeling of administrators and faculty as well as specific programming.

And just a word more yet about integrity. As Yale's Stephen Carter reminds us, "The word integrity comes from the same Latin root as integer, and historically has been understood to carry much the same sense, the sense of wholeness: a person of integrity, like a whole number, is a whole person, a person somehow undivided."[18] Parker Palmer has called educators to a deep sense of that good Lutheran term *vocation*, linking it to the need to live "divided no more." Integrity to our traditions must start with inner integrity. Palmer calls the integrated teacher the product of an "undivided self," which he defines as a state of being in which "every major thread of one's life experience is honored, creating a web of such coherence and strength that it can hold students and subjects as well as self."[19]

To the extent that we as teachers have been shaped by the faith and learning tradition of our institutions and by other professors and students deeply shaped by them, we bring a set of beliefs and experiences into our lives and into our work that are as vital to our growth as teachers and scholars as graduate education itself. If our institutions are to be "undivided," we shall have to learn how to stimulate conversations among all professors, including those who are not Lutheran and not Mennonite on our campuses, so that they can connect their prior experiences to the ones they now share with us. Palmer's advocacy of teaching from within and leading from within gives all religious traditions equal opportunities to discover the "hidden wholeness," a phrase Palmer borrows from Thomas Merton, and to use that vision of wholeness to extinguish fears. Every religious tradition produces its own set of fears. The role of education ought to be to confront those fears with love. Lutherans call it "grace." Mennonites call it "peace" or "discipleship." The larger name which connects us to each other and all of faith to all of learning is "love."

Though we too often fail, as teachers and administrators at a Mennonite institution, we seek to model and foster such integrity—a wholeness that is concerned not only with intellectual acuity but with honesty, consistency, character formation, spiritual growth, emotional stability, and interrelational sensitivity. At Goshen, "faculty" is a designation given not only to those of us who teach but to administrators and campus counselors and admissions personnel and student development team members and resident dorm directors, a recognition that teaching and learning happen across the campus, in both the visible and the invisible curriculum, the ethos of the place.

In a world peopled by radical individualists living fragmented lives, we—like you at St. Olaf—want our students to be whole, to recognize the interrelationship of their various dimensions, to make commitments and to acknowledge their dependence on their Creator, the earth, and their companions on the journey. One way this interdependence is best symbolized on our campus is in our frequent hymn-sings, consistently the best attended chapels of the year. A music ritual performed at times of crisis by the Mbuti, the pygmy hunter/gatherers of Zaire, is the molimo. In the molimo the singers employ a technique known to musicologists as hoquet, in which "the individual notes of any melodic line are ascribed to individual singers, so that no one singer carries the entire melody but each carries an essential part of it and all are therefore equally necessary."[20]

Our four-part singing in chapels, singing of hymns borrowed from many other denominations and cultures, embodies this reality: all parts are essential for the beauty of the hymn, and we carry each other into this self-transcending, communitarian moment. As Mary Oyer, Goshen College Professor of Music Emerita, has said, "We Mennonites sing our theology." The words are only part of the theology (we can borrow freely), but the sound we make together is an aural expression of a spiritual reality. The message is not lost on students. And so we sing.

You at St. Olaf sing also. In fact, our college radio station WGCS carries the weekly program of sacred music "Sing for Joy" produced on your campus. Music is another tradition that binds us together. As we celebrate the past 125 years with you, we leave you with the challenge we give ourselves—to find new ways to sing, to come to voice in the twenty-first century. We need to understand the metaphor of sound. According to Walter Ong, the noted Jesuit scholar and author of *Orality and Literacy*, hearing involves a knowledge of interiors: it is therefore a wonderful metaphor for integrity itself. Knowledge based upon hearing is wholistic—it involves intimacy, potency and subjectivity.[21] Ong makes the case for sound as the "process sense par excellence" because "sound better represents another world, of dynamism, action, and being in time (sound necessarily signals the present use of power as no other sensible phenomenon necessarily does although it exists only when it is going out of existence)."[22]

Our institutions have created great music, a tradition in which everyone partakes, not just music faculty and music majors. Let us invite those who enter our communities to study our traditions but not to rest on them. Let us invite them to tell us their stories and listen to ours, let us listen together for the music of the spheres, that original sound at creation, still audible in the highest and lowest ranges. Let us fashion new conversations and remember old ones. Let us listen to the wisdom of Lutheran pioneers and Mennonite martyrs and let us bring into our songs the wisdom of village elders from around the world. If education means to draw out, and what we draw out is a new sound remembered from the past, we will not stop with singing. We will dance.

We pray that St. Olaf, and Goshen College, and other church-related colleges and universities, can remain authentically rooted in our own traditions, and that we also can humbly learn from each other in such exchanges. We have learned much from reading about St. Olaf's heritage, the deep wells from which the institution draws. We pray that in the future we all may be faithful to our callings as administrators, teachers, and supporters of this holy, transformative practice of higher education.

NOTES

1. Richard W. Solberg, "What Can the Lutheran Tradition Contribute to Higher Education?" in Richard T. Hughes and William B. Adrian, eds., *Models for Christian Higher Education: Strategies for Success in the Twenty-First Century* (Grand Rapids, Mich.: Eerdmans, 1997) 78. Solberg taught at St. Olaf College as well as several other Lutheran schools.

2. We are struck by the contrasts we note between the St. Olaf pictured in this volume and the school described in, e.g., James Tunstead Burtchaell's *The Dying of the Light: The Disengagement of Colleges and Universities from Their Christian Churches* (Grand Rapids, Mich.: Eerdmans, 1998). In his "St. Olaf College" section, Burtchaell has such subheadings as "The Blahs" and "A Faculty Indifferent."

3. Theron F. Schlabach, "Goshen College and Its Church Relations: History and Reflections," in Hughes and Adrian 217.

4. Susan Fisher Miller, *Culture for Service: A History of Goshen College, 1894–1994* (Goshen, Ind.: Goshen College, 1994) 35.

5. Darrell Jodock, "The Lutheran Tradition and the Liberal Arts College: How Are They Related?" 19.

6. Jodock 25.

7. St. Olaf College Self-Study Committee, *Integration in the Christian Liberal Arts College*, 2 vols. (Northfield, Minn.: St. Olaf College, 1956), as cited in Mark Granquist, "Religious Vision and Academic Quest at St. Olaf College," in Hughes and Adrian 89.

8. Panel, "The Expectations and Responsibilities of Conferences and Local Congregations vis-à-vis Mennonite Higher Education," in *Mennonite Higher Education: Experience and Vision: A Symposium on Mennonite Higher Education*, by Ken Hawkley (Bluffton College, 1992) 137.

9. Erik Hetle, *Lars Wilhelm Boe: A Biography* (Minneapolis: Augsburg, 1949) 101, as cited in Granquist 86.

10. Rodney J. Sawatsky, "What Can the Mennonite Tradition Contribute to Christian Higher Education?" in Hughes and Adrian 195. The incarnational motif also is important for valuing the material world: if God comes to us in the flesh, as the Christian tradition has affirmed, one must take seriously earthly matter. Such a perspective provides at least some theological warrant for earth-keeping as well as the arts.

11. Richard T. Hughes, "How the Lutheran Worldview Can Sustain the Life of the Mind," in *From Mission to Marketplace*, papers and proceedings of the 83rd annual meeting of the Lutheran Educational Conference of North America (Washington, D.C., 1997) 12.

12. John Richard Burkholder, "Pacifist Ethics and Pacifist Politics," in Michael Cromartie, ed., *Peace Betrayed? Essays on Pacifism and Politics* (Washington, D.C.: Ethics and Public Policy Center, 1990) 198.

13. Ann Kelleher, *Learning from Success: Case Studies in International Program Development* (New York: Peter Lang, 1996) 209.

14. "The Study-Service Trimester Abroad," March 1971: 10. Available in the Mennonite Historical Library, Goshen College.

15. Wilbur Birky, "SST: Vision, History and Ethos," 1997–1998 *SST Faculty Handbook*, Goshen College; emphasis in original.

16. For a fuller analysis of Goshen's SST program, see Keith Graber Miller, "A One-Armed Embrace of Postmodernity: International Education and Church-Related Colleges," in *Talking Out of Place: Professing in the Postmodern Academy*, ed. by Stephen R. Haynes and Corrie E. Norman (forthcoming, 2000).

17. Michael B. Aune, "'Both Sides of the Hyphen'? The Churchly and Ethnic Heritage of St. Olaf College" 38.

18. Stephen L. Carter, "Becoming People of Integrity," *Christian Century* (March 13, 1996): 297.

19. Parker J. Palmer, *The Courage to Teach: Exploring the Inner Landscape of a Teacher's Life* (San Francisco: Jossey-Bass Publishers, 1998) 15.

20. Colin Turnbull, "Liminality: A Synthesis of Subjective and Objective Experience," in Richard Schechner and Willa Appel, eds., *By Means of Performance* (New York: Cambridge University Press, 1990) 81. We are indebted to Tom F. Dri-

ver, *Liberating Rites: Understanding the Transformative Power of Ritual* (Boulder, Colo.: Westview Press, 1998) 152, for this reference.

21. We are indebted to Goshen Professor David Mosley for this summary of Ong's thought in response to Shirley Hershey Showalter's speech "Discovering an Anabaptist Voice: A Philosophy of Education," given April 18, 1998, at Goshen College.

22. Walter Ong, *Interfaces of the Word* (Ithaca, N.Y.: Cornell, 1977) 136.

31. THE FUTURE OF ST. OLAF: A VIEW FROM OUTSIDE

Nicholas P. Wolterstorff

How can a college with a history and background such as St. Olaf's best serve students in the present world? That is the question before us.

It's not collegiate education in general that is our topic. It's not even *church-related* collegiate education in general. It's the education offered by "a college with St. Olaf's history and background." That gives our question a great deal more specificity than it would otherwise have. What also gives it specificity is that St. Olaf occupies a position within the incredibly pluralistic and decentralized system of *American* collegiate education.

Nothing like the American system exists anywhere else in the world. In particular, the church-related college is virtually unknown elsewhere. A college or university is free, in the American system, to give itself whatever stamp it wishes, subject only to the relatively tolerant judgments of accrediting agencies and the relatively intolerant demands of market forces. Even the relatively tolerant judgments of accrediting agencies can be dismissed or rejected by colleges and universities if they wish to do so; there's no Minister of Education requiring accreditation on pain of license being withdrawn.

St. Olaf is a player in this pluralistic and decentralized American system. As such, the question of what distinctive features it should aim at is not only much more open-ended than it would be in any other national system of education; it's up to the governing officials of St. Olaf to make the decisions. Some parameters are given, however. St. Olaf is not going to repudiate its "history and background"; that comes through clearly in the earlier essays in this volume. Accordingly, the question is how, *given its history and background*, St. Olaf should face the future. It goes without saying that one can embrace one's history and background without being enslaved to it.

Before setting out I should perhaps make clear what sort of "outsider" I am. Over the years I have visited St. Olaf a good many times, and come to know a good many of its faculty, past and present. But I am not a graduate of St. Olaf, nor have I ever been on its faculty. Neither am I Lutheran. I locate myself in the Reformed/Presbyterian tradition of Christianity. But that tradition is close to the Lutheran. Together these two traditions constitute the so-called "magisterial Reformation" emerging from western Europe in the sixteenth century. Furthermore, I taught for many years at a college located in the Reformed/Presbyterian tradition, namely Calvin College. There I found myself reflecting on the same sorts of issues that confront St. Olaf as it seeks to find the position that fits it in that anarchic complex which is the American system of higher education. In short: an outsider who's about as close to being an insider as an outsider can be!

The Distinctive Project of the Christian College

Two things especially struck me in reading the essays in the first three parts of this volume. For one thing, the extraordinary loyalty of present and former faculty, and of former students, to St. Olaf—a loyalty grounded, as the writers make clear, in the fact that they experienced St. Olaf as doing something that they found, and continue to find, of great worth. What also comes through, however, is an anxiety. Most of the time the anxiety is just below the surface, or just barely above it. It protrudes above the surface most clearly in the essay by Professor Robert L. Nichols. "Today," says Nichols, "the college's older Norwegian Lutheran animating spirit seems largely eroded." Later, speaking more elaborately about the Lutheran rather than the Norwegian aspect of this animating spirit, he says that

> for a college of the church one might have expected a stronger assertion of the Christian faith that we are, in all our diverse parts, actors in the meaningful story of God's continuing efforts on behalf of our salvation, and that this assertion would provide a steady force for greater coherence and integration in the advancement of knowledge and in the teaching about it. The character of higher education at St. Olaf should differ from that of other liberal arts colleges because its educational mission is rooted in the conviction that the Triune God actively strives for the perfection of a fallen humanity: God's great never ending love story that unfolds in an intelligible and meaningful universe.

There's a wide-ranging discussion going on nowadays among church-related colleges concerning their mission and future. A great many important issues are being raised in these discussions: how should these colleges take account of the increasing globalization of our society and culture?

How should they take advantage of new educational technologies? How can they form authentic academic communities? How can they shape, and how should they shape, the "hidden curriculum"? Should they promote research? If they should, how can they do that without endangering their commitment to good teaching? How can they survive financially? All of them, important questions.

A college comes about when a faculty and a student body are assembled with the purpose of bringing those students into contact with that faculty so that that faculty can "educate" those students. From all the important issues that I cited, it's that goal of the collegiate enterprise—the faculty's (intentional) education of students—that I want to focus on in this essay. I realize that once the enterprise is under way, a great deal of *unintentional* education of students by faculty takes place, along with education of students by staff, of students by students, and even of faculty by students. I also realize that a great deal of education of students by "media" other than faculty and staff takes place—by books, for example. Each of these dimensions of collegiate education is worth reflecting on, as is the fact that American colleges have a good many goals ancillary to the central one mentioned—like fielding winning sports teams! But on this occasion, I want to talk only about the education of students by faculty. And I want to focus all my attention on the content of that education, neglecting the pedagogy.

I would say—now using some of the words of Robert Nichols—that one of the fundamental ways in which "the character of higher education at St. Olaf should differ from that of other liberal arts colleges" is in the content of the education offered by its faculty to its students. It should differ in a good many other ways as well; but definitely in this way. More specifically, I would say—again using words of Nichols—that the education offered should differ because St. Olaf's "educational mission is rooted in the conviction that the triune God actively strives for the perfection of a fallen humanity: God's great never-ending love story that unfolds in an intelligible and meaningful universe." I would say that this "difference" is the essence of what the present-day St. Olaf has been bequeathed by its (Norwegian) Lutheran history and background. And now, more specifically yet, I want to propose that the most appropriate expression of this "difference," when it comes to the content of the education of students by faculty, would be for St. Olaf to commit itself to the project of what I shall call "Christian learning." Obviously some explanation is called for, and some rationale.

But first, the following observation. I understand the proposal of Professor Darrell Jodock to be quite different from the one I have just made.

As I understand him, he does not locate the "difference" of the Lutheran college in the content of its instruction; it teaches what everybody else teaches. Neither does he locate the "difference" in the goals of the education and the virtues cultivated; plenty of other colleges strive for the goals and virtues he cites: academic excellence, freedom of inquiry, commitment to the ideal of the liberal arts, and so forth. He locates the "difference" in the *reasons* offered by the Lutheran college for its embrace of those shared goals and virtues. And the reasons he offers do indeed strike me as constituting a distinctively Lutheran "take" on the goals and virtues he defends. Accordingly, whether or not I agree with Professor Jodock that St. Olaf's "difference" is appropriately confined to having reasons of a Lutheran sort for doing what lots of other good liberal colleges do, what strikes me when reading his essay is that it is a specimen of *Christian learning*, as I understand it. Specifically, it's a specimen of *Lutheran* Christian learning. My question is whether such learning as he exhibits can long endure if no college anywhere commits itself to the project of Christian learning—not to mention, Christian learning in the Lutheran tradition. Or perhaps the issue isn't so much endurance as nurturance. Who knows under what conditions such learning can endure? The question is how can it be nurtured. It seems clear to me that, in our present American situation, the best way to nurture such learning is for colleges such as St. Olaf to commit themselves to engaging in the sort of learning exhibited in Professor Jodock's paper.

The Role of Faith in Learning: Augustine versus Locke

What do I mean by "Christian learning"? Perhaps a good place to begin is with the well-known Augustinian formula, *credo ut intelligam*—I believe in order to understand. We must hear Augustine as packing two distinct points together into this compact formula. The goal of believing is understanding; understanding is the telos of believing. But conversely, believing is *the condition* of understanding; if I wish to understand, then first I must believe. It was of course Christian faith that Augustine was thinking of: faith is both the condition and the goal of understanding.

What did Augustine have in mind? How was he thinking? Though Augustine's thought on the matter is not difficult, his presentation is extremely diffuse. So rather than expounding Augustine, let me turn to that most Augustinian of theologians, Anselm, and to that most Augustinian of Anselm's books, his famous *Proslogion*. Anselm opens his work with language that unmistakably echoes Augustine: "I have written the following treatise in the person of one who strives to lift his mind to the contemplation of God, and seeks to understand what he believes." What then follows is an extraordinarily plaintive passage in which Anselm, referring to himself but speaking in the name of humanity, over and over laments humanity's lack of understanding. We wander in a foreign country, exiled from our homeland, "from the joy of immortality into the bitterness and horror of death." What is the cause of this exile? Our sin, our wrongdoing, is the cause. We were created in the image of God so that we might be mindful of God, understand God, love God. But "the smoke of our wrongdoing" has so obscured and wasted away that image that "it cannot achieve that for which it was made" unless God renew it. To Anselm himself, God has been gracious and granted him that reorientation of self away from sin, and that renewal of the *imago Dei*, which comes with faith. Yet faith does not automatically yield the understanding for which Anselm longs. In Anselm's own words: "I long to understand in some degree thy truth, which my heart believes and loves. For I do not seek to understand that I may believe, but I believe in order to understand. For this also I believe—that unless I believed, I should not understand." Anselm then addresses God in prayer, pleading that God will give him the understanding for which he longs and which his faith has made possible.

The thought, to put it ever so generally, is this: one's understanding and lack of understanding are intertwined with one's convictions, one's commitments, one's affects, one's orientation. One's loves and hates, one's beliefs and disbeliefs, one's determinations and rejections contribute to shaping one's learning—contribute to enabling understanding.

Now, as contrast, let me describe that understanding of properly conducted learning which, until recently, has been dominant in the Western universities throughout the modern period. When we approach the university, we each bring with us our particularities: some of us are male, some female, some white, some African-American, some Native American, some Norwegian, some Canadian, etc. In the narthex of the university we are to strip off all such particularities, so that we can enter the halls of the academy as nothing more than generic human beings. Academic learning is to be a generically human enterprise. There is no place for Christian philosophy, feminist political theory, African-American sociology, Norwegian psychology; all such modes of learning are biased, prejudiced. There's place only for generically human philosophy, human political theory, human sociology, human psychology. The great proto-Enlightenment philosopher John Locke recognized that, by virtue of our tendency to believe what others tell us, we are all embedded within tradition. Such embeddedness obscures the facts from us. Tradition is bias, prejudice.

The metaphor I used, of stripping off our particularities in the narthex of the academy, isn't quite fair to Locke. Locke was not actually of the view that we can empty our heads of all that we have come to believe by way of induction into a tradition. One cannot get rid of one's Lutheran beliefs, one's Catholic attitudes, one's feminist sensibilities, just by *deciding* to get rid of them. Locke did think, however, that it's possible, when engaging in the academic disciplines, to place in cold storage all that one has come to believe from life outside the academy—not in any way to appeal to those beliefs, or allow them to influence one's results.

Think of it like this: what one believes, by virtue of induction into a tradition, is what might be called a "contingent particularity" of oneself: *particularity*, because not everybody believes what those in one's tradition believe, *contingent*, because one might not have been inducted into that tradition. The essence of Locke's proposal was that in our practice of the academic disciplines we are not to allow any of our contingent particularities to play a role; only what belongs to us qua human beings should be allowed to function. One's gender identity, one's national identity, one's racial identity: all are to be put in cold storage. To allow such identities to shape one's learning is to engage in *biased* learning. In the academy we are to practice unbiased, objective learning—that is, purely human learning.

The religious allegiances of human beings are obviously "contingent particularities"; not everybody is Lutheran, and those who are, might not have been. Our religions then are among those "contingent particularities" which are to be put in cold storage when we engage in learning. We don't actually shuck off our religion; we don't even pretend to do so. We just make no appeal to it, nor do we allow it to influence us in any way in our academic endeavors. The difference from the Augustinian vision is startling. Faith enables understanding, says Augustine; faith obstructs understanding, says Locke.

One of the most fascinating aspects of John Locke's great work, *Essay concerning Human Understanding*, is that, in its penultimate chapter, Locke himself delivered the death blow to this vision of academic learning as a generically human endeavor. A child reared in Catholicism, says Locke, will believe the doctrine of transubstantiation as firmly as anything. As a consequence, when that child apprehends some truth which contradicts the doctrine, the child won't come out believing that truth and disbelieving the doctrine; instead the child will continue to believe the doctrine and will disbelieve the truth which he has apprehended. He'll say to himself some such thing as, "It certainly *seems* true; but it can't be." (The example indicates that Locke regarded the Catholic doctrine of transubstantiation as false.) All of us can think of similar examples: if some trusted friend of mine in mathematics tells me that some mathematical proposition which I have always believed has just been proved false, I will no longer believe that proposition—even if it is true—but will say to myself, "It certainly *seems* true; but I guess it isn't."

Notice what is going on. Previously Locke held that, when entering the academy, we could put into cold storage whatever we had come to believe in our everyday lives, and employ only what we bring with us as human beings—our eyes, our ears, our "reason," our introspection, and so forth. Now he admits that this is much too simplistic a picture. The beliefs we already have function as part of our present belief-forming self. Our belief-forming selves are constantly being formed and re-formed. The belief-forming self that one is, at any time, is a blend of one's inherent human capacities plus what one already believes. If I believe that I'm looking at a cleverly painted stage set, then, even if I'm not, I won't come out believing that I'm seeing a chair but that I'm seeing a very cleverly painted image of a chair.

The conclusion to be drawn is that learning is unavoidably *perspectival* in character. We cannot toss off, in the narthex of the academy, our "contingent particularities" of tradition, religion, and so forth; neither can we put those particularities into cold storage, rendering them nonfunctional while we're working in the academy. They have become part of who we are, part of our identity, part of the belief-forming self which engages in the disciplines. We function *inside* the traditions into which we have been inducted—not alongside or outside.

Two ancillary observations are called for. The example Locke offered, as he understood it, and the examples I offered, were examples in which a belief one already has serves to *obstruct* the acquisition of a new correct belief. But it's definitely not the case that the beliefs one already has all function obstructively. Sometimes they function to *enable* us to get in touch with reality. That is the essence of much of the case for feminist learning; having the beliefs, affects, sensitivities, etc., typical of a woman *enables* one to see things that otherwise one would most likely not see. That is likewise the essence of the Augustinian vision: the particularity of Christian faith *enables* understanding.

The other ancillary point to be made is this: a good many people nowadays would agree with my point about the inevitable and proper role of our "contingent particularities" in the conduct of learning. They would agree that one's contingent particularities may enable as well as inhibit. But many, if not most, of those who would agree on this point would go on to affirm metaphysical antirealism. That is to say: they would insist that there's not a ready-made world waiting to be explored by us, but that it's only relative to a particular conceptual scheme that things are a certain way. Relative to your conceptual scheme, there are thirty-three kinds of snow, and this before us is one of them; relative to my conceptual scheme, there are only three kinds of snow, and this before us is one of those three. So who's to say who's right? What would it be, to be right? Why suppose that there is any such thing as being right? Reality is a social construction.

The issues are complicated, and here is definitely not the place to explore them. Let me simply say that I see no reason at all for not combining a *perspectivalist* understanding of academic learning with the ontological position of metaphysical *realism*. There is a ready-made world out there, created by God. But the hope of acquiring some generically human, completely objective, access to it, is a vain hope.

What Is Christian Learning?

I take it that to be a Christian is, for one thing, to acknowledge God as creator of the universe, as having dwelled among us in Jesus Christ, and as working within us in the person of the Spirit; and then to place one's faith in God as thus acknowledged. I take it that to be a Christian is, secondly, to participate in the life of the church and to make one's membership therein part of one's narrative identity—part of who one is. And I take it that to be a Christian is, thirdly, to accept the Christian Scriptures as canonical. Faith of a specific sort, interwoven with identification with a specific community, interwoven with acceptance of specific scriptures as canonical—I take those things to single out Christians from other human beings. These constitute the Christian "particularity." Additional things as well: Christians carry the mark of baptism. But at least those three things.

To engage in Christian learning, then, as I understand it, is to allow that faith, and that communal identification, and those Scriptures, to shape one's learning in whatever be the relevant and appropriate way. To allow them to shape one's judgments as to what is *legitimate* to investigate: for example, one's judgment as to whether it is legitimate to engage in research on aborted embryos. To allow them to shape one's judgments as to what is *important* to investigate: for example, one's judgment as to whether it is important to find out why the disparity between rich and poor in the United States has been increasing over recent decades. To allow them to shape one's convictions as to the conditions which a theory on a certain matter must satisfy if it is to be acceptable: for example, one's convictions as to whether a theory of jurisprudence is acceptable if it thinks entirely in terms of maximization of utility and not at all in terms of justice and rights. To allow them to shape how one treats one's fellow scholars: for example, one's willingness or unwillingness to speak abusively of women, or of men, of blacks, or of whites, of conservatives, or of liberals. To allow them to shape how one thinks about faith and church and Scripture themselves. And so forth, on and on. To allow the metaphors of the psalmist, St. Paul's fruits of the Spirit, the parables told by Jesus, the narrative of Christ's resurrection, the pathos for the social outsiders preached and exemplified by the prophets, the prayers of the Eucharist, the philosophy of Anselm and Aquinas, the theology of Bonaventure and Barth, Luther and Calvin, the hymns of Wesley and of the American slaves, the etchings of Rembrandt, the music of Bach and Messiaen, the poetry of Dante and Eliot—to allow all of these, each in its own way, to shape one's learning, after one has oneself been formed by them. That, I say, is what I understand by Christian learning. Put it just a bit differently: Christian learning is faithful learning. Learning faithful to faith in the triune God, learning faithful to the Christian community and its tradition, learning faithful to the Christian Scriptures. A piece of Christian learning may or may not be different in its content from the learning of those others with whom one participates in the practice of scholarship. It will, in any case, be faithful learning. And its fidelity will make it distinctive enough.

Christian learning is also learning *whereby* one is formed by Christian faith, by the Christian community and its tradition, and by the Christian Scriptures. Anthropologists have powerfully made the point that, unlike other animals, the biological component in the makeup of us human beings is woefully insufficient for our flourishing—insufficient even for our continuing existence. If we are to survive and flourish we have to be cultured—or better, *en*culturated. But there's no human culture in general—no human culture *allgemein*. There are only human *cultures*. The enculturation undergone by a member of the Benin tribe in West Africa in the seventeenth century was profoundly different from that which you and I have undergone. Thus it is that there is such a thing as *Christian* culture—or more precisely for my purposes here, Christian *en*culturation. Always a person's Christian enculturation will intersect and interact with other modes of cultural formation: with twentieth-century American modes, twelfth-century Byzantine modes, and so forth. But if to be a Christian is to exhibit a specific sort of faith, to identify with a specific community, and to accept specific scriptures as canonical, then, perforce, whatever else may go into being a Christian, being a Christian will incorporate a certain identifiable cultural formation. And for the acquisition of that formation, education is indispensable. Not necessarily academic learning, admittedly. But it would be pointless, here in this particular volume, to argue that it is indispensable for the health and survival of the Christian community in our part of the modern world that Christian enculturation would take the form, for many of us, of academic learning.

In summary: Christian learning is both learning *shaped* in whatever be the appropriate ways by one's Christian cultural formation, and learning which is the *medium* of that Christian formation. An implication of the latter is that the canon, in a college with a history and background such as St. Olaf's, will differ from the canon to be found in a "secular" college. Whereas the philosophers in the secular college may think Augustine and Aquinas can be ignored with impunity, those in a college with a history and background such as St. Olaf's will find them indispensable parts of the canon—while also, let me be clear, finding Plato and Kant indispensable parts. I would go so far as to say that it would be appropriate for the canon at St. Olaf to have a distinctly "Lutheran" contour.

Two explanatory points must be appended, lest I be misunderstood. Christian learning, I have said, is both learning which is shaped by one's Christian formation, and learning which is the medium of such shaping. It is by no means, however, *dogmatic* learning. The practitioner of Christian learning listens to objections; and often, having listened, changes her mind. Christian learning is *dialogic* learning. To be a person of Christian enculturation is to know not only that Christians are not the sole possessors of truth but that, on many points, what they "possess" is not truth but falsehood.

A closely connected point is that Christian learning, as I understand it, is not some hole-and-corner exercise. The learning in which the Christian scholar participates is the learning of humanity in general: all together we seek the truth. But once we recognize that the Enlightenment ideal of learning as a generically human enterprise is illusory, once we realize that our common human practice of learning must be understood instead as a dialogue among perspectives, then the challenge for the Christian scholar is to participate with Christian fidelity in that shared dialogue.

Christian Learning Is More than Theology

Professor Michael Aune, in his contribution to this volume, seconds the suggestion made by Professor William H. K. Narum, in 1960, that it is theology that holds the entire educational enterprise together in a college such as St. Olaf. I agree that if the Christian formation of which I have spoken is to occur at a college such as St. Olaf, theology must be an important part of the curriculum—part of the "canon." The fact that it is not part of the canon in the average secular liberal arts college is not a reason for St. Olaf's not making it part of its canon. But Christian learning, as I have tried to set it forth here for the consideration of the reader, is not to be identified with theological learning. It will, I am persuaded, disappear in the absence of theological learning; theological learning is a condition of Christian learning. But it's not the same.

Let me explain with an example. An important theme in the church fathers and the medieval theologians was that the poor have a *right* to adequate means of sustenance. The moral significance of poverty for John Chrysostom, to name just one of many, was not that the poor provide an opportunity for the wealthy to exercise their obligations of charity, but that the poor have a *right* to fair access to adequate food, clothing, and shelter. It is my view that we as contemporary Christian scholars should take seriously this part of our tradition; though we should not just "swallow" it unreflectively, we should also not ignore it. We should reflect critically on it. That's part of the Christian formation which I am recommending. But if the outcome of our reflection is that we conclude that John and all the others were right about this—which is where I myself come out—then the thesis that the poor have a right to sustenance will not only be an interesting and challenging item that turns up in a course on the patristics; it will shape the thought pattern of our philosophers, our political theorists, and our economists.

Speaking, then, as an outsider who is almost an insider, I propose, for the consideration of the reader, that the best way St. Olaf can serve students in the present is by offering them what is recognizably *Christian* learning—even, *Lutheran* Christian learning. Thereby it will not only honor its history and background; it will occupy a distinct and significant niche within the diversity of American higher education. If that niche is not occupied, something important for all of us will be missing from the picture.

ACKNOWLEDGMENTS

The editors are grateful to many people for help with this book. First of all to the Lilly Fellows Program at Valparaiso University for approving the grant proposal that gave us the mentoring program for new faculty and the seed money for this collection of essays. To the varied group of faculty members and administrators who have made up the St. Olaf Forum these past few years, for their general support of this project, and for reading and discussing the background essays in Part I and offering the writers suggestions for revision.

To the writers of the essays in the book, 33 of them, who graciously accepted our invitations, in due time sent forth their essays, and even more graciously revised them again and again, without murmur. To Steve Edwins for the map, and to John Maakestad for the cover painting, the final version of which he began three days after cataract surgery. To the members of the St. Olaf Communications Division who have generously given us advice and help in preparing the manuscript, particularly with the graphics: Carole Tillisch, Sandra Gilderhus, Lisa Graff. To John Gorder, Director of Church Relations at the college, who arranged an early morning photo shoot on campus for the two of us (and in the process he gave me a short course in observing the details of the chapel windows). To Sue Oines, Secretary to the English Department, who supplied expert clerical and technical help with this manuscript in the midst of her regular duties. Thanks also to Susan Carlson, the Paracollege Program Assistant, who cheerfully and competently pitched in a year ago when Sue Oines was out of town and we had a complete manuscript to assemble from the separate essays and a deadline for mailing it, To Joan Olson, St. Olaf's recently retired archivist, who read through the biographical essays and offered advice and correction. To Tim Whipple, Gary DeKrey's assistant in the Archives and a 1999 St. Olaf graduate, who helped put together the original set of photographs from which we made our final selection. To Jean Ditmanson, Evelyn Flaten, Robert Flaten, Judith Hong, and Ella Valborg Tweet for lending us family photographs.

To Phyllis Larson for helping her mother, Judy Hyland, who is legally blind, with the practical aspects of producing a manuscript and its revisions.

To all the colleagues, students, and alumni who encourage on-going conversations about the relationship between church and college—we are well aware and grateful that this book arises out of such a rich dialogue. To those who have written books of history to commemorate St. Olaf's previous anniversaries, from which we have drawn heavily in planning this very different anniversary volume: William C. Benson, *High on Manitou: A History of St. Olaf College 1874–1949* (1949); Joseph Shaw, *History of St. Olaf College 1874–1974* (1974) and also his *Dear Old Hill: The Story of Manitou Heights: The Campus of St. Olaf College* (1992). And last of all, to St. Olaf's president, Mark Edwards, who offered this faculty-born project encouragement and support before we asked for it, who set aside money for our use during a year of tight budgeting and attached no strings to it, who was willing to discuss the book in its larger aspects and in its details but granted us complete editorial discretion.

Such widespread and generous support have made the book a pleasure to plan and bring into being.

CONTRIBUTORS

KATHRYN ANANDA-OWENS has been teaching piano in the Music Department at St. Olaf since 1997. She was born in Chicago and grew up in California and Bethesda, but mostly Madison, Wisconsin. She received a B.A. in economics from Oberlin College, along with a B.Mus. in piano performance from Oberlin Conservatory. At Peabody Conservatory, where she earned her graduate degrees, she studied with Julian Martin. She won first prize in the 1993 Neale-Silva Young Artists Competition, and while at Peabody, she made her Lincoln Center debut. She performs with two chamber groups, and in the summer of 1998 she toured Europe with the St. Olaf Orchestra as the featured soloist.

MICHAEL B. AUNE is the Academic Dean at Pacific Lutheran Theological Seminary in Berkeley, where he has taught for many years. He grew up in Elbow Lake and Thief River Falls, Minnesota, and graduated from St. Olaf in 1966. He studied at Luther Theological Seminary at St. Paul and then received his graduate degree at Notre Dame in theology, with a concentration in liturgical studies, New Testament, and pastoral theology. He has served as a parish pastor in western North Dakota. He says that after all these years in California, he is still a Minnesota Vikings fan.

ROBERT BENNE is the Jordan-Trexler Professor of Religion at Roanoke College in Salem, Virginia. He is also Chair of the Department of Religion and Philosophy and directs his college's Center for Church and Society. He grew up in West Point, Nebraska, and graduated from Midland Lutheran College in Fremont, Nebraska. He received his graduate degrees from the Divinity School at the University of Chicago, specializing in ethics and society. For seventeen years, he taught at the Lutheran School of Theology at Chicago until moving to Roanoke in 1982. In 1999–2000 he will be Senior Fellow in the Lilly Fellows Program in Humanities and the Arts at Valparaiso University. He tells us that he is "a tennis fanatic and addict."

KRISTINE CARLSON is a pastor at First Lutheran Church in Fargo. She grew up in Brooklyn, where her father was a pastor. She graduated from St. Olaf in 1974, and then studied at the University of Minnesota and at Luther Theological Seminary in St. Paul, where she is now working on a doctorate in New Testament. She has taught English at the University of Regina in Saskatchewan and served Minnesota parishes in Richfield and in Northfield. She is married to Morris Wee, also a Lutheran pastor, and they have three sons. Recently, with her family and father, she visited the island of Madagascar, "where my grandparents were missionaries, my father was born, and my grandfather is buried."

GARY DE KREY has taught in the History Department at St. Olaf since 1988. He grew up in Bismarck and Linton, North Dakota, and graduated from St. Olaf in 1971. He received his graduate degrees from Princeton and for several years taught at Colgate University. He has published extensively on seventeenth-century British history and recently was awarded a Guggenheim Fellowship, the first St. Olaf faculty member to receive this honor. He never met the fabled Agnes Larson, but he says that he has always felt her as a definite presence in the History Department, increasingly since he has become its chair, a position that she filled with great majesty for two decades.

MARK U. EDWARDS, JR. has been President of St. Olaf since 1994. He was born in Oakland and grew up in Southern California. He received undergraduate and graduate degrees from Stanford University and has taught history at Wellesley College, Purdue University, and Harvard University, where he also served as Acting Dean of the Divinity School. He has served on the governing boards of Wittenberg University in Ohio, a sister school of St. Olaf, and Holden Village, a Lutheran retreat center in the Cascades. He cofounded a software company and designed a software system. He has written four books on Martin Luther, and his present research is on historic Christianity and the environment.

STEVEN EDWINS is a partner in the Northfield firm SMSQ, Architects, and teaches in the Art Department at St. Olaf. He grew up in Southern California and St. Louis Park, Minnesota, graduated from St. Olaf in 1965, and earned a degree at Yale School of Architecture. He worked in community development in Appalachia in Kentucky and taught at the University of Kentucky. He has worked on many building projects at St. Olaf, particularly as a color consultant, and he designed the renovation of Studio A in the Radio Building, the organ recital room, one of the campus showpieces.

He enjoys photography and concerns himself with issues of historic preservation in Northfield. He and his wife Jennifer have two sons.

JAMES FARRELL teaches in the History Department and Paracollege at St. Olaf and directs its program in American Studies. At the college, he has taught a wide variety of courses, including such topics as Environmental History, the Clarence Thomas Affair, and Walt Disney's America. He has published extensively on American culture and was selected as the first holder of a three-year endowed post at St. Olaf, the Boldt Distinguished Teaching Professor in the Humanities. He was born in Washington, D.C., grew up in Danville, Illinois, graduated from Loyola University in Chicago, and received graduate degrees at the University of Illinois. He lives in Eden Prairie, Minnesota, with his wife Barb and two sons.

ALBERT E. FINHOLT taught chemistry at St. Olaf from 1949 to 1985, and served as its Academic Dean for seven years. He grew up in Chicago and Oak Park, Illinois. He graduated from Knox College, and during World War II he worked at the University of Chicago on the Manhattan Project. He earned his doctorate from Chicago, doing research in inorganic chemistry under the direction of Herbert Brown, who won the Nobel prize in 1977. Finholt helped initiate several important programs at St. Olaf including the Paracollege and Great Conversation. "It was my goal, as a professor and as a dean, to improve the academic stature of St. Olaf in every way possible." He is retired and lives in Northfield with his wife Marion.

ANGELA GOEHRING, a 1993 graduate of St. Olaf, has been working at the college since 1996, as an Admissions Counselor and as Adviser to International Students. She grew up mostly in Brunswick and Topsham, Maine, but also "anywhere and everywhere and wherever the navy takes families." She spent a year in Paraguay as a volunteer missionary teacher of music and English, and she has also taught at an international boarding school in Arizona. She enjoys sea-kayaking and "can do an Eskimo roll."

PATRICK CABELLO HANSEL is a Lutheran pastor. His present call is a five-year-old mission congregation in Hispanic North Philadelphia, Nueva Creación/New Creation Lutheran Church; he also directs a community center for youth and families. Before this, he worked in the South Bronx for several years, as director of a coalition of inner-city Lutheran congregations and as a pastor of Fordham Lutheran Church. He grew up in Austin, Minnesota, and graduated from St. Olaf in 1975. He studied at Christ Seminary-Seminex, St. Louis, Missouri, and at Pacific Lutheran Theological Seminary in Berkeley. His wife Luisa and daughter Natasha are both natives of Santiago, Chile. He is a poet.

JUDY SKOGERBOE HYLAND served as a Lutheran missionary to China from 1940 to 1945 and to Japan from 1950 to 1980. She grew up in Erskine, Minnesota, and graduated from St. Olaf in 1934, with majors in English and Latin. She did graduate work at the University of California at Berkeley in Chinese language and linguistics. At age eighty-six (and legally blind) she teaches a Bible class, speaks to church gatherings and civic organizations, and is finishing her second book, on her years in Japan. Her first book describes her experiences in a Japanese internment camp in the Philippines during World War II. She lives in Northfield, where her daughter Phyllis Larson teaches Japanese language and literature at St. Olaf.

DARRELL JODOCK has taught in the Religion Department at Muhlenberg College in Allentown, Pennsylvania, for twenty-one years; in September 1999 he becomes the Drell and Adeline Bernhardson Distinguished Professor of Religion at Gustavus Adolphus College in St. Peter, Minnesota. He graduated from St. Olaf in 1962, and studied at Luther Theological Seminary in St. Paul, Union Theological Seminary, Columbia, and Yale, earning his doctorate there. He has taught at Luther Seminary and served as a parish pastor. He grew up on a farm near Northwood, North Dakota, and is married to a graduate of Concordia College; they have two sons. He collects toy tractors and farm equipment from the 1930s to 1960s.

DEBORAH LIV JOHNSON grew up in Ridgecrest, California, in the Mojave Desert. She graduated from St. Olaf in 1980 with a music major and is now the president and owner of a record company in San Diego, as well as a composer, producer, and full-time touring musician. Over the years she has accumulated a well-rounded work portfolio: freelance editing, teaching school, laying tile, bartending, clerking at a shipyard. She also managed the Art and Advertising Department for Adventure 16, an outdoor company, for seven years and edited their outdoor publication. She tells us: "I love fishing, old trucks, hiking, and all my friends in Minnesota, and I'm still doing my damnedest to get on 'A Prairie Home Companion.'"

L. DEANE LAGERQUIST is Senior Tutor of the Paracollege and has taught in the Religion Department at St. Olaf since 1988. She grew up mostly in Ames, Iowa, and graduated from California Lutheran College in Thousand Oaks. Her graduate degrees are from Luther Theological Seminary in St. Paul and the Divinity School at the University of Chicago. She taught at Valparaiso University before coming to St. Olaf. Her interest is the history of Christianity, and her latest book is on women in the American Lutheran church. She explains that "although I did not attend St. Olaf, I studied the school as part of my doctoral dissertation," directed by Martin Marty.

JOHN MAAKESTAD grew up in Rochester, Minnesota, where his father was a pastor, and graduated from St. Olaf in 1950 with majors in art and English. He earned an M.F.A. at the State University of Iowa in Ames and returned to his alma mater in 1956, where he taught studio art and art history in the Art Department for thirty-eight years. He has continued to draw and paint and sculpt throughout his life; in the year of his retirement, 1994, a retrospective exhibit of his work was shown at Steensland Art Gallery at St. Olaf, with artworks lent by many private and corporate owners. Though he has traveled and studied all over the world and painted what he saw, he has lived his entire life in southern Minnesota and "wouldn't have it any other way": "spirit of place" is primary. He and his wife Bobbi live on a farm south of Northfield

NORMAN E. MADSON is an architect. For twenty-eight years he was a partner in architectural firms, including the Sövik firm in Northfield, then called Sövik Mathre and Madson. In 1974 he joined the St. Olaf staff, serving for almost twenty years as Director of the Physical Plant as well as Staff Architect. He grew up in Stanhope, Iowa, and attended Waldorf College and Iowa State University, where he received a degree in architectural engineering. In his retirement, he lives in Burnsville, Minnesota, and stays involved in the design and construction industry as an arbitrator with the American Arbitration Association.

KATHY WILKER MAGYERI has taught high school English for thirty-four years, at present in Sandy Springs, Maryland. She was born in Madison, Wisconsin, grew up in Owatonna, Minnesota, and graduated from St. Olaf in 1965. She has master's degrees in English and in gerontology from George Washington University. She has taught in the Ukraine and won a Fulbright to study in Malaysia. In 1995 St. Olaf presented her with its Distinguished Alumna Award. She swears that "none of these awards compares to skiing down double back diamond runs at Jackson Hole" or "flying a small plane over the Florida Everglades gazing at 'gators below" or "speaking to two greats during my last trip to Minnesota—theologian Martin Marty and Jesse 'The Body' Ventura."

MARTIN E. MARTY is the Fairfax M. Cone Distinguished Service Professor Emeritus at the University of Chicago and also the chair of the St. Olaf Board of Regents. He grew up in Nebraska, in West Point, and Battle Creek, and attended "an old-worldly combination of prep school plus junior college" at Concordia College in Milwaukee. He continued at Concordia Seminary in St. Louis and did graduate work at the Lutheran School of Theology at Chicago and the University of Chicago, where he later taught theology. He was a parish pastor for eleven years, and for forty-three years he "moonlighted" as an editor at *The Christian Century*. He has spoken at five hundred colleges and universities, and for four decades has made the church-related liberal arts college a special interest.

KEITH GRABER MILLER teaches in the Bible, Religion, and Philosophy Department at Goshen College. He grew up in Kokomo, Indiana, and graduated from Franklin College in that state, with majors in journalism and prelaw. He studied at the Associated Mennonite Biblical Seminary in Elkhart, Indiana (where he now teaches one or two courses a year in ethics), and at Emory University, receiving a doctorate in Christian ethics and sociology of religion. In the past he has worked as an editor and general manager of a weekly newspaper in Howard County, Indiana, as a pastor at a rural Mennonite church, and as Campus Minister at Goshen. He and his wife Ann are the parents of two children, with a third to be born in November 1999.

WILLIAM H. K. NARUM taught in the Philosophy and Religion Departments at St. Olaf for forty-four years. He grew up in Fargo, the son of a Lutheran pastor, and graduated from St. Olaf in 1943. He received a doctorate in theological ethics from Princeton Theological Seminary and returned to teach at his alma mater in 1947. He was a visiting professor at the University of the Philippines and at Iowa State University. In 1963 he was given the Danforth Foundation's Harbison Award for Distinguished Teaching. Toward the end of his teaching career, he developed an interest in C. S. Lewis, and since his official retirement in 1991, he has taught many courses on Lewis, to students at St. Olaf and to adults in Northfield, where he lives.

MARK L. NELSON is a 1974 graduate of St. Olaf. He earned a master's degree at Luther Theological Seminary and an M.B.A. at the University of St. Thomas, both in St. Paul. At present he is the Executive Director of LifeTrac Transplant Network and Assistant Vice President for Allianz Life Insurance in Minneapolis.

ROBERT L. NICHOLS has taught in the History Department at St. Olaf since 1972 and also served as its chair for several years. He grew up in Poulsbo, Washington, and received his undergraduate and graduate degrees from the University of Washington. He taught at the University of Washington as well as several other colleges in that state before coming to St. Olaf. He does research on the Russian Orthodox Church and has published widely in the field. He has a summer home on the Kitsap Peninsula in Puget Sound.

DAVID J. O'BRIEN is Loyola Professor of Roman Catholic Studies at the College of the Holy Cross, Worcester, Massachusetts. He also directs the Peace and Conflict Studies Program at Holy Cross, where has taught for thirty years, with time off to teach at Stonehill College and to work for a year as a consultant to the National Conference of Catholic Bishops. He was born and raised in Pittsfield, Massachusetts, and graduated from Notre Dame. He received graduate degrees from the University of Rochester in U.S. political and social history. He has written several books on American Catholic history, and in recent years he has written and lectured on Catholic higher education.

JAMES L. PENCE has been the Academic Dean at St. Olaf since 1996. He grew up in Denver and earned B.A. and M.A. degrees from Colorado State University. He received his doctorate from the University of Arizona, specializing in Renaissance literature, Elizabethan comedy, and rhetoric. He taught at several colleges and held administrative posts at the University of Southern Colorado and at Wartburg College in Waverly, Iowa. He was raised a Roman Catholic and became a Lutheran by Affirmation of Baptism while at Colorado State. He has been an active member of church congregations, serving as president of church councils as well as teaching Sunday school and singing in choirs. He and his wife Janet have two daughters.

TOM PORTER taught in the Physical Education Department at St. Olaf and served as Head Football Coach for thirty-three years until his retirement in 1991. He grew up in Bayport, Minnesota, and graduated from St. Olaf in 1951. He taught high school in Neenah, Wisconsin, and did graduate work at the University of Minnesota, the University of Colorado, and Pennsylvania State University. In 1958, upon Ade Christenson's retirement from coaching, Porter succeeded his former teacher and coach at St. Olaf, where he has also coached baseball, hockey, and track. Although he called himself "a cookbook track coach," in his first season his team won the conference title. He and his wife Gloria live in the country near Northfield.

SIDNEY A. RAND served as President of St. Olaf for seventeen years and as Ambassador to Norway. He grew up in Rothsay, Minnesota, and graduated from Concordia College in Moorhead and Luther Theological Seminary in St. Paul. He studied church history at the University of Chicago. He has served as a pastor, Executive of the Board of Education for two Lutheran church bodies, and president of three other Lutheran colleges (Waldorf in Iowa, Augustana in South Dakota, and Suomi in Michigan). He has been awarded honorary doctorates by eight colleges, and was decorated by the King of Norway on three occasions. He and his wife Lois live in Minneapolis and continue to be active members of St. Olaf College.

JACK SCHWANDT was born and raised in Enderlin, North Dakota. He graduated from Concordia College in Moorhead and received his graduate degrees from the University of Minnesota. He taught for two years at Oklahoma State University before coming to St. Olaf in 1963. There he taught courses in political philosophy, American government, literature, and writing, and he retired in 1996. He has been a lifelong reader of Kierkegaard and in the early stages of his graduate work studied under Paul Holmer. For the first four years of his married life, he was a tenant at the Hong House on Heath Creek.

PAMELA SCHWANDT taught in the English Department at St. Olaf for twenty-six years. She grew up in two small towns in southern Minnesota, Petersburg and Redwood Falls. She graduated from St. Olaf in 1961, and from the University of Washington and the University of Minnesota, specializing in eighteenth-century British literature. She retired in 1996, and now lives in Northfield with her husband Jack, four cats, and a large woodland garden.

JOSEPH M. SHAW taught in the Religion Department at St. Olaf from 1957 to 1991. He wrote the college's history for its centennial celebration, and since then he has written two further books about St. Olaf's history, one on the campus of the college and one on the St. Olaf Choir. He has also published books on his primary teaching interests, Bible and Christian humanism. He grew up in Estherville, Iowa, and received his bachelor's degree from St. Olaf in 1949. He graduated from Luther Theological Seminary and from Princeton Theological Seminary, concentrating on New Testament. He and his wife Virginia, both now retired from working at St. Olaf, live in Northfield.

SHIRLEY HERSHEY SHOWALTER is the President of Goshen College in Goshen, Indiana, where she was earlier Professor of English and Department Chair. She grew up in Lititz, Pennsylvania, and graduated from Eastern Mennonite College. She received her graduate degree in American civilization from the University of Texas at Austin. She was Senior Fellow for the Lilly Fellows Program in Humanities and the Arts at Valparaiso University. Of her present job, she says, "I love my work. I view my job as President to be another form of teaching. I continue to teach one course at least every other year. I also believe that interaction with people of other cultures and other faiths deepens awareness of and commitment to one's own faith."

E. A. SÖVIK was born in central China of American missionary parents and grew up there. He graduated from St. Olaf in 1939, studied at Luther Theological Seminary in St. Paul, and took a degree in architecture at Yale University. He taught in the Art Department at St. Olaf for many years. In 1949 he cofounded (with Arnold Flaten) a firm in Northfield now named SMSQ, Architects, whose specialty is church architecture. Sövik and his firm have been responsible for twenty-eight building projects at St. Olaf, including the Christiansen Hall of Music, which contains one of the college's most beautiful rooms, Urness Recital Hall. In World War II he served as a Marine pilot. Now retired, he lives in Northfield with his wife Genevieve.

WALTER STROMSETH taught for forty years in the Religion and Philosophy Departments at St. Olaf. He grew up in Atwater, Minnesota, and graduated from St. Olaf in 1950. He earned degrees at Yale Divinity School, and at Yale University in philosophical theology. He has been a visiting professor at Wilfred Laurier University in Canada and in the Graduate Program of Religious Studies at Princeton University. He has led several St. Olaf international study programs in Asia, and during the 1999–2000 school year, he will teach at Fudan University in Shanghai. Since retirement in 1996, he and his wife Betty have divided their time between Naples, Florida, and Northfield.

WALTER C. SUNDBERG teaches church history at Luther Theological Seminary in St. Paul. He was born in Brooklyn and grew up in Long Island and northern New Jersey. He graduated from St. Olaf in 1969, received a doctorate from Princeton Theological Seminary, and served as a pastor at Como Park Lutheran Church in St. Paul. He has written on many topics in theology; his book *The Bible in Modern Culture* (1995), co-written with Roy A. Harrisville, is coming out in a second edition. He is an editor of *The Rose*, a "Gospel-centered, practically oriented magazine meant for pastors, Christian leaders and laypeople." He is an avid collector of CDs. He and his wife Virginia have two daughters.

NICHOLAS P. WOLTERSTORFF is the Noah Porter Professor of Philosophical Theology at Yale University. He grew up in Bigelow and Edgerton, Minnesota, and graduated from Calvin College in 1953. He received his graduate degree from Harvard in philosophy and taught at his alma mater, Calvin, for thirty years. For half of each of five years he taught at the Free University of Amsterdam, and has been Visiting Professor at Princeton, Notre Dame, the University of Michigan, the University of Texas, Temple University, and Haverford College. He has published extensively on aesthetics, metaphysics, epistemology, and philosophy of religion. He comes from a long line of woodworkers, and woodworking is one of his loves.

SOLVEIG ZEMPEL has taught in the Norwegian Department at St. Olaf since 1976 and is its chair. She grew up in Roseau, Minnesota, and graduated from St. Olaf in 1969. Her graduate degrees, in Scandinavian languages and literature, are from the University of Minnesota. She has written extensively on Ole Rølvaag and translated several of his novels as well as his letters, and most recently a collection of his essays. Her mother, Ella Valborg Tweet, who lives in Northfield, is the daughter of Ole Rølvaag.

CREDITS FOR PHOTOGRAPHS

Most of the photographs in this volume come from the St. Olaf Archives or from private individuals and are credited beneath the print.

The following photographs of Arnold Flaten's carvings come from *Arnold Flaten, Sculptor* (Minneapolis: Augsburg, 1974):

p. 1, "I Am the Door"
p. 71, "I Am the Light of the World"
p. 136, "The Vines and Branches," "Teacher," "Jacob's Ladder," "King Olav"
p. 137, portrait head of Evelyn Flaten, "I Am the Way," "Esthete"
p. 161, "I Am the Bread of Life"
p. 213, "I Am Alpha and Omega"